UKRAINE

UKRAINE

A NATION ON THE BORDERLAND

KARL SCHLÖGEL

English translation by Gerrit Jackson

REAKTION BOOKS

Published by Reaktion Books Ltd
Unit 32, Waterside
44–48 Wharf Road
London N1 7UX, UK
www.reaktionbooks.co.uk

First published by Reaktion Books in 2018
First published in paperback 2022
English-language translation by Gerrit Jackson
Translation © Reaktion Books 2018
Preface to the New Edition © Karl Schlögel 2022

Original title *Entscheidung in Kiew. Ukrainische Lektionen*
© Carl Hanser Verlag München 2015

The translation of this work was supported by a grant
from the Goethe-Institut, which is funded by the
German Ministry of Foreign Affairs

GOETHE
INSTITUT

Printed and bound in Great Britain by
Clays Ltd, Elcograf S.p.A.

A catalogue record for this book is
available from the British Library

ISBN 978 1 78914 677 6

CONTENTS

PREFACE TO THE NEW EDITION

FOR YOUR AND OUR FREEDOM!

'We couldn't have imagined it,' was the rhetorical formula of our powerlessness and bewilderment after the Russian attack on Ukraine. And we cannot imagine what is yet to come.

The images of the new Ukraine that have lingered in our minds since the Maidan revolution are now drenched in blood and littered with rubble. Since the end of the Soviet Union, Ukraine had become a different country, despite the difficulties it faced. A country that had got down to work, that wanted nothing but to be left alone. The new splendour of Kiev, a modern Kharkiv, Odessa as a place of longing, Lviv on a wave of tech and tourism booms: a nation so long on the fringes of European perception had finally found its place on European horizons, at last emerging from the shadow of the Soviet Union and Russia.

Now all of that is to be undone. Putin has already demonstrated what he intends to do with Ukraine. During the Chechen war he razed Grozny to the ground; in Syria, he reduced the more than 4,000-year-old Aleppo to rubble and ashes. But he doesn't stop at urbicide. Unimaginable until recently, nuclear facilities have become a war target. Zaporizhzhia, the largest nuclear power plant in Europe, is located where the Dnieper dam, at the time Europe's largest dam, was built in the 1920s. During the Second World War, the dam was blown up twice, and the surrounding industrial landscape was bombed back to the Stone Age. Kharkiv, twice conquered and destroyed by the Germans, is now being destroyed by Russian missiles. The countryside around it, which was devastated by the starvation of millions in the 1930s, has become a countryside in which sowing seeds is no longer possible this year, so there will also be no harvest. We could not imagine that the cathedrals of the cave monastery high above the Dnieper could be blown up again. In the old photographs we recognize the train stations with hundreds of thousands of people fleeing; from there, millions of Ukrainian men and women were once transported to the German Reich for slave labour. And we could never have imagined that debris from the Kiev TV tower would fall on the Babi Yar site, where more than 33,000 Kiev Jews were murdered in September 1941. These pictures of German crimes in Ukraine are now followed by the images of Russian war crimes today. Every Ukrainian knows what it means when cities are surrounded and starved in blockades.

We've watched the chronicles of a prophesied war for far too long. It was more comfortable to look the other way, despite the fact that we had all learned never to do so again, to look on when evil happens. It was always said that one should not demonize Putin. What he intends to do in Ukraine, and how he wants to destroy Ukraine as an independent state, as an independent nation, can be studied in Russia these days. A new type of totalitarianism prevails in Putin's Third Empire, which is intended to succeed the Russian and the Soviet. Myths, censorship and hate speech have taken the place of the historical memory that the country so desperately needs. A great exodus has begun. Putin has led the country into an impasse and is evidently ready to take it down with him. But it wouldn't be the first time a senseless, costly, criminal war has brought down a regime. It is highly unlikely that the madness of this war will leave Russia unscathed. What is certain, however, is that it is currently the Ukrainians who are putting a stop to Putin's war. They have already thwarted his calculations for a small, quick invasion, and they are paying the price that the Europeans, the West, or what the West once was, was unwilling to pay. The least we can do here today is listen to the Ukrainians in the moment of mortal threat and to help wherever we can.

SLAVA UKRAYINI!

> The text is based on the speech at Bebelplatz in Berlin
> on 6 March 2022.

UKRAINE, OR REMAPPING EUROPE:
PREFACE TO THE ENGLISH EDITION

HISTORY DOES NOT take breaks and rarely concludes with a happy ending. Still, the fall of the Wall and the Iron Curtain in 1989 inspired hopes, especially in Central Europe, that the decades-long Cold War dividing Europe into enemy blocs had been an extended state of exception now followed by a return to normal. Things turned out differently: Yugoslavia's disintegration spawned new wars; the initial euphoria faded as nationalist and authoritarian regimes gained strength; corruption was endemic; Russia suffered from post-imperial phantom pains and proved ready to bully and attack neighbouring states.

Ukraine is where, in the twenty-first century, war has returned to Europe. Crimea, annexed in 2014, is still occupied by Putin's troops; pro-Russian separatists have established a reign of terror in the Donbass. The territorial integrity of Europe's second-largest country is violated day after day, and in this situation of perpetual aggression the implementation of urgently needed reforms has slowed to a crawl. All of this is playing out no more than a few hours by plane from Warsaw, Berlin or London. It sometimes seems that Europe has resigned itself to the permanent military incursion on its periphery – the continent is overwhelmed as it is by the many concurrent crises: the Euro crisis, Greek crisis, Brexit, terrorism, the refugee crisis.

For the longest time, Ukraine as an independent nation with its own culture and history was non-existent on most Europeans' mental maps. Many regarded it as a province and backyard of far larger entities – Russia and, earlier, the Soviet Union. Ukraine's political and cultural identity and the Ukrainian language were thought of as variants of their Russian counterparts. This incuriousness became untenable with the 'Revolution of Dignity' that erupted in Kiev and other major cities in

2014, and especially with the undeclared war Putin's Russia has waged against Ukraine. Europeans had to admit to themselves that they had only the haziest notions of the country and nation – if they had any idea at all. So a portrait of Ukraine and its people, of its cities, towns and landscapes, of the manifold cultural and historical influences that moulded them, remains an acute desideratum. The essays on Ukrainian cities collected in this volume represent an attempt to apprehend this diversity in selected examples. They were written at different times between 1987 and 2015 and so also trace a shift of perspective: from a Russian-centric view in which Moscow was the unquestioned vantage point and Ukraine part of the periphery, to a keen appreciation of the ways in which Ukraine is an autonomous and distinctive nation. This shift did not come easily for a writer whose academic socialization took place in Moscow and Leningrad, now St Petersburg, but it has certainly been instructive.

In its particular interests and concerns, this book is recognizably the work of a German historian. Wherever the traveller goes in Ukraine, he encounters traces of German involvement in the country's history, of positive contributions as well as atrocities. In the German perspective, Ukraine has rarely figured as more than a part of the Russian Empire ('Little Russia'), a colonial possession and Eastern European breadbasket, or a battle zone and occupied territory where millions became victims: Soviet prisoners of war, forced labourers, Jews. With Belarus, Ukraine was the main theatre of war and the single largest source of forced labourers from Eastern Europe; scattered across it are innumerable mass graves from the genocide against the Jews of Eastern Europe. It took Germans a long time to acknowledge that Russia was not the only target of the Third Reich's campaign of conquest and annihilation, and to accept the special responsibility for the fate of today's independent Ukraine this history implies.

The situation after the end of the Cold War's division of the world and the demise of the Soviet Empire is reminiscent of the period after the First World War, with its numerous newly independent states and newly formed alliances, its shifting boundaries, minority conflicts and volatile domestic politics. The disaffection of ethnic and linguistic minorities was harnessed for revisionist foreign policy schemes; governments flouted the rules of peaceful dispute resolution. The experience of Munich 1938 exemplifies the illusion of appeasement – 'Peace for our time' – in the face of a political strategy in which the annexation of Sudetenland was but another step towards the devastation of Europe.

Europe and the West more generally have a hard time defining their place in a changed world. They are virtually unprepared for the new kinds of hybrid and asymmetrical warfare and slow to respond to the novel instruments of today's 'information war'. They seem stymied by the intellectual challenges these forms of aggression pose, not to mention by the need to rethink the West's military defence capabilities.

No end to the Ukraine crisis is in sight. The war rages on, and the danger that Ukraine will be destabilized remains very real. This is not just about Crimea or the Donbass: the larger question is whether Europe will close ranks and make a stand against the International that Putin is forging with allies from the far left to the far right. One prerequisite for effective and sustained support for Ukraine is a better understanding of its emergence as a nation and its natural and cultural diversity. The most obvious tokens of this complexity are the multiple names by which most places are known, each of which stands for a different historical period and political affiliation: Leopolis/Lwów/Lemberg/Lvov/Lviv, Kharkov/Kharkiv. More than in virtually any other European country, bilingualism and multilingualism are an unremarked-upon fact of daily life in Ukraine – which is why, depending on the historical context, some places appear under different names in the essays collected in the following pages.

I am most pleased that the book, which has been published in Ukrainian, Russian and Spanish translations in addition to the German original, is now coming out in English. My gratitude goes to Michael R. Leaman, publisher at Reaktion Books, and to Gerrit Jackson, who has translated it with his usual diligence.

AUTHOR'S NOTE

ONE TECHNICAL-EDITORIAL remark: in preparing essays for print that examine Russian-Ukrainian issues, the usual quandary of how to transliterate personal names and toponyms – the choice is between reader-friendly and scholarly variants – is compounded by the question of which name to use in a country in which most names exist in Russian and Ukrainian versions. I have sought to chart a middle course between the familiarity of the Russian forms, which were long dominant in the literature, and a gentle Ukrainianization; it is not my intention to engage in linguistic affirmative action. Striking a balance between longstanding tradition and contemporary sensibilities has not always been easy. I have avoided cluttering the text with footnotes or source references – information on the cited literature and tips for further reading may be found at the end of the book.

Anti-government protest in Ukraine, 20 February 2014, in Maidan square.

EUROPE'S *UKRAINA*:
AN INTRODUCTION

I T IS IMPOSSIBLE to tell how the struggle over Ukraine's future will
end. We cannot know whether the country will stand up to Russian
aggression or fall to its knees; whether the Europeans, the West, will
defend or abandon it; whether the European Union will close ranks or
disintegrate. What is certain is that Ukraine will never again fade from
our mental maps. Not so long ago, this state, this people, this nation
barely existed in the general consciousness. In Germany in particular,
it was widely thought of as somehow part of 'Russia', of the Russian
Empire or the Soviet Union, and that its inhabitants spoke a language that was a kind of subspecies of Russian. With the 'Revolution
of Dignity' Ukrainians ignited on Maidan, and in their resistance to
Russia's attempts to destabilize their state, they have demonstrated that
an evolving reality has long made this view obsolete. The time is ripe
to take a fresh look at the map and review what we think we know.

That is certainly how I felt. Writing a book on Ukraine was not part
of what I had planned for this stage in my life. But there are situations
in which developments make a mockery of our plans and compel us
to join the fray. Putin's surprise conquest of Crimea and the ongoing
war in eastern Ukraine left me no other choice. Not because I believe
I am especially competent; in fact, on the contrary: I realized that I had
spent a lifetime studying Eastern Europe, Russia, the Soviet Union without ever knowing much about Ukraine – and I was not the only one
in my field who came to this realization. The general public was even
more clueless. The non-stop media talk was almost entirely about Putin's
Russia, which was described not as a political subject and active player
but as a victim that responded to the initiatives of the West. People rarely
spoke to Ukrainians, preferring to talk about them and their country.

Many participants in the debate were recognizably ignorant of the nation they were opining on and saw no need to go there to learn more about it. In Germany, which had occupied and ravaged Ukraine not once but twice in the twentieth century, many of the same speakers who were eloquently empathetic with the 'Russian soul' had nothing to say about the Ukrainians beyond the stereotype of inveterate nationalists and anti-Semites. I felt largely impotent in the face of this ignorance and arrogance of armchair generals who, to make matters worse, smugly regarded themselves as occupying the progressive position. Week after week, German television audiences can choose between dozens of films about Russia, mostly river-journey travelogues and historical documentaries. By contrast, a full year after Ukraine was turned into a theatre of war, at least the public broadcasters have not managed to give the country a face beyond the images from Maidan: no documentary about Odessa or the Donbass or the history of the Cossacks, no tour of Lviv or Chernivtsi – places that might in fact mean something to some Germans thanks to the poets old and recent among their sons and daughters. In short, Ukraine remained a blank on our horizon, a vacant spot that was at most a source of vague unease.

This book is an attempt, my attempt, to form a picture of Ukraine. It is not a history of Ukraine, for which the reader is directed to the works of several eminent historians (the Further Reading section lists the studies I found the most helpful). Nor does it try to narrate and comment on current events in the country; that is the task of journalists and reporters, some of whom do their jobs with positively heroic dedication. I get to know a country by exploring its historical topographies. My way of familiarizing myself with a nation's or a culture's history and distinctive character is to travel to its places and survey its spaces. I have described this method in my book *In Space We Read Time: On the History of Civilization and Geopolitics* (2016, originally published in German in 2003). One can 'read cities', decrypt them as textures and palimpsests, uncover their strata in a kind of urban archaeology, in order to make their past speak. Cities are documents of the first order, and they can be parsed and decoded. In the perspective I propose – as an alternative to the macrocosmic-global and microcosmic views – cities then reveal themselves to be the points in which the spaces of history and historical experience attain their maximum density.

Portraits of Ukrainian cities, the fruits of this form of urban archaeology, form the core of the present volume. Their mesoscopic perspective offers advantages that cannot be overstated, especially for the study of the history of Ukraine, a nation defined not in ethnic but in political terms whose territory bears the imprints of the history and culture of very different empires. The fragmentary, the particular, the regional are the crucial registers in which the specific nature of Ukraine's emergence as a nation and nation state finds expression. The collection of city portraits in the following pages is far from complete: I should very much have liked to include Vinnytsia and Chernihiv and the Ukrainian village, so horribly devastated by the Holodomor; a visit to Uman or Drohobych, where I could have gleaned the remaining traces of the shtetl, the centre of Eastern European Jewish life annihilated in the Shoah, would arguably have been essential; and I should have gone for a stroll on the DneproGES dam, that icon of Soviet modernization. Despite these and other regrettable gaps, I believe that the studies presented in this book can open readers' eyes to the extraordinary complexity and richness of today's Ukraine. We have only just begun to explore this European borderland and 'miniature Europe'.

The portraits of Lviv and Chernivtsi date from the late 1980s, while those of Odessa and Yalta were sketched in 2000. They are now outdated, the cities they paint thoroughly altered by recent events. Still, they capture a perspective and a shift of perspective that are themselves quite illuminating: Lviv and Chernivtsi appeared on our radar when Central Europe, the Europe that was neither East nor West, resurfaced; so Ukraine was not altogether beyond the European horizon even then. 'The centre lies to the east,' I had argued in the 1980s, before the fall of the Wall. Now we realize that this eastward expansion of our field of view was incomplete, that we need to enter cities like Kharkov, Dnepropetrovsk, Donetsk on our maps. The accounts of Crimea and Odessa, meanwhile, bring home another important insight: the imperial history that informs the post-Soviet space – though both were part of Ukraine during the Soviet period – will remain palpable for a long time, with effects that no decree can undo from one day to the next.

Ukraine has decided to pursue its own path and defend the way of life it has chosen, to resist the Russian aggression. The blue-and-yellow flag of Ukraine flew over the Maidan uprising, but so did the blue European flag with its golden stars.

KARL SCHLÖGEL, Vienna, June 2015

Russian journalists on their last day at work for the independent news website Lenta.ru, based in Moscow.

ONE

INFORMATION WAR

I N NORMAL TIMES, a writer can choose the circumstances of his work. He sets the rhythm in which he turns to his various tasks, works through a stack of books he has accumulated, constructs chapter after chapter. Everything has its time; the entire process is structured and manageable. But then there are moments, situations, that wreak havoc on a writer's plans; he is thrown off balance and must remake his arrangements and find a new footing if he hopes to keep up with his times. The pacing of his projects is then determined by outside events. He is compelled to react, devise some sort of response, not because he wants to get in on the game, make himself heard, 'raise his voice', but because he has been struck, because everything – the concerns of a lifetime's worth of study – is suddenly at stake, because he feels that, in some sense, he himself has been dealt a blow. He has no choice but to fight back – 'strike back' would perhaps be too strong. I found myself in such a situation when protesters were massacred on Kiev's Maidan Nezalezhnosti or Independence Square, generally known in the West simply as 'Maidan', and when Vladimir Putin spouted the bald-faced lie that there was no annexation of Crimea even as we watched it happen with our own eyes.

'Situation Room': an English phrase that entered general parlance at some point during the last year, presumably thanks to the popular format pioneered by CNN: 'You're in the Situation Room, where news and information are arriving all the time. Standing by: CNN reporters across the United States and around the world to bring you the day's top stories. Happening now . . . I'm Wolf Blitzer, and you're in the Situation Room.' The set-up is supposedly modelled on the White House Situation Room created under President Kennedy: a central control post where incoming information is collated and condensed in real time to provide a view of the world at a single glance.

When the world is so much with you that you can no longer go about the work you had set yourself to do, much, though perhaps not everything, is different. You stop trying to keep the news at bay; on the contrary, you depend on it, you hunger for it. If, like me, you have not given up resistance to the Internet and the pressure to be available at all times, you must rush to familiarize yourself with the web's technologies and techniques if you want to stay current. Not out of a penchant for visual thrills or as an idle pastime but because everything rides on the next piece of news, the next event: will the chain of violence be broken, will the machine come to a halt, or will the escalation continue? Disasters are not just conceivable but real at every moment. You are sucked into the maelstrom of information, which is now available in unlimited quantities, innumerable snippets of news that are infinitely diverse, contradictory, each giving the lie to the other. Casting about for something to hold on to, you turn to the summaries, analyses, editorials, opinion pieces that follow each other in rapid succession. But they do not let you catch your breath either, as developing events make their conclusions moot before the printer's ink has dried. You are a thousand miles away and yet right there, for thousands of eyes watch from thousands of vantage points throughout the space in which history unfolds. You are on a windowsill in a corner building overlooking an intersection in Donetsk's Leninsky District, observing everyday life in the occupied city: armoured vehicles are moving over there, but workers are also busy building bicycle lanes, while shelling can be heard in the distance. You see the pictures from the basements that have become bomb shelters and the press conferences of the warlords who have made themselves at home in the offices of the oligarchs. The interim director of the Donetsk Opera gives interviews about the season's repertoire. The sociologist who is forced to leave his university submits a final report on the new lines of social conflict in the city: a scholarly autopsy from the war zone.

All of this floods the study, coming in through a wide variety of channels: broadcasts on television, on Russian, Ukrainian and many other stations, and reports in newspapers that are available online – the *Donetsk Times*, the *Kharkiv Times*, the *Kyiv Post*, Moscow's *Novaya Gazeta*. You can watch as commentators make sense of the events on the discussion programmes: Savik Schuster's, in Russian and

Ukrainian, from Kiev; the one on Dozhd, the Moscow cable channel that is surprisingly still on air; interviews on *Ekho Moskvy*; and the unending and virtually unchanging ritual of the talk shows on the German stations. In Germany, people somehow still do not seem to grasp what is happening in Ukraine. Then there are pictures, letters, op-ed articles, démentis – everything accumulates in the study where a writer is usually at work on books that examine the history of the space in which these news stories originate. And you know that you will never be able to keep up, and know, too, that for the time being and perhaps for a long time, you will be powerless against the gravitational pull of habit, of ignorance, of proliferating and self-perpetuating prejudices. It is a feeling of boundless impuissance. In this situation room, where the news and images from Ukraine, primarily from the contested areas, converge, it is difficult to stay cool and hold your nerve.

Destabilization is not an abstract idea: a destabilization campaign of the sort conducted by Russia is directed against the 'authority', the 'sovereignty' of a state. But the true target of destabilization is the integrity of the adversary under attack, the country's society or, more precisely speaking, its people. The ultimate goal of a destabilization campaign against a state, a society, is to break people. To bring a country to its knees, one must bring its citizens to theirs. To force a government to surrender, one must force those who elected that government to submit, to accept submission. Escalation dominance is not something that is asserted against an abstract entity – a nation, an army, a government – but a form of *ad hominem* violence. Rules are dictated to someone, someone's will is imposed on someone, someone is given an ultimatum and must respond one way or another. Of course, those on whom this conflict has been forced can opt out, choosing resignation, indifference, cynicism, defeatism. All these attitudes are material factors in the ongoing struggle over Ukraine; in the past, they have sometimes been crucial, contributing to the escalation of wars, even triggering their outbreak. One thing they have never done is prevent a war.

It is never quiet in the situation room. Breaking news is announced around the clock. Time itself has a different cast. What is happening calls for commentary, even for an intervention, but those are hardly the historian's strengths. His métier is the *longue durée*, the completed series of events. He is competent when it comes to the past, to history, but his grasp of current affairs can be shaky. Current affairs are the business of the man of action who commands the tanks to advance or retreat and produces the next breaking news. He does not pause to offer explanations; those will come when all is done. The only antagonist who is a match for him is one who stands up to him – yet beyond the Ukrainians, who have no choice but to fight, such men are nowhere to be seen.

One effect of the new media is that we are always up to speed, that we have access to live images and can watch almost in real time as frontlines shift, villages and towns are captured, bridges and railway tracks are blown up. Thanks to Google Maps and satellite-based information systems, we can make out Donetsk's main thoroughfare, the football stadium, the culture park, the airport that has been reduced to rubble. We zoom in on a steppe crossed by European route E40 and the fields into which the Malaysian passenger plane crashed. The table in my study that is usually reserved for the maps on which I locate the scenes of historic events are now covered with charts that let me navigate the theatre of the current war: Gorlovka, Enakievo, Torez, Debaltsevo, Artyomovsk and on and on. We can follow the ongoing military operations and mark the new frontlines on our maps. We read the messages and letters from the war zone on the blogs, read about what is going on in the basements and the prisons. We become mere witnesses, onlookers, observing with our own eyes and ears a battle whose outcome others determine and others pay for with their lives.

To be in the situation room is to be lonely. Every one of us must make his own sense of the flood of images and news. The world of shared certainties falls apart, and our power of judgement is challenged, a test we had hoped we would never again be subjected to. The shells that explode in the cities and towns also shatter the portraits of their urban fabrics. The present does not allow us to study the past as it ought to be studied: from a distance. In a time of war, how could one paint the sweeping view of the Dnieper from the hill on which Kiev's Monastery of the Caves stands without opening himself to the charge of sentimentality? Portraits of cities are not wanted when the bombs fall. It is the war reporter's time and even more the war photographer's. Details that would otherwise be indispensable now sound like chatter, as if the speaker had more time than he knew what to do with, as if he were trying to cover up his embarrassment, as if he were oblivious of the world around him. It is an unfamiliar experience, being an eyewitness when the gloves come off. Describing battles is a craft we have never learned. Observers who offer their accounts from a distance, we are no longer needed. Our opinions have long divided us into stable camps that respected each other's cherished commonplaces, but that stability is disintegrating, and each one of us must stake out his position in light of a new set of circumstances. This realignment requires us to make decisions. It is an individual, a molecular process: it is not an anonymous 'society' that positions itself anew, that confronts an unwonted situation; everyone must make his own choice. The build-up of defensive capabilities against a war fomented by others comes after a protracted and agonizing period of destabilization, fragmentation, atomization. Destabilization is how the transition to a different Europe takes place. Will we endure, will we weather this storm? These anguished questions may already be obsolete by the time the book appears in print. Notes from yesterday.

TWO

FAREWELL TO EMPIRE,
FAREWELL TO RUSSIA?

THE ANNEXATION OF CRIMEA was, for me, the proverbial bolt out of the blue. Could we not have seen, or at least suspected, that it was coming? How was it possible that certain unequivocal portents were ignored or dismissed? Which mechanism of self-protection against a reality we felt to be menacing was in play? I had travelled to the Soviet Union and later to Russia on a regular basis for decades, but never once had I heard anyone say that Crimea was a 'festering wound', a source of constant pain for Russians. Had I been in denial, had I closed my eyes to what I did not want to know? But then in all those years, acquaintances and I had talked about all sorts of things that were on our minds. I do not remember a single conversation in Moscow or elsewhere in which Crimea was mentioned as a sore spot. It came up as a literary topos: antiquarian booksellers hawked Baedekers from the pre-revolutionary era and Soviet guides to the 'Red Riviera', and over time I compiled a small collection. But as a bone of contention, a controversial issue? Only one case comes to mind. I must confess that I was initially an admirer of Yury Luzhkov, the mayor of Moscow, whose gumption impressed me. I saw him as a legitimate heir to the city's great leaders before 1917, such as Pavel Tretyakov, a patron of the arts and benefactor; Luzhkov went about Moscow's transformation into a twenty-first-century global city with formidable energy. And so, although I knew that he was paying visits to Sevastopol, giving speeches about Crimea, collecting dona-tions, I did not take these activities entirely seriously until my friend, the sociologist Lev Gudkov, drew my attention to the mayor's Russian patriotism. He thought of it as dangerous, a steady campaign of prov-ocations and challenges stabbing at Ukraine. I realized that there was a flip side to Luzhkov's track record of success. But beyond this one instance, I never sensed the slightest concern with Crimea, let alone passionate interest in its fate. People who could afford to travel – and as the scene at Moscow's airports showed, many people could – went on holiday not in Crimea but in Paris, Florence, the Canary Islands, Greece, the Turkish Riviera around Antalya, or Sharm el-Sheikh. What struck me on my visits to Crimea was something else: the dilapidated infrastructure once I arrived in Simferopol; the palatial Soviet-era hotels that, far from being fully booked, often sat largely deserted; the brusque tone – another holdover from the Soviet era – with which the staff at the reception desk handled guests; the cheap fireworks on the promen-ade in Yalta; but also the city of Sevastopol, built of white stone, spread out in the brilliant sunlight just as in Alexander Deyneka's magnificent pictures from the 1930s. And I remember the shanties clinging to the hillsides, the settlements, I was told, of the Crimean Tatars who had recently returned in large numbers from Central Asia, where Stalin had had them deported in May 1944. So Crimea was an enchanting place out of time, a corner of the earth forgotten by history, rather than a hot spot of internal conflict or international embroilments. It was Putin who suddenly put Crimea on the map, who gave it a central part in Russian mythology and, more importantly, made its future a matter of war and peace.

Saying No to Putin

The annexation and especially Putin's brazen denial that it had taken place made it impossible for me to receive the Medal of Pushkin, which the President of the Russian Federation has given out since the 1990s for significant contributions to promoting the study of Russian culture abroad. I wrote to the Russian ambassador in Berlin, for whom I had the highest respect, that in light of the events I found myself unable to accept the award, which I was to be given in recognition of my work (I had first been notified in November 2013). Was that a cop-out? Was I giving in to the pressure of public opinion, which was outraged by Putin's *coup de main*? Was I being disloyal to Russia, even 'betraying' it? At the moment of supreme disappointment over the actions of the Russian leadership, would it not have been more imperative than ever to 'keep faith' with Russia?

Yet Russia's policy towards Ukraine – fomenting war against her quintessential 'sister nation' – threatened to undo everything that had been accomplished in German-Russian relations. For me, and I think for everyone who has studied it, Russia is more than a subject of research; it is deeply woven into our personal lives. And so, the so-called Ukrainian crisis was a moment of truth, challenging us to reconsider deeply held convictions and how we had arrived at them. It called for more than a review of the scholarship of the past and the evolution of the cultural, diplomatic or business relations between the countries. It struck to the core of our dedication to dialogue, and more was at stake than merely a position that might be revised or amended. What was cast in doubt was an undertaking to which we had devoted ourselves with heart and soul, an engagement that could not have remained without consequences, that might almost be called an enchantment or entanglement. In short, this was about Russia as an integral part of our biographies; the events in Ukraine called a major part of our life's work into question. However important and fruitful it may be to revisit the succession of felicitous German-Russian encounters as well as dramatic clashes between the countries over the past centuries, the very efforts at objectivity of such historical surveys, usually presented in chronological order, are a source of obfuscation. The main themes, the literary leitmotifs, the authors and their characters make their appearances, but the reader is left in the dark about the true mainsprings and forces of cohesion that operated and still operate in such relations. They proffer specious explanations rather than genuine illumination. These might be questions fit for private soul-searching if they did not have implications for society at large. For the stakes are considerable; clarity is needed on which stance one should take – which stance the Germans should take – on Russia's Ukraine policy. To gauge the gravitational pull exerted by the 'Russia complex', we must first acknowledge it, and rather than draw up an abstract sketch of an abstract history of ideas, we might as well start with ourselves. Its power grows out of experiences no less than ideas, out of impressions no less than readings.

Growing up in the 1950s in a village in the Allgäu, a rural area in the far south of Germany, possibly the remotest corner of a country that was in some ways cut off from the wider world, I thought of Russia as a faraway land. But the graves in the cemetery and the plaque in the chapel dedicated to the memory of the village's dead soldiers spoke a different language. They bore the names of families I knew and, next to them, those of towns or, much more often, vague and imprecise information, as though specifications of place and time had no traction in that enormous space: 'Killed in Russia, Winter 1942'. Russia, that was war and war captivity, the subjects of conversations we children overheard, especially when, once a year, father got together with fellow soldiers who had made it out alive. Russia – more specifically, Stalingrad, Siberia – became what, using a later coinage, we would call a literal *lieu de mémoire*, a space fleshed out in the imagination by what I found rummaging through the not altogether very well-stocked library of the boarding school run by Benedictine monks: *So weit die Füße tragen* by Josef Martin Bauer, a writer who had attended my own school, and *Die Armee hinter Stacheldraht* by Edwin Erich Dwinger, an author I would later identify as a monumental figure of German light fiction and manufacturer of 'Siberia as a landscape of the German soul'. At home, Russia was rarely ever spoken of. Father had 'taken part' in the war from 1 September 1939 – the beginning of the 'Polish campaign' – until the end in the spring of 1945, spending most of that time on the eastern front as a simple soldier and driver, as he said. That was where the jagged-edged black-and-white pictures came from that he kept in a tin box, pictures of the sort that German squaddies had brought home by the hundreds of thousands, even millions: blown-up bridges; pillars of smoke rising from towns whose names were sometimes recorded on the back of the photographs and which I recognized when I visited them decades later; river sceneries – the San, the Dnieper – and market squares, pigs and geese being slaughtered, the crew taking a bath in a river, the *Rollbahn* stretching towards an infinitely vast space. There were, too, the names of towns and transportation hubs that got stuck in the child's mind, configuring a mental map that I retain today: Lviv, Lublin, Orsha, Kremenchuk, Kramatorsk, Stalino. Later, after my father's death, I was able to reconstruct the entire journey that had taken him from the Allgäu to the eastern front and the wider world. It turned out that I had unknowingly travelled along the same routes.

I sighted my first 'Russians' on the transit motorway from Bavaria to West Berlin. The political socialization of West German pupils of the late 1950s and 1960s would not have been complete without these obligatory educational trips with funding support from the Federal Ministry of the Interior. Here lies a major difference between the experiences of growing up in East and West Germany. In the East, citizens lived in a sort of cohabitation with Russians, with barracks, athletic facilities, officers' villas, special shops, and trains labelled 'Wünsdorf–Saratov' in Cyrillic letters. However hermetically sealed the world of the Soviet armed services may have been, these were part of the interior of the East German lifeworld, just as GIS, jeeps and the malls of the U.S. Army were in the West. So I encountered 'Russians' first in a car park outside a service area near Leipzig and then, a little later, in the 'Druzhba' bookstores in East Berlin, in Prague, Sofia and all the other cities I visited when I started travelling in the Eastern Bloc in the mid-1960s. There was an allure to everything Russian: the director Benno Besson's production of Evgeny Schwartz's *The Dragon* at the Deutsches Theater had an aura of non-conformism; Evgeny Evtushenko came to Munich with his poems 'Babi Yar' and 'The Heirs of Stalin', an event prominently featured in *Die Zeit*, which also printed the complete texts, a clarion call of de-Stalinization. The reading left me spellbound, the epitome of something that has never ceased to mesmerize me: the poet declaiming on the stage; I later experienced something similar when Joseph Brodsky came to Berlin, or when I listened to a physicist reciting Esenin's poetry in the hills above the beach at Sochi – the gravitas of the spoken word, people knowing entire poems by heart, a cultural practice that, back home, had already fallen out of fashion when I went to school. It was probably also in these experiences that my fascination with the phenomenon known as the 'intelligentsia' was born, that small and marginal group of people who believed in their moral right and fought for their convictions, risking to sacrifice everything and bending the course of history.

Nothing in life is preordained, and it took a series of coincidences to put me on the Russian track. A Bavarian grammar school – and one run by Benedictines! – in which Russian was taught was uncommon enough. It was there that we rehearsed our first Russian songs, under the tutelage of a teacher who was actually a Pole; a native of Białystok, he had ended up as a 'displaced person' in the American occupation zone when the war ended. Our teachers, the priests, were receptive to novel ideas. We saw their war wounds – one had taken a shot through the cheek, another's leg was smashed – and could tell that they were infinitely grateful for having escaped with their lives, not least thanks to the mercy simple people had taken on them that they had had no right or reason to expect after everything that had happened in 'Russia'. They spoke a distinctive idiom: the Russian of war prisoners. The environment was presumably also informed by the new open-mindedness of the Church – this was the time of the Second Vatican Council, which our abbot played an important part in preparing: he was prominently involved in ecumenical dialogue and the Church's relations with the patriarchs of Constantinople and Moscow. And Munich was nearby, a city that (unlike the endangered island of West Berlin) was then home to a considerable community of Russians in exile. Rumour later had it that the philosopher, sociologist and writer Fyodor Stepun – who had been exiled from Soviet Russia in 1922, taught in Dresden before the war, and then had become the embodiment of the 'Russian spirit' at the University of Munich after 1945 – spent his summer holidays at our school, a stranger whom we espied only from afar, recognizing him by his beret over a shock of snow-white hair.

In this environment, it was not entirely absurd that I would write a letter to Khrushchev – or was it merely to Radio Moscow? – and receive, a few months later, a reply: two bulky parcels of books, wrapped in the sturdy coarse paper that is now part of the material culture of a distant era. I first saw the world behind the Iron Curtain during my final years in school, on a journey to Prague, which became my *porta orientis*: the outwardly unscathed metropolis of Central Europe – an almost incomprehensible sight for me, who knew only cities ravaged by bombing – and scene of the budding Kafka myth, it was also the breeding ground of a political movement that would blossom and go to its demise only a few years later under the name the 'Prague Spring'.

My earliest physical encounters with 'Russia' – a shortcut that always referred to the Soviet Union – occurred the year before I graduated and then after I enrolled at Freie Universität in Berlin. I wrote down the story of the school trip in my first extended essay, titled 'Russisches Tagebuch' (Russian Diary), which I published under a pseudonym, Paul Tjomny (in part out of coquettishness and in part due to the lingering fear of repercussions in the Cold War era). Reading it today, I am struck by how carefully the excursion was prepared – we had attended seminars on historical materialism inspired by the leading expert of the period, the Jesuit professor Gustav A. Wetter, on collectivization in Soviet agriculture and the planned economy, but also on Russian literature and the Thaw. The trip itself was organized by our class with financial support from local businesses, including Hipp, the makers of baby food, and it took us to Moscow via Vienna, Budapest, Uzhhorod, Mukachevo, Lviv, Kiev, Kharkov and Kursk, concluding – we were, after all, a Catholic boarding school – with a visit to the town of Zagorsk, a centre of the Russian Orthodox Church and pilgrimage destination, which has since discarded its revolutionary-era eponym and is once again known as Sergiev Posad. Two years later, we crammed into a Renault 4 and drove from West Berlin via Stockholm, Helsinki, Vyborg, Leningrad, Moscow, Kursk, Rostov-on-Don, Grozny, Ordzhonikidze, Tbilisi and Yerevan to the Soviet-Iranian border and then back via Sochi, Kiev, Slovakia and Prague – this was a year after the invasion by Warsaw Pact troops – to Berlin.

The lasting impact these and later trips criss-crossing the map of the Soviet Union had on me is of interest for our context only insofar as it has bearing on my attempts to come to a better understanding of an experience that now, decades later, appears to have been called in question, even confuted. Looking back, it is tempting to think that a wish to promote German–Soviet or German–Russian reconciliation was the mainspring behind my interest in Russia. But that would be to cast my curiosity in narrowly political terms, and to claim the mantle of a moral mission 'to overcome stereotypes of the enemy'. In 1950s and 1960s West Germany, the choice of Russia was for many an expression of their desire to see and do something completely different. At a time when everyone longed to go to France or England, why not head off in the opposite direction, towards the East rather than the West, to the Soviet Union? The fascination of the very foreign was no doubt part of it, but so was the wish to be different, to do something or be someone out of the ordinary, and the more pushback we encountered – from our parents or schools – the better. To immerse oneself in Russian culture and history was to take a stance that was perhaps not outright combative but certainly a cautious proclamation of difference, of dissension. It would be disingenuous not to acknowledge that it set us apart and let us feel special.

Fascination

Taking an interest in the East did not require any sacrifices from us (in contrast with those communists who faced persecution in the Federal Republic and even went to prison for their loyalty to the 'fatherland of the workers'). On the contrary, abundant rewards beckoned: the discovery of a universe that had disappeared behind the Iron Curtain, of another European history we had lost sight of when the world was divided. To travel to the Eastern Bloc and especially to the Soviet Union was to explore a world unto itself, a space of experiences and histories waiting to be unearthed. It has become fashionable to talk about the fascination of the 'foreign', the 'invention of the other', but what drew me in was the opportunity to get to know and study a history that to us – I am thinking of West Germans – had gradually become unintelligible. I cannot say that the Soviet Union as a political system ever appealed to me. It was an entirely different dimension that captivated me, and presumably others as well. How should I sketch its outlines here if not in the form of an autobiographical narrative?

Arriving in the Soviet Union, one entered into an unfamiliar temporal horizon, bidding farewell, at least for an instant, to an era defined by speed and strained nerves. Time stood still in Russia, time had no value, making every visit a relaxing experience; the maxim that 'time is money' – an English phrase that is proverbial in German – was suspended. One felt this unwonted sense of timelessness acutely in days and nights spent on trains and in nocturnal kitchen-table conversations during which the hours ceased to matter. A journey into a lost past, into the time of childhood? Others, of course, suffered the same standstill of time as painful and debilitating stagnation, spending their lives in endless queues.

Another aspect of travelling in the Soviet Union was the country's vast expanse, undivided by boundaries once one had passed the great boundary that enclosed and sealed off 'one sixth of the earth'. To leave the compartmentalized geography of Western and especially Central Europe was to have a sort of epiphany: here – no less than in the United States, where I and others sensed something similar around the same time – was a great wide world. It was thrilling to be able to look back towards Europe, with its narrowness and provincial ways, from the 'Russian space'. To escape the insularity of their divided native land, some Germans roamed southeastwards, to Istanbul and on to Tehran, Kabul and Goa, while others flew to the United States to drive down Highway 66, and yet others – though we were fewer – felt the allure of Russia, the immensity of an empire in which trains travelled between Moscow and Tashkent, between Leningrad and Odessa, a space in which the visitor might lose his way, might disappear from the radar, beyond the reach of anyone trying to contact him. The empire: it was in the great rivers that the Trans-Siberian Railway bridged, in the Georgian Military Road across the Caucasus, in the smelting works scattered across the steppes like Cyclopean sculptures. And the determined traveller undeterred by some discomfort was free to roam this land in its entirety. We quickly figured out that there was an official reality in which stamps, outer offices and permits were all-important and another in which all that bureaucracy could be ignored with impunity. Yes, there was a peculiar imperial charm in the homogeneity – uniformity is a less kind word – of the Soviet way of life, which did not vary between Minsk, Novosibirsk and Vladivostok, and beneath it a much older stratum: classicist buildings, governors' palaces, merchant villas, railway stations, the architectures that had transformed that wide and heterogeneous space into the 'one and indivisible' space of empire, all the revolutions, wars, disruptions, modernization campaigns, and disasters wrought by technology notwithstanding.

I am not sure there is such a thing as the quintessential Russian, but I know that Klaus Mehnert's book *Der Sowjetmensch*, a portrait of Soviet man, which came out in the late 1950s, made a powerful impression on me. I could tell that the author – born in Moscow, he had studied in Germany before moving to the Soviet Union in the early 1930s, filled with youthful enthusiasm – had understood something about the country and its people. I also know that, on my first trips, I met people who conformed to the positive stereotype about Russians in every respect. In the streets and railway stations one still saw the war invalids, double amputees who sat on wooden platforms on castors, using their hands wrapped in sackcloth to propel themselves forward. On camping grounds I ran into veterans in their blue-and-white striped sailor shirts who welcomed a young German visitor, and moreover one from the divided country's western part, as though nothing had happened: no war, no mass casualties, no scorched earth. Their heartfelt friendliness and generosity – and I know I am not the only one who encountered it – was casual and almost intimate, not at all a display of moral superiority, not a conscious effort to bury the past in silence in the presence of the enemy's descendant. Much has been said about the warmth and hospitality of 'the Russians'; I have always thought of it as a holdover from the village community, or as a characteristic way of people who needed to stick together in hardship if they hoped to pull through. And so virtually everyone who 'went to the other side' felt welcome and among friends; many who were alienated by the relentless pace, the indifference and 'coldness' of the West found in Russia a sort of second homeland. This refuge, it seems, has crumbled in the harsh climate of the post-Soviet world.

The Other Russia Was Real

As I try to get to the bottom of the peculiar attachment that formed over many years, the fondness that makes it so difficult for many of us to see Putin's Russia for what it is, there are other aspects that come into play. When I was a student in West Berlin, the Wall was a tangible reality; I came face to resentfully joyless face with the border officials at the checkpoint at Friedrichstraße and saw the Warsaw Pact tanks in Prague in 1968. For people who raved about the Chinese Cultural Revolution without knowing much of anything about it, Soviet communism was without interest. For a radical leftist, however, the history of twentieth-century Russia was an inexhaustible treasure house of role models, intriguing characters and heroic gestures, of innumerable tragedies and personal as well as collective fates, all bound up with a 'betrayed revolution'. Beyond all the imitations, disguises and travesties, there was a pervasive fascination or certainly an apprehension that this 'Russian century' had been an era of positively biblical grandeurs and horrors. There was a kind of hot core that had still not gone cold, a legacy for later generations to unriddle. Choose your obsession: the Russian Revolution, the Silver Age, Budyonny's Cavalry Army, Trotsky's intellectual physiognomy, Serge Diaghilev's Ballets Russes in Paris, the Soviet avant-garde, Constructivism, El Lissitzky, Sergei Eisenstein's cinematic aesthetic – elements of a history that deserved to be remembered but remained incompletely understood, that was truncated or misrepresented to fit political expediency, as in the GDR, that needed to be brought back to light. Even more importantly, after the devastations of Stalinism, something was astir in the Soviet Union itself: dissidents, civil rights activists, an underground press, writers as the 'conscience of the nation', the rebirth of the intelligentsia and the intelligentsia myth. However little interest the Soviet Union under Brezhnev and the men who followed him in quick succession, their health already failing when they assumed office, held for the Western left, the figures who emerged from the underground and took on the powers that be were fascinating. They were people we identified with, they deserved our solidarity, they gave us new hope that history would continue. Meeting the dissidents – first, in the mid-1970s, in the centres of the new diaspora, in Paris, London, Copenhagen, Munich, then, in the early 1980s, in the Moscow and Leningrad scenes – we felt that we were witnessing a revival of the heroism and self-sacrifice of Russia's historic radical and revolutionary movement. That was the context in which I wrote my studies of labour opposition in the Soviet Union, Petersburg as the laboratory of modernism, the discourses of the Russian intelligentsia, the Russian Berlin of the 1920s, and the Great Terror of 1937 in Moscow.

It would be altogether strange to describe my work as an effort at reconciliation or rapprochement, as a mission or a sacrifice that needed to be offered. It was something far more modest and yet infinitely more: the opening of a continent the explorer gradually came to know, with the horrendous fates it had inflicted on some of its people, sufferings that we who had grown up in an orderly world of peace and prosperity could scarcely imagine. It was this discovery of another universe, another history, that we were taken with and that we sought to share with our countrymen at home. The sometimes self-important chatter that has become so fashionable today about the 'need to deepen' or 'maintain the dialogue' is the privilege of people who have never taken part in the adventure of these encounters or have made the organization of dialogue the lucrative business of an ostensibly high-minded profession. The dialogue never broke off, it continued across the Wall and underneath the Iron Curtain; it did not need to be invented by diplomats or staged by politicians looking for their stab at immortality. The kitchens of 1970s and 1980s Moscow were the birthplace of an unceasing conversation about anything and everything, a conversation that came out into the open during Perestroika, into the public sphere, television, the squares of the major cities, and parliament – only to be marginalized or driven into exile once more by Putin's regime and the media it has brought into line.

A Fresh Start and a Dead End

When the Soviet Union was disbanded, there was ample reason to fear disaster; few empires had ever left the stage without violence. But there was just as much reason to hope that the new states emerging from the disintegrating empire, the Russian Federation among them, would eventually stabilize in new forms and establish their internal legitimacy as sovereign nations. Looking back from the Putin era, in the perspective of those who have (for the time being) prevailed, the 1990s can be neatly summed up as a period of 'troubles', the years in the wilderness, a time of robbery and murder, of utter disorientation and the unscrupulous embezzlement of state property, of mob rule and oligarchy, of looting and capital flight. Theorists of transition look back on the failure of a programme that was, they say, appropriate in and of itself but could not be implemented properly due to a lack of qualified personnel.

Among the causes for cautious optimism was the fact that the end of the empire also put an end to the burdens of empire; that Russians, racing with almost disturbing alacrity to make up for lost time, underwent learning processes that would have been impossible in the entrenched structures of Western societies; that millions of people shunned no risk and spared no sacrifice to remake their lives – from the phenomenon known as *euroremont*, in which they remodelled their apartments to bring them up to Western European standards, to the establishment of entire new professional fields. There was much to suggest that the country, though exhausted and strained to its limits, would avoid collapsing into civil war and find a new balance, that it was improvising while lives were being rebuilt, a process that was inevitably messy and defied central control. The wildness of those years – in the streetscapes as much as in the country's intellectual life, in people's private relationships as much as in the institutional chaos – was appalling, but equally baffling was that Russia somehow mustered the strength to endure the wrenching changes that were manifest everywhere, in the so-called provinces no less than in the cities, without falling apart. The stability Putin promised has turned out in retrospect to have been a mirage: sustained by wealth flooding into the country thanks to oil and gas exports, it was never matched by genuine modernization and hinged on a single individual who lives in the dangerous illusion that his fortunes are inseparable from Russia's.

For those of us who have long taken an active interest in Russia's present and future, watching Putin manoeuvre the country into a dead end by picking a fight with Ukraine has been more than just one of those disappointments that adult life inevitably brings. However, once we have resigned ourselves to the humiliating defeat this unexpected turn of history has inevitably dealt to our hopes, with consequences that will extend beyond our lifetimes, we can recognize that, like any act of destruction, it brings a new freedom: here is an opportunity to think again and afresh about Russia.

Perplexity and Sentimentality

People in the West are bewildered by the new situation, especially in Germany. Putin has dared to do the unthinkable – a war against the 'sister nation'! Territorial integrity no longer matters; troops and materials are being shipped across the border; thousands have been killed; hundreds of thousands have become refugees; Donetsk, a city of a million people only yesteryear, is a ghost town terrorized by irregular militias recruited from criminals, former Chechnya fighters, Russian high-tech experts, Spetsnaz agents and career public relations specialists. What began as a lightning operation against Crimea has transitioned into an undeclared war whose end is nowhere in sight. Putin has not brought Ukraine to heel, at least not yet – on the contrary his actions have unwittingly helped to catalyse a process of nation formation that, in less dramatic circumstances, might well have taken decades or generations. Yet not only has his plan not worked out, but he has steered Russia into a dead end worse than anything that embargoes, containment strategies, sanctions or the evil deeds of an Evil Empire could have inflicted on his country – a situation in which no one can tell what will happen next.

It has been a shocking development, especially for those of us who have dedicated our lives to studying Russia and helping improve relations between Westerners and Russians. We all wonder whether there were signals we failed to hear or see, whether we even deceived ourselves and others and now face the ruination of all our efforts. There are those who claim that they saw it all coming. I am not among them. Many still recall Putin's speech before the German parliament in September 2001, perhaps not without a certain emotion. Then, in 2005, Putin described the dissolution of the Soviet Union as the 'greatest geopolitical catastrophe of the twentieth century', which took some observers aback, and his speech at the 2007 Munich Security Conference has been characterized by attendees as a slap in the audience's face and indeed a 'relapse into the Cold War'. These speeches have been analysed a thousand times, each of their rhetorical qualities and semantic nuances held up to scrutiny, and deservedly so. The address in the Bundestag, delivered in a building whose walls are graced by meticulously restored graffiti by Red Army soldiers who took part in the final battle for Berlin, captured a dynamic in which many strands of history converged. There was the simple fact that a Russian president addressed the German parliament.

A native of Leningrad, a city still deeply marked in his childhood years by the German army's blockade, the city in which his brother had died, he nonetheless chose to speak in the language of Schiller and Goethe. Here was a Russian president who seemed to refute at a single stroke all the prejudices that many harboured because he had worked as a spy in Dresden. His very physique made him the diametrical opposite of the rhetorically inept gerontocrats who had dominated the Soviet Union's functionary class. Speaking where he did, he reminded his listeners of the German-Russian tragedies of the twentieth century and derived lessons from the two countries' experience of twofold totalitarianism before sketching an open future in which all conflicts could be resolved at long last and the great challenges of the next decades would be tackled, delineating a programme that entrepreneurs, engineers, bankers, artists and museum directors had dreamt of for decades. He cut an imposing and winsome figure. All contradictions and antagonisms seemed to dissolve in an atmosphere of the earnest wish and ability on both sides to understand the other.

It is not difficult to grasp, even in retrospect, why the address was interrupted several times by applause that finally grew into standing ovations. A sense of gratitude for Russia's role in making the reunification of Germany possible was part of it, always tinged with the German feeling of guilt towards 'the Russians'; so were the readily understandable longing for peace after a century of horrendous violence and the idea that all problems, however daunting, could be resolved in dialogue. These are the broad outlines of the ensemble of dispositions and expectations that remains operative today like an erratic block of the mind, now solidified by nostalgia often admixed with sloppy sentiment, producing in some the firm conviction that the Germans and 'the West' squandered the future by rebuffing Putin when he 'wooed' them.

Putin's appearance at the Munich Security Conference in 2007 was perceived as a self-confident, even swaggering, comeback of Russia on the international stage: he gave the West a stern talking-to, accusing it of applying moral double standards, breaking its promises and flouting international norms with increasing abandon. He castigated the United States in particular for aspiring to global dominance in a unipolar world order. A great power that had difficulties enough adapting to the end of the old bipolar world and the new global disorder, America was an easy target for these charges; exhibit A was the Iraq War, waged by an alliance led by George W. Bush, whose government had deceived

An armed unit marches outside a Ukrainian military area, in a village outside
Simferopol, Crimea, 7 March 2014.

the global public. Ever since, Putin has been the man who 'is teaching those Westerners' and especially 'the Americans' who are allegedly pulling the strings; the man rallying all those who stand against the arrogance of power, against America, and more generally against globalization and its consequences. He is the avenger of self-perceived victims of all stripes – casualties of the pressures of consumerist societies, of Hollywood movies, of the NSA, and perhaps even of a German reunification gone awry. These are the ingredients for the narrative that 'the West' bears responsibility for the 'Ukraine crisis' and that Russia is the victim of the West's and NATO's aggressive policies.

Humiliation and Failing Man

But the great Russia is not the victim, however much Putin makes himself out to be the defender of a beleaguered nation. The sense of debasement and humiliation he foments and exploits for demagogic effect is not the result of an encirclement by menacing outside forces; it springs from the disgraceful situation within the world's largest country, which, under his rule, has proven incapable of taking the steps necessary to bring it into the twenty-first century.

No one who witnessed the chaos of 1990s Russia, which resembled a Darwinian fight for survival, could fail to sympathize with the population's yearning for discipline and public peace. In a wealth grab without precedent in history, the so-called elites were busy seizing whatever public property they could get hold of and stashing their wealth abroad – the oligarchs of the 1990s would be superseded in the 2000s by secret-service men and the self-declared 'new aristocracy' that manned the apparatus of power. Cyprus, the City of London, real-estate agents on the Côte d'Azur, and other offshore financial centres all profited handsomely from these flows of money. Yes, one could tell that something was off about the new stability that went hand in hand with the enforced conformity of the media. Nowhere was the wealth on more brazen and immoderate display than in Moscow. Conditions in the country resembled those familiar from developing nations: mind-boggling luxury in the metropolis as the vast countryside slowly reverted into a trackless wilderness. But having read our Marx, we were aware that 'the West', too, had gone through a bloody and dirty primitive accumulation of capital, that it had taken generations to 'civilize' private wealth. Visiting Russia on a regular basis, we also saw how progress was being made here and there, how it was becoming a 'normal' country, and it was from these observations that we drew encouragement that the rest of the country would get there, too – by its own efforts and without the prescriptions of the Chicago Boys.

But the wealth that poured into the country thanks to a felicitously timed boom in the oil and gas markets did not fuel its modernization, the renewal of massive infrastructures like the Trans-Siberian Railway, or the building of high-speed rail links, technology parks and communication networks. More people have left Russia over the past decade than at any time in its history – an unprecedented exodus of highly qualified young workers who see no opportunities for themselves in their own country. Not even the wave of emigration after 1917 constituted a comparable brain drain. Millions of people – primarily residents of major urban areas – have travelled abroad as tourists or on business in the last twenty years and seen with their own eyes the infrastructures, services and business culture that can be created in a decade; the Chinese economic miracle, in particular, left Russian visitors aghast. The 1990s were a period of turmoil in which all certainties melted away, with meteoric careers and dramatic falls from power. Rage, frustration, disorientation, the need to identify enemies were widespread in a country in which oligarchs and bureaucrats acted or sat on their hands as they pleased with impunity, in which 'stabilization' was tantamount to state control, vertical hierarchies of power and the redistribution of property in favour of an unbridled kleptocracy. Hatred and envy were rampant. Pollsters have correctly noted the deep-seated feeling of humiliation and indignity, but those have little to do with distant forces like NATO or the EU or Obama's unnecessarily cutting remark that 'Russia is a regional power' and everything with life in a country that offers no opportunities to capable and energetic people with good qualifications. They leave because the prospects for more participation in decision-making and a fairer and more predictable legal system are non-existent. The so-called Ukraine crisis is a Russian crisis first and foremost, brought on by a government that was never up to the task of a century: modernizing a nation. Occupying Crimea in a small operation executed with surgical precision turned out to be easier than finishing the Moscow–St Petersburg motorway. The internal situation in Russia rarely comes up in the Western discussion, even though the knowledge, expertise and literature are readily available. It is easier to interpret Putin's policies as an outcome of and reaction to outside threats (encirclement, containment, the enlargement of NATO and so on) and the understandable decisions of a country tormented by 'phantom pains' – in short, as the fault of others, the West, led by America. An added advantage of this view is that one does not need to know the first thing about Russia to chime in.

The West Out of Its Depth: Ukraine – Terra incognita

Nor does one need to know anything about Ukraine – when it is even so much as mentioned in the debate. Europe's second-largest country by area, a nation of 45 million, Ukraine has been independent since 1991, but until lately it barely existed on most Europeans' mental maps; most thought of it as a formerly Russian and then Soviet province. Not at all long ago, Ukrainian was regarded not as a distinct language but as a slightly defective variant, a dialect, of Russian. Germans, in particular, were somehow unable or unwilling to understand how someone could be a Russian-speaking Ukrainian, or to recognize that the country is more thoroughly bilingual than almost any other in Europe. They know a great deal about the crimes their ancestors perpetrated in the Soviet Union, but their feelings of guilt are directed solely towards 'Russians' – as though there had not been millions of Ukrainian Red

Army soldiers, millions of Ukrainian forced labourers in the Reich, not to mention the Shoah on Ukrainian territory. Until recently, Ukraine figured in most Germans' worldview as mere periphery, a backyard, glacis, sphere of influence or buffer zone, an object for others to handle, not a subject with its own vision of its history and the right to organize its life as it sees fit, a right that is accorded to any other nation, no strings attached. The historical experiences of the peoples living between Russia and Germany – most saliently, the Polish and the Baltic nations – still count for little in this discourse or are even dismissed as an idiosyncrasy, a sort of hysteric reaction that makes them incapable of engaging in realpolitik.

If there is a reproach that the West or the EU deserve, it is not that they were overzealous in their commitment to the interests of their Eastern neighbours. On the contrary, the latter were perceived as a burden, threatening the cohesion of Europe and the European Union with their impertinent pleas, especially at a time of internal crisis. The High Representative of the Union for Foreign Affairs, Lady Ashton, was not the only one who was out of her depth in the 'Ukraine crisis' of 2013. For too long, Westerners reassured themselves with the mantra of the society-in-transformation, the automatic and inevitable transition from planned to market economy, from dictatorship to democracy, even years after the actual trajectory of history, in a period of 'troubles', had diverged widely from this predetermined course. For decades, the mere mention of geopolitics had elicited knowing smiles – its insights were allegedly obsolete – but suddenly, in a phrase that was widely bandied about, 'geography mattered'. Caught by surprise, too, were those critical critics who had long bid adieu to the 'history of great men' and now found themselves confronted with the ascent of a man who demonstrated 'escalation dominance', put the world's most powerful military alliance on the defensive, and played the media with great skill and an unerring sense of timing.

Not only was Europe unprepared for this new kind of warfare, but it is still trying to catch up with Putin's comprehensive information war. There is talk of a 'return to the Cold War', while the small, local, non-linear, so-called hybrid war is already on. No one on the talk shows has the military expertise to explain what is happening. Looking for information, one learns more in the depths of the Internet than from the bulletins of the intelligence services, whose – taxpayer-funded – business it should be to stay abreast of the developing conflict.

European experts are beginning to discover geopolitics when in reality this is already about something unheard-of and yet strangely familiar: the old and new conjunction of 'people and soil', of territory and *ethnos*, a national-imperial mixture that has exploded with devastating force before. That is in fact exactly what Putin proclaimed on 18 March 2014: Russia, he said, believed that it had the right and the obligation to intervene wherever Russians and Russian-speaking people lived. It was the sort of thing one had heard from Germany's Freikorps in the interwar years – 'wherever we are is Germany.' We can all only guess which other places Putin might have referred to: the Baltic republics, Moldavia, Georgia, perhaps even Germany, which has over 3 million Russian-speaking residents and hundreds of thousands carrying Russian passports.

Information War

Since the occupation of Crimea, the brazen lie proffered with perfect sangfroid has become a staple of Russia's television channels. Worse, we are expected to believe that the difference between fact and fiction, between truth and lie, no longer obtains. Putin's media people are not only well-versed in the idiom of postmodernism, they have also internalized the values of Holy Russia. They ridicule the European Union with its 28 members as a heterogeneous construct incapable of concerted action and too weak to stand by its values and defend itself militarily. In his address to the nation, Putin presented himself as the champion of the real European values and spokesman and leader of a new International that has room for German leftists as well as the nationalist right in France, a coalition of all forces that display sufficient anti-European and, more importantly, anti-American animus, a movement that does not balk at inviting notorious anti-Semites and neo-Nazis to Moscow even as the state-owned television channels drum up support for the fight against the 'fascist junta' in Kiev.

Everyone has the choice: between Putin's Russia and another Russia that is still out there, despite all the nationalist and chauvinistic mobilization, a Russia that struggles to retain the few channels and spaces to which it has been relegated and withstand the onslaught of the mob unleashed against 'agents' and 'traitors to the fatherland'.

The Other Russia Speaks Up

The annexation of Crimea acted as a catalyst for the tensions within the Russian intelligentsia. Representatives of the country's educated class responded with two public appeals, one approving of and one rejecting the military intervention. Even before Putin's major speech on 18 March 2014, in which he justified the annexation at length, representatives of Russian cultural life published a statement in support of the president's position on Ukraine and Crimea. They wrote:

> In these days when the fate of Crimea and our countrymen is being decided, the Russian arts community cannot remain cold-hearted and indifferent observers. Our common history and roots, our culture and its spiritual sources, our fundamental values and language have always united us. We would like the shared identity of our peoples and cultures to have a solid future. This is why we strongly support the position of the President of the Russian Federation on Ukraine and Crimea.

The letter was signed by over five hundred prominent figures, including numerous artists and culture professionals whose renown extends beyond Russia's borders: people such as the violist Yury Bashmet; the conductor Valery Gergiev; the documentary film-maker Stanislav Govorukhin; Iosif Kobzon, a crooner who had been popular throughout the Union; and the Moscow-based architect Mikhail Posokhin. Some added individual statements elaborating on their reasons for supporting Putin's policies: many grew up in the multi-ethnic Soviet empire's mixed families, many recalled personal negative experiences with Ukrainian nationalism and many decried the 'fascist policies' of the leadership in Kiev.

A letter by the writer Lyudmila Ulitskaya and the human-rights activist Lev Ponomaryov published in the 13 March 2014 issue of *Novaya Gazeta* expressed a different position. The two argued that,

> Our country has become embroiled in a highly risky venture. Crimea has effectively been annexed already, under cries of, 'Let us defend the Russians in the Crimea and all Ukrainians from the new illegitimate fascist powers in Ukraine!' International law has been gravely violated and the principles of European

security and stability have been shattered. Russia is hurtling headlong towards a new Cold War with the West that would have unforeseeably grave consequences. All state-owned mass media in Russia flood the country with streams of lies and disinformation, and a no less well-orchestrated and deafening propaganda campaign targets everyone who attempts to call the lawfulness of the authorities' actions into question and point out their baleful consequences for the country and the people. Those who disagree are vilified as 'Fifth Columnists' and 'fascists'. And there are many who dissent. A quick review of the uncensored mass media or the numerous comments on the social networks shows that political scientists, economists, foreign-policy professionals and people who simply have a shred of social sensitivity left are warning that Russia is headed toward a veritable catastrophe – an economic, political and humanitarian disaster. Writers of the Russian pen Centre, the Human Rights Council – which unites the most important leaders of the major civil rights organizations – as well as filmmakers, scientists, ecologists, rock stars (Grebenshchikov, Makarevich, Shevchuk, Butusov) and many others have spoken out against the war.

The appeal was signed by around 250 representatives of Russian cultural life, including numerous members of the Academy of Sciences; well-known civil rights activists such as Lyudmila Alekseeva and Sergei Kovalyov, veterans of the dissident movement; the writer Alla Bossart; the poet Alina Vitukhnovskaya; Vladimir Sorokin, Vladimir Voinovich, Alexander Genis and Viktor Erofeev; the sociologist Boris Dubin; the publisher Irina Prokhorova; theatre and film directors like Mark Rozovsky and Eldar Ryazanov; the economist Irina Yasina and the literary scholar Marietta Chudakova. The large number of prominent writers and representatives of the old civil rights and dissident movements among the signatories is noteworthy. Many of them had taken part in the Bolotnaya Square protest campaign against election fraud December 2011, and many remained actively involved after signing the letter, for example by participating in a conference of Russian and Ukrainian intellectuals in Kiev organized by the businessman Mikhail Khodorkovsky. An essay by Ulitskaya in *Der Spiegel* exemplifies the mood among these intellectuals and their courage:

I live in Russia. I am a Russian writer of Jewish origin, was brought up in a Christian culture. Now my country is at war with the culture, the values of humanism, freedom of the individual and the idea of human rights, the fruits of the entire development of civilization. My country is sick with aggressive ignorance, nationalism and imperial megalomania. I am ashamed of my ignorant and aggressive parliament, of my aggressive and incompetent government, of the political leadership – supporters of violence and treachery aiming at the role of supermen. I am ashamed of all of us, of our people, who have lost their moral compass. Culture in Russia has suffered a heavy defeat, and we artists and writers cannot alter the suicidal political course of our nation. Our country's intellectual community is divided: as in the early years of the century, only a minority speaks out against the war. With every passing day, my country pushes the world closer to the brink of war. Our militarism has sharpened its claws in Chechnya and Georgia, now it is training in Crimea and Ukraine. Farewell, Europe – I am afraid we will never become part of the European family of nations. Our great culture, our Tolstoy and Chekhov, Tchaikovsky and Shostakovich, our artists, actors, philosophers and scientists were unable to prevent the policies of the religious fanatics and the communist ideas of the past, and they are unable to stop the actions of today's power-crazed madmen. For the past three hundred years we have drawn strength from the same sources – they were our Bach and our Dante, too, our Beethoven and our Shakespeare – and never gave up hope. Today, we, the representatives of Russian culture, the small part to which I belong, can only say one thing: Farewell, Europe!

The best-selling writer Boris Akunin similarly repudiated Putin's Russia and even moved to France for a while. He wrote:

Everyone has his own Russia, but I have nothing in common with Putin's, everything about it is alien to me. And being here in an age of widespread clouded thinking is difficult for me. I don't want to emigrate, but I will spend the great majority of my time outside Russia. A sober man will never be easy sharing a roof with a drunkard. I will stop by from time to time to see whether the carousal is coming to an end.

As more and more artists and intellectuals have moved abroad, a growing number of exiles such as Vladimir Sorokin and Mikhail Ryklin, who live in Berlin, have denounced the developments in Russia. The answers came promptly: slandering independent minds as Fifth Columnists has become a standby on the state-owned media, and since the murder of Boris Nemtsov on 27 February 2015, death threats have not been uncommon.

Ukraine on the Russian Intelligentsia's Mental Map

As far as I can tell, the critical Russian intelligentsia did not see the aggression against Ukraine coming any more than other observers. The publisher Irina Prokhorova has expressed her bafflement: 'Those who kept a cool head have asked themselves the same agonizing questions a hundred times: How did this happen to us? How can educated and cultured people euphorically exclaim "Crimea is ours!"? How did we allow two friendly nations to become mortal enemies?' The media propaganda alone, she noted, did not explain this transformation; the crisis had 'struck hidden emotional chords in today's society', a collective trauma born of the fear of civil war and the clash of fundamentally different mentalities. It is not like Russian intellectuals had kept a close eye on Ukraine's fate since its independence, studying the new state and emerging nation and everything that process entailed. On their mental maps, I suspect, Ukraine figured as a country, a swath of land and a people with a distinctive dialect, but not as a fully sovereign state. Unlike the Baltic republics – which stood on the cultural difference signalled by their non-Slavic languages – Ukraine, although it has its own language, somehow felt linguistically open.

Personal ties were close. Most Russians knew of a Ukrainian connection of some sort somewhere in their family histories. The space of empire had allowed for a kind of 'natural' familial cohabitation: careers, biographies and educational trajectories had woven across the border, networks of personal relationships had spanned the entire Union. And just as Ukraine was not seen as a truly independent state, Kiev was not perceived as a genuine capital; the country's other major cities were thought of as regional centres, provincial conurbations. To travel to

Kiev, one passed through Moscow, still the gateway to the empire. In Kiev, Odessa, Kharkov and other cities, majority populations speak Russian, so Russian visitors never needed to feel like they were actually abroad. What remained were the different landscapes, a shift of tonality and atmosphere that Russian intellectuals – and not only they – relished: Crimea was the quintessential dream destination for Russians, though after the end of the Soviet Union, Antalya, Tenerife or the Côte d'Azur beckoned. For intellectuals, Crimea was also a *lieu de mémoire* of the first rank, in, among others, Maximilian Voloshin's Koktebel, Chekhov's summer home in Yalta and Vasily Aksyonov's utopian novel *The Island of Crimea* (1979); the erstwhile Jewel of the Empire and Red Riviera, with scenic charms to rival those of the Mediterranean coasts; and Sevastopol, a scene of military glory first in the Crimean War and then in the Second World War. The trains to the peninsula had not stopped at the boundaries between the republics, and people had been familiar with the names of the destinations even as children; Artek, the Young Pioneers' model camp, was one of them. Usually absent from this picture was the population of Crimea, which, far from being Russian pure and simple, was a characteristic blend that also included Tatars, Jews, Greeks, Italians and Ukrainians. Also sorely missing was the much longer history of Tatar Crimea and the collective deportation of the Tatars to Central Asia in 1944.

For intellectuals in Moscow, western Ukraine – Lviv, Chernivtsi – was the West, a piece of Central Europe, with all that the Russian Empire had never had, such as Magdeburg rights, Polish cemeteries and magnates' mansions. Kiev, in their perspective, was the city gorgeously set high above the Dnieper, with the Cathedral of St Sophia, the Monastery of the Caves and the Khreshchatyk – a city risen again after the ravages of the war. The Donbass, the remnants of its erstwhile glory as the centre of heavy industry first of the empire, then of the Union, still tangible and visible everywhere, was actually part of this picture, though less as the fertile ground from which a lively proletarian culture had once sprung than as an irredeemably antiquated and dilapidated industrial colossus, the dinosaur of a bygone era. On the Soviet citizen's mental map, the grand construction projects – the Dneproges dam, the Kharkov Tractor Plant, the irrigation facilities – were not primarily associated with Ukraine; they were milestones of Soviet industrialization. And just as discussion of the Soviet-era terror and violence was avoided and actively discouraged in post-Soviet Russia, it was certainly felt that there was no need to talk about the Holodomor as a specifically Ukrainian experience, when millions of Russian peasants and Kazakh nomads had likewise been killed by collectivization and famine. Yes, there was Babi Yar, but the genocide of the Jews had been almost unknowable for decades, veiled by the formula of 'fascist crimes against peaceful Soviet citizens'. I would go so far as to say that in the minds of the intelligentsia (and the Soviet populace in general), Ukraine did not exist as a separate nation with its own history and statehood: it was no more than a region where people spoke a slightly peculiar dialect. And there was an unspecific suspicion that any insistence on a distinctive Ukrainian identity, on Ukrainian-ness, was noxious and nationalistic – not even a mind as subtle and independent as the dissident poet Joseph Brodsky's was unaffected by this prejudice, as his poem 'On Ukrainian Independence' (1994) revealed.

Russia's aggression against Ukraine has not only wantonly wrecked the once close relations between Russians and Ukrainians – it will take generations to undo the damage, if it can ever be undone – but Putin is also the great destroyer of the work of reconciliation undertaken by Russians as well as Germans after the catastrophe that arose from German soil. Germans must now choose: will they make common cause with Putin's Russia, or will they hold faith with those who, in defending the integrity of Ukraine and the 'Revolution of Dignity', defend also the Russia that will come after Putin?

THREE

SEEING FOR OURSELVES: DISCOVERING UKRAINE

WHEN WRITERS, INTELLECTUALS and artists from several European countries arrived in Kiev in May 2014 for a conference that Timothy Snyder and Leon Wieseltier had initiated under the title 'Ukraine – Thinking Together', it was, for most of the participants, their first visit to the capital of Europe's second-largest country. The symposium's meticulously prepared hearings and debates were held at the Diplomatic Academy. A lyceum before the revolution of 1917, the building with its Neoclassical facade – some of the embellishments on the inside are Neo-Gothic – looks out over the square in front of St Michael's Monastery, a complex painted in blue and white that was demolished in the 1930s and rebuilt after Ukrainian independence. At the other end of the square is the court building where the notorious Beilis trial took place in 1913; the proceedings attracted enormous attention and concluded with an acquittal that was perceived by the bourgeois public as a victory over the anti-Semitism of the late tsarist era. Remnants of Maidan's barricades and tent city could still be seen outside the monastery, which had been converted into a makeshift hospital for wounded protesters during the days of violence. Tourists gathered around the monument to Saint Olga; Tatars staged a demonstration in solidarity with their compatriots in Russian-occupied Crimea. Spring was in the air over the wide square and people sat in cafés; scorch marks from the fires remained and the burnt smell had not dissipated, but life seemed to have returned to normal. Some of the conference's events were held at a second venue, the Petro Mohyla Academy in Podil, Kiev's other old town down by the Dnieper; independent until the nineteenth century, it had been the town of artisans and merchants and a centre of Jewish Kiev and is now one of the capital's most lively areas, popular with students, artists and the 'middle class' – one could tell that it would pass through the various stages of gentrification in the near future. Walking down from the upper to the lower town, the visitor had a breathtaking view of the river and the neighbourhoods on the eastern bank.

With its rich programme, the conference was a highly instructive introduction to the concerns that had preoccupied many Europeans since the outbreak of the 'Ukraine crisis': What were they to make of the accusations that Russians and Russian-speaking citizens faced discrimination in Ukraine? Which role did the nationalist and extreme right-wing factions play? Where did things stand in the Donbass? Which view did Ukraine's religious communities, and especially the Jewish community, take of Maidan? In Kiev, the visitors from afar encountered highly competent interlocutors who addressed these burning questions: Iosif Sissels of the Jewish community; representatives of the Ukrainian Orthodox and Catholic Churches; journalists who had travelled to Kiev from Lugansk and Donetsk; civil-rights activists from Kharkov. The discontent fomented by separatists in eastern Ukraine had already erupted in violence; presidential elections were to be held a few weeks later. 'Thinking Together' revealed how much even those who were usually well-informed and involved in global affairs still had to learn – among the panel speakers were the former Swedish minister for foreign affairs Carl Bildt; Roger Cohen, who had covered the wars in the former Yugoslavia for the *New York Times*; the pugnacious and indefatigable activist of the Polish civil-rights movement Adam Michnik; Bernard-Henri Lévy and Bernard Kouchner from Paris; Václav Havel's erstwhile close adviser Karel Schwarzenberg; Wolf Biermann; Slavenka Drakulić, whose writings had captured the nationalist fury in Yugoslavia; and from Moscow the writer Viktor Erofeev and the veteran of the civil rights movement Alexander Podrabinek.

It was odd: although Ukraine had in the preceding few months emerged as the flashpoint of an escalating international crisis, it was effectively still a vast, unknown country, a blank spot on the map, a clean slate on which marks, places and boundaries were now being entered one by one. We were taken aback to find that this country in Europe's eastern reaches had no 'image', no 'face'. How – if the impression is correct – is one to explain this curious void?

Ukraine: So Close and Yet So Distant

Most Germans and Austrians have yet to pick up on the fact that they have not needed a visa to travel to Ukraine in years. All they have to do is buy a ticket and board the bus or plane. The lifting of the visa requirement – which, to this day, Europe has not reciprocated – was a kind of second fall of the Wall, considering the formidable barriers the bureaucratic aspects of preparing a trip to the former Eastern Bloc had long constituted. The flight from Berlin to Kiev's Boryspil International Airport is a mere two and a half hours, although there is only one plane a day. Before hostilities broke out in the Donbass, there were direct flights from Munich to Kharkov and Donetsk. If time is not of the essence, you can take the bus that departs from the terminal near the Funkturm in Berlin and reaches Lviv after fifteen hours and Kiev-Dachna after 23 hours. Austrians have it even easier. Flights connect Vienna to five Ukrainian cities: Kharkov, Dnepropetrovsk, Kiev, Lviv and Odessa. Again, the cheapest way to go is by bus: a Eurolines coach leaves Erdberg, a stop on Vienna's U3 underground line, at 6 p.m., arriving in Uzhhorod after just over nine hours and then at the bus terminal on Lviv's Stryiska Street after less than thirteen hours; from there it is several hours more to Rivne, Zhytomyr or Kiev. A slightly faster alternative are the *marshrutki* or privately operated minibuses, which cover a dense network and originally served the needs of small traders. This web of connections, which also includes budget airlines, has long sustained molecular movements – I call them creeping currents – that have sutured Ukraine to the rest of the world. The vans are popular with Ukrainian students, businessmen, tourists and labour migrants, predominantly women, who earn money abroad to keep their families afloat and hope that at least their children will have a better life.

Having arrived in Kiev and made his way to the city centre, the visitor is right in the middle of the action: the escalator of the Khreshchatyk-Maidan underground stop hauls him from the cavernous station 100 m (330 ft) below the surface up to the square. We are now all familiar with it from our television screens, though mostly in the perspective of the cameras that were posted on the Hotel Ukraine's 'Sky Desk', looking out over an enormous urban space framed by the monumental buildings that went up when the Khreshchatyk was rebuilt after the war. Thanks to these images, it feels like Maidan is nearby, like the other urban settings where history was made in recent years

– Cairo's Tahrir Square, Istanbul's Taksim Square, the urban canyons of Hong Kong, all the great arenas in which citizens who, to paraphrase Lenin's definition of the revolutionary situation, no longer wanted to live in the old way clashed with authorities that no longer could.

The live broadcasts that made us eyewitnesses to history unfolding have hardly turned us all into experts on Ukraine overnight, but at least we now know a little bit about a country that was terra incognita for most of us. It was not educational programmes that taught us basic facts about it, but pictures and coverage delivered into our homes every night, the news of the events as they were happening, shocking scenes that plunged us into an unfolding crisis of which, on some level, we wanted no part. Since then we have read up on the most important geographical and historical facts. We had always known that Kiev was a major European city, but it was only with the reports from Maidan that its skyline impressed itself on our memory, with the bell tower of St Sophia's Cathedral, the domes of the Monastery of the Caves and the view towards the Dnieper. A new geography gradually took shape in our minds as we learned the names of places that suggested something about the immense linguistic, cultural and historical breadth of this European country. Who of us had had more than the haziest notions about Crimea? Citizens of the GDR, maybe, who had been on holiday there, or lovers of Russian literature who were aware that Anton Chekhov had had his summer home there and that the intellectual bohemians of St Petersburg's silver age had gathered at Maximilian Voloshin's Koktebel. We were there with the reporters and correspondents, those professional minute-takers of history in the making, as they pushed towards the frontlines, as they criss-crossed a rapidly changing scenery of checkpoints and lines of demarcation where only yesterday no boundaries had existed. We watched live as masked gunmen, anonymous combatants without any insignia, crossed the border of a European nation. We became acquainted with the steppes of the Dyke Pole, the 'Wild Field', for it was there, near a town in the Donbass called Torez – the name sounds French and indeed honours Maurice Thorez, the leader of the French Communist Party – that a Malaysia Airlines Boeing 777 with 298 people on board was downed on 17 July 2014. Seared on our minds is the sight of Donetsk's hypermodern airport, named after the composer Sergei Prokofiev, who was born nearby in 1891; completed just in time for the 2012 European Football Championship, it was shot to pieces during the fighting in 2014 and now resembles a post-apocalyptic scene straight out of a Hollywood phantasmagoria. We became familiar with this topography just as other generations had memorized the names of embattled cities in the Spanish Civil War or the Vietnam War. Rather than Teruel, Madrid or Saigon, the matrix in the minds of those living today presumably features Donetsk, Lugansk, Mariupol, Odessa, Ilovaisk, Debaltsevo, perhaps also Minsk I and Minsk II. We were beset by swarms of images that reached us day after day, hour after hour; smartphones, digital cameras, social networks, bloggers and television broadcasters transmitted a constant real-time stream of them that were supposed to help us form an idea of the situation in the field.

But perhaps I was hasty in calling this country a terra incognita; perhaps it is closer to home than I suggested? We might look at it from the Austrian perspective: Vienna occupies a privileged position from which, for reasons historical as well as contemporary, Eastern and southeastern Europe, including Ukraine, are less remote. The Viennese still maintain relationships rooted in family traditions, documented in photo albums, and refreshed by visits to the numerous 'little Viennas' of the erstwhile Habsburg monarchy; and, more saliently, there is a familiarity mediated by the literary tradition: Joseph Roth, Karl Emil Franzos, Paul Celan, Gregor von Rezzori and others come to mind. The perceptual horizon is different than in, say, Berlin or Paris. Vienna has also long been a base for the professional observers, the correspondents, journalists and reporters, who have kept us abreast of what was going on 'behind the Iron Curtain'. As early as 1984 Martin Pollack's *Nach Galizien* opened a door to a region that had vanished from sight, and in 1989 Christoph Ransmayr edited a volume bearing the programmatic title *Im blinden Winkel: Nachrichten aus Mitteleuropa*, or *In the Blind Angle: News from Central Europe*. Karl-Markus Gauß has spent years roaming these spaces of historical experience that were lost to us. Visiting Vienna today, you hear a lot of Ukrainian on the underground, and you can tell that these young Ukrainians are seasoned border crossers and know their way around the foreign capital. Events and exhibitions that turn the spotlight on Ukraine are everywhere: a show of pictures from Maidan by Oleksandr Ratushniak, documentary films, numerous panel discussions and workshops, the opening of an exhibition exploring the 'Myth of Galicia' that was compiled in Kraków. A gallery in the Leopoldstadt neighbourhood presents wartime photographs taken by German soldiers; one series dating from 1942 is titled 'From the Donets to the Don' and surveys the same territory that has now again become a scene of the ravages and crimes of war. In the academic world, the University of Vienna stands out as one of the few institutions of higher education in the German-speaking countries where Ukrainian history is an established subject, with prominent teachers who contribute to the public debate. Vienna – like the City of London and Switzerland – has also attracted Ukrainian oligarchs looking for a new home in the West for themselves, their families and their business empires; Azarov, Yanukovych and Firtash are here. The latter – an American extradition request has long hung over his head – has recently launched an initiative to raise billions in support of Ukraine, though oddly without coordinating with the Ukrainian government.

Berlin has no history of cultural relations with Ukraine to match Vienna's, but there is scattered evidence: the actor Alexander Granach launched his career on the stages of Berlin soon after arriving at the city's Schlesischer Bahnhof railway station; Martin Buber came here from Lviv; during the interwar years, Ukrainian emigrants set up an institute for the scholarly study of their native country; Pavlo Skoropadsky, whom the Central Powers had installed as hetman in Kiev in 1918, spent the decades after his evacuation from the Ukrainian capital near Berlin. Certain circles in the Reich always toyed with the idea of playing the 'Ukrainian card' – first against the Russian Empire, then against the Soviet Union. The history of German involvement in Ukraine is one of violence first and foremost, recorded in the hundreds of thousands of snapshots taken by Wehrmacht soldiers and the newsreels of the advances across the Bug and Dnieper, remembered by the millions of Ukrainians who were deported to Germany as forced labourers, seared on the minds of posterity with pictures from places like Babi Yar. There are few instances of positive interaction in the twentieth century to counterbalance this history of terror, whose traces have been gathered in imposing works of documentation and scholarship on the Shoah. But things have begun to change; Ukrainian writers are frequent visitors in Berlin, and the country's young literature almost has a second home in the city, where it finds an audience far beyond the sizable local Ukrainian community.

A road sign pierced by shrapnel stands at the new terminal of Donetsk airport.

The Imperial Gaze: Ukraine's Absence from the Contemporary Observer's Horizon

I cannot say that I knew nothing about Ukraine. I first visited it in the 1960s, during a fascinating trip organized by my Bavarian grammar school that brought us to Uzhhorod, Lviv, Kiev and Kharkov. But these were stopovers on a voyage whose true destination was Moscow. I came away with powerful impressions of the landscapes, the cities – I even remember the sublime 1920s Bauhaus-style complex in Kharkov – and the Dnieper. Still, this was a journey to the Soviet Union, and the language we spoke when we met people was Russian. I returned as a university student, but always on excursions from a centre: we stayed in Moscow and ventured out 'into the provinces', a slightly dismissive term that we applied not only to Ukraine. The role of Russian as the Union's lingua franca was apt to make us forget that there were other languages (although the peoples along the Baltic seashore and in the Caucasus sometimes used theirs as barriers to keep strangers at arm's length). It took us a long time – until quite recently, really – to apprehend and appreciate Ukraine as a historical subject unto itself, with its own language, culture and history. It existed less as a political and cultural entity in its own right than as a collage of regions and places: Kiev was the erstwhile capital of Kievan Rus'; Lviv exemplified the Central European-Polish-Habsburgian world, a cultural sphere we

Westerners found more easily accessible; Odessa stood for the intersection of southern Russian, Mediterranean and Jewish cultures that had produced the urbane and cosmopolitan literature of legendary writers such as Isaac Babel, Konstantin Paustovsky, and Ilf and Petrov. Ukraine had something for everyone, and you picked what suited your interests: Central Europe, the Jewish shtetl, Soviet modernism and of course also the myth of Crimea, the 'Pearl of the Russian Empire'.

But this picture always had an imperial focus; its vanishing point was forever located outside the territory and country we now know as Ukraine. We envisioned it from Vienna, or from Kraków and Warsaw, or from St Petersburg and Moscow, or from the Sublime Porte. In the German view, Ukraine was primarily the granary coveted in the First World War and the Second World War, a projection of colonial fantasies and designs. Seen from these imperial centres, Ukraine was always peripheral. There was a Polish-centred, a Habsburg-centred, a Russian-centred and then a Soviet imperial perspective, raising the question of whether there even existed such a thing as a distinctive Ukrainian history. I was struck to find that I was not the first and certainly not the only one who was abruptly confronted with this question, and it seems that it took the post-Soviet, anti-imperial and anti-colonial articulation of Ukraine's rebellion to crack this intractable and highly effective imperial complex, to challenge it and spur its critical examination. Such Ukrainian self-assertion, meanwhile, prompted the reflexive suspicion that it could not be anything other than Ukrainian nationalism, possibly laced with right-wing extremism and anti-Semitism.

The imperial complex also extended to the darkest chapter in German-Ukrainian relations. And it is at work to this day; witness the television talk shows in which experts and non-experts exchange ideas and, when the conversation turns to the war Nazi Germany waged on the Soviet Union, speak without further ado of 'Russia'. It is implicitly understood that the crimes Germans perpetrated in the occupied areas of the Soviet Union were crimes against 'Russians' and 'Russians' alone. All feelings of responsibility and guilt – and Germans have every reason for such feelings – are projected onto 'the Russians'. In this perspective, in which the Second World War usually commenced not in 1939 but on 22 June 1941, Belorussia and Ukraine, countries overrun in their entirety by the war machine, occupied as 'breadbaskets' and exploited as sources of slave labour, are invisible. There is no Kiev, a city that was laid waste, its population reduced from almost a million to no more than 180,000. The destruction of thousands upon thousands of villages; the flooding of mines and demolition of dams and generating stations; the deportation of 2.1 million Ukrainians to the Reich for forced labour (out of a total of 2.8 million Soviet forced labourers); the facts that 5.3 million people – one out of six citizens living in Ukraine – died, that the centre of Eastern European Jewry before the war lost 2.5 million of its Jewish citizens, 60 per cent of all Jews in Soviet Ukraine, 90 per cent of Galicia's Jewish residents: all these are swept under the carpet in the German discourse on Ukraine. It does not matter that 2.5 million Ukrainian Red Army soldiers fought against Hitler, that many thousands fought both Hitler and Stalin. Instead, the Ukrainian *Hiwis* and collaborationists in the occupied areas, the pogrom that Stepan Bandera's nationalist and anti-Semitic OUN (Organization of Ukrainian Nationalists) unleashed in Lviv after the city was evacuated by the Red Army, and the two Ukrainian ss divisions levied towards the end of the war define Ukraine's image in the German consciousness. Rarely does someone try to explain that Ukraine faced twofold oppression from two sides and that many saw the conflict between Hitler's Germany and Stalin's Soviet Union as an opportunity to achieve independence. Germans are so proud of their efforts to come to terms with their past, but what Arnold D. Margolin, Ukraine's Jewish representative at the 1919 Paris Peace Conference, said of the Americans might as well be said of today's Germans: 'They are as uninformed about Ukrainians as the average European is about the numerous African tribes.'

All competitive tallying of casualties and ideology of victimhood aside, it is clear that twentieth-century Ukraine was a scene of horrendous carnage. The evidence can be found in almost every city and town and in thousands of villages. To travel in Ukraine is to tour a veritable topography of violence, terror and catastrophe: the staggering numbers of civilians and soldiers who died in the First World War; the mass graves in which the victims of the civil war, anti-Jewish pogroms and the first famine of 1920–21 lie; the remaining traces of the deportations from the areas subject to collectivization; the mass graves for the victims of the Holodomor in 1932–3; the wave of suicides triggered by the repression against the Ukrainian national cultural elite in 1934–5; the victims of the mass operations during the Great Terror of 1937–8; the systematic extermination of Ukraine's Jewish citizens at sites such as Babi Yar, Drobytsky Yar, Odessa, Kamianets-Podilsky, and the Janowska camp in Lviv; the millions of dead Soviet prisoners of war; the victims of the 'civil war within the war' that did not end until the 1950s, and, lest we forget, the liquidators of the Chernobyl nuclear disaster. Add to these the more than 6,000 people who have now died in the war fomented by Russia in the eastern parts of Ukraine.

In Germany, and perhaps in other countries as well, the public is still largely ignorant of why Ukrainians had little reason to feel any sort of loyalty towards Stalin's regime. Hundreds of thousands of Ukrainian peasant families had been deported, millions had perished in a famine that was perhaps intended and certainly allowed to continue, the nation's elite had been decimated and any anti-Soviet resistance had been rooted out in a war waged with merciless cruelty.

Ukrainian intellectuals who travel to the West find that people they meet, if they ask questions at all, expect them to take a stance on nationalism and anti-Semitism; there is little interest in how Ukraine brought off the miracle of resisting the temptations of nationalist fervour under extraordinary outside pressure and uniting Orthodox, Catholic, Jewish and Muslim citizens in a movement that transcends religious and ethnic factionalism. Others, like the Polish, Lithuanians, Latvians and Estonians, show greater sympathy. They experienced occupation by two murderous systems in succession for themselves, so it is easier for them to understand why Ukrainians today think and act the way they do.

Because of the German fixation on Russia, Ukraine, like other countries in Central and Eastern Europe, is always cast as derivative and secondary. These nations are assigned the status of non-subjects, undeserving of a seat at the table when Germans seek an understanding with a counterparty they stubbornly call their 'neighbour' even though there has not been a German–Russian border in a long time.

Charting the 'Grand Narrative'

Ukraine was missing from the European and perhaps more widely Western mental maps, and this absence marred the understanding of not only the general public. One scholar who would know, the German expert on Russian history Dietrich Geyer, noted in his introduction to a history of Ukraine edited by Frank Golczewski: 'For Western and especially German educated circles, the culture and history of Ukraine have remained terra incognita. Even most trained historians have only a faint idea.' Andreas Kappeler, one of the few scholars in the German-speaking countries to have focused on the history of Ukraine, confirms that research and teaching on the country have been 'modest at best'. The 'confession' the American historian of Russia Mark von Hagen offered back in the 1990s – that Ukraine had always been on his scholarly agenda, but only as an element in the framework of other histories, those of Russia and Poland – is illuminating and may point a way forward for a renewed study of Ukraine. He noted that in his career as a historian it took him quite a while until he felt compelled to ask: 'Does Ukraine have a history?' In other words, what is it that constitutes the country's as a genuinely 'Ukrainian' history? In the eyes of his colleagues in a Russian-centred field, he added, merely raising the question aroused suspicion that he was a nationalist deviationist, while Ukrainian historians who presupposed an ethnic-national Ukrainian identity, including representatives of the large communities of Ukrainian exiles, sometimes viewed him as an agent of a historiography infected with Russo-centrism.

The various national historiographies relegated the Ukrainians to a place on the periphery. Golczewski has shown how easily the resulting projections could be harnessed to political agendas.

> Many Russians thought of Ukrainians as 'Little Russians' speaking an outlandish dialect; Polish nationalists, meanwhile, regarded them as a peasant people that was stuck in a lower stage of cultural evolution and, provided better education, would naturally be absorbed by their own culturally superior nation. Who has not heard of the Cossacks? But who has a reasonably specific idea of what the term designates? The National Socialists believed that the Cossacks were an ethnicity that could be defined by racial criteria; the Soviet communists saw them as the sword of reaction; Polish farmers and Jews feared them as murderous bands; and Ukrainian romantics extolled them as Europe's first democratic society. Depending on one's political interests, each of these distorted portraits was eminently useful, while no side cared to examine the historical record.

Even the Austrian overlords in Galicia, who took a friendly view of Ukrainians, primarily sought to bolster their identity 'as a counterweight to Polish dominance, whereas Russophobes in Poland and Germany hoped to weaken Russia – the Ukrainians themselves did not matter to them. The moment the political constellations shifted, interest in Ukraine quickly faded.' Golczewski sums up the regrettable, though hardly surprising, result: 'To this day, a reader who would learn about the history of a country that is among Europe's largest must assemble it from books on Polish and Russian history and will inevitably arrive at impressions and conclusions that are informed by the perspectives of those two nations.'

Considerable progress has been made in charting new approaches to a modern historiography in the past two decades – Mark von Hagen highlights the greater openness of Polish historians in particular, which was hardly to be expected given the centuries-long complications in Polish–Ukrainian relations. On the other hand, there is widespread consensus that the unhistorical and essentialist construction of a Ukrainian 'core nation' is untenable. And while the view that there is such a thing as a Ukrainian history *sui generis* is now largely undisputed, even the broad outlines of that history, the grand narrative that will accommodate the historical experiences of the people living on the territory of today's Ukraine, remain contentious. The work on such a historical narrative, Andreas Kappeler argues, must steer a course between Scylla and Charybdis, between the negative stereotypes of the Ukrainian as an incorrigible nationalist and anti-Semite, of the traitorous Cossack and partisan (from Khmelnytsky and Mazepa to Petliura and Bandera), of the peasant speaking a corrupted Slavic dialect, and the 'myths of national Ukrainian historiography', which would project the genesis of the Ukrainian nation into a distant past, claiming that it has existed for over a thousand years.

Ukrainians are not the only people that, for the longest time, had neither a state of their own, nor a fully developed social structure or distinct literary language. Almost everywhere in Europe, nation formation and the consolidation of a unified territory were a complicated process repeatedly disrupted by setbacks. 'This discontinuity,' Andreas Kappeler writes, 'is a crucial reason why Ukrainians to this day present the picture of a comparatively insecure and perpetually vulnerable community. Its instability, which is exacerbated by the traditional sense of superiority among Russians and Poles vis-à-vis the so-called "unhistorical" peasant people, in turn prompts some Ukrainians to adopt a defensive posture, making them unusually sensitive to criticism and occasionally spurring them to compensate with an excessive sense of national identity.'

Ukrainian historians, especially younger ones such as Yaroslav Hrytsak and Heorhy Kasianov, have recognized the danger of a narrow ethnic-national lens on Ukrainian history and have struck out in new directions. In the past two decades, the process of nation building itself has inspired the genesis of studies that complement the classic scholarship, from the oeuvre of the father of Ukrainian historiography, Mykhailo Hrushevsky, to the contributions of members of the diaspora such as Orest Subtelny, Roman Szporluk and Paul Robert Magocsi. These recent works sometimes suggest that Ukraine's might in fact be an exemplary European history: one that is constitutively transnational and cannot be reduced to a national story.

For an illustration of how rich, but also how enormously complex and intractable, this history is, take any attempt to spin it into a narrative thread, be it a compact exposition or textbook, be it an art-historical treatise or the sequence of exhibits in a history museum of national or local significance. The reconstruction of the plural 'local histories' may in fact turn out to be an especially helpful way to do justice to the heterogeneity of the skeins of history that are interwoven in Ukraine. Visiting and revisiting a museum such as the National Museum of the History of Ukraine in Kiev, one also vividly senses that history is 'in flux', that exhibits change as interpretations vary and emphases shift, that certain objects disappear and others take their place. History is a contested field, and so are museums with their mission to inform and educate, especially in times of radical change.

The first chapter that is indisputably essential to any history of Ukraine concerns Kievan Rus', the most significant political entity formed by the East Slavic tribes and one of the largest in medieval Europe. It persisted from the ninth to the thirteenth centuries, and its flourishing heart was Kiev, on the middle reaches of the Dnieper, the 'route from the Varangians to the Greeks'. Ukrainians, Russians and Belorussians all later invoked it as their distant ancestor, although these modern ethnicities did not come into existence – let alone congeal into nations in the modern sense – until much later. Contact with Byzantium brought Eastern Christianity and its culture to the Kievan state. Kiev lost its status as the capital of the Eastern Slavic world when Rus' fell to the Mongol invasion after 1236.

Starting in the fourteenth century, political and cultural predominance shifted towards new centres. The rise of the Grand Duchy of Lithuania and its union – first personal, in 1386, then real, in 1569

– with the Kingdom of Poland had consequences that inform the political landscape even today: the influence of Polish culture and the Polish language, the ascendancy of the churches united with Rome, and, not least importantly, the forms of self-government made possible by the awarding of town privileges. In 1648 the revolt of the Dnieper Cossacks living along the southern border of the Kingdom of Poland against their Polish overlords, the 'greatest popular movement in early modern Eastern Europe', according to Andreas Kappeler, which was accompanied by horrendous pogroms against Jews, led to the establishment of the Cossack Hetmanate, which some regard as a precursor of the later Ukrainian nation. The second pole that determined the fate of the Ukrainian lands emerged with the ascent of the Grand Duchy of Moscow, or Muscovy, and the expanding Russian Empire. The hetmanate soon lost its independence to Muscovy and vanished from the map in the eighteenth century with the Partitions of Poland and the complete integration also of right-bank Ukraine into the Russian Empire. Moscow would rule over most of contemporary Ukraine's territory until the late twentieth century.

Starting with the First Partition of Poland in 1772, the third centre of power that left traces visible in Ukraine today was the Habsburg Empire. When the Habsburg monarchy disintegrated, Galicia, where the Ukrainian national movement first gathered strength in the nineteenth century, achieved short-lived independence as the West Ukrainian People's Republic, only to fall to the recreated Polish Republic in 1919.

Along the northern shores of the Black Sea and in Crimea, the Golden Horde was succeeded in the fifteenth century by the Crimean Khanate, which was annexed by the Russian Empire in 1783. As an independent power and vassal of the Ottoman Empire, the khanate had been a major factor in the struggle between its two powerful neighbours. Crimea has remained the homeland of the Crimean Tatars despite rigorous Russification programmes in the nineteenth century and their collective deportation under Stalin after the end of German occupation in 1944.

Another significant consequence of the Partitions of Poland was that the Polish crown's Jewish subjects now found themselves living within the boundaries of the Russian Empire. Established in 1791 and enforced until 1915, the so-called Pale of Settlement, which extended from the Baltic to the Black Sea, by the end of the nineteenth century had around 5 million Jewish residents, most of them in areas that are now part of Ukraine, making the country the centre of Eastern European Jewry until its almost complete extermination by Nazi Germany.

Europe's Frontier: Ukraine as a Laboratory of Boundaries

In light of this history, it is clear that the territory of today's Ukraine comprises regions that have absorbed very different influences, and a 'history of Ukraine' worthy of the name must integrate all these heterogeneous histories: the diverse traditions, historical experiences and religious beliefs, the various languages and literatures. No history whose narrative follows a single ethnic, linguistic or religious community can do justice to the complexity of the process in which Ukraine emerged as a nation and state.

Ukraina is generally thought to mean 'borderland'. Ukraine has been a paradigmatic land of borders, and not only because it once bordered the steppes; it is a territory criss-crossed by boundaries. Ukraine – to summarize and, inevitably, simplify – encompasses the central region on both banks of the Dnieper around Kiev, the erstwhile hetmanate; eastern Ukraine with the Donbass; the south, which, after the demise of the Crimean Khanate, was settled and developed as Novorossiya, and Crimea; Galicia and Bukovina, which were under Habsburg rule for well over a century; and Carpatho-Ukraine, where Hungarian cultural influence was strong. There can be no history of Ukraine without the plurality of denominations – the Eastern Orthodox Churches under the patriarchates in Moscow, Kiev and Constantinople, the Ukrainian Greek Catholic Church, which is in communion with Rome, as well as Protestants, Jews and Muslims. Ukrainian literature includes texts in Ukrainian, Russian, Polish, Yiddish and German. It is not an exaggeration to say that this *ukraina* is a true laboratory of boundary landscapes, which is to say, a Europe in miniature. No grandiosely proclaimed 'paradigm shift' is needed to understand that Ukrainian history cannot be shoehorned into the format of a neatly self-contained and narrow-minded story of tribal origin and national continuity.

Many readers will know that the concept of the 'border' or 'boundary' is the subject of a long-running debate and a considerable body of scholarship. The two words cover an extraordinarily wide and differentiated spectrum of phenomena. There are hard and soft, permeable and hermetically closed borders; real and virtual boundaries as well as phantom boundaries that have been effaced and yet continue to have palpable effects; unfenced 'green' borders and fortified ones with troops stationed to defend them; territorial boundaries and lines drawn by social distinctions. We know natural borders imposed by the physical-geographical relief as well as diffuse zones of transition, borderlands and shatter zones, lands in between and buffer zones. The border fortified with barbed wire and trenches is the hardest demarcation conceivable, where encirclement, attack and defence are matters of life and death. This phenomenal diversity has given rise to an entire 'boundarology'. As Georg Simmel and Friedrich Ratzel – and others before them – pointed out, borders are among humanity's most elementary experiences of space and time.

Most recently, Ukraine has once again become a scene of the violent redrawing of borders. Virtually before our eyes, trenches were dug where none had been, lines of demarcation were drawn where residents had moved freely and unencumbered by restrictions, urban spaces were subject to initially symbolic, then violent, occupation, areas were transformed into enclaves held by armed forces, into occupation zones, corridors and frontlines. Internationally recognized national boundaries were simply ignored and violated; men with guns cut off the previously unchecked flow of people. Regions disintegrated into no-go areas, no-man's-lands, fields of fire – a part of Europe became a laboratory in which an experiment in the liquidation of existing and the making of new boundaries was undertaken.

All of this happened and is still happening in a country defined by transitions more than almost any other in Europe. Intermixture, here, is the rule rather than the exception. Almost every Ukrainian has relatives in Russia; after many generations of labour migration – as well as forced migrations – the Russian-Ukrainian marriage and family is an unalterable fact of life. For generations, academic and political careers took Ukrainians to St Petersburg and Moscow; back home, Russian was the language of schools, universities and the media, a custom sometimes enforced by prohibitions and discrimination. Russian in public, Ukrainian among family and friends: a bilingual reality that, in the zones of the most intensive linguistic contact, even gave rise to a specific hybrid known as Surzhyk. Multilingualism probably functioned and still functions more smoothly in Ukraine than in any other European country, more smoothly even than in Belgium or Switzerland – that was on display in the talk shows, where the guests communicated in both languages without raising an eyebrow, or during football broadcasts, with sports commentators switching back and forth between the two languages, not as a symbolic gesture of goodwill but as an everyday practice that felt perfectly natural.

Turning linguistic into ethnic difference and an ethnic distinction into a social, political and ideological contention was the work of political forces whose sole capital consists in their ability to foment antagonism and open hostility. Ukrainians also prove their ability to communicate in the different languages and the registers of different cultures within their country and even their city when it comes to issues of faith and religious affiliation: the existence of several Orthodox and Catholic denominations has ingrained in them a habit of mutual acceptance, a lived pluralism that is incompatible with notions of a quasi-national church favoured by some Russian Orthodox clergy.

Once we stop conceiving of Ukrainian history as tied to an ethnic group and understand it as the entire ensemble of traditions that evolved and are lived in the territory of today's Ukraine, the question of 'Ukrainian-ness' – the question of Ukrainian identity – is revealed to be a potentially explosive unresolved problem: how can a nation, a polity, absorb and integrate such divergent and indeed contrarian experiences? As the multi-ethnic and transnational historiography of Ukraine produced in the past two decades has shown, the history to be written would have to incorporate the full plurality of perspectives and narratives and accomplish an enormous work of synthesis. Such a history would feature not only the representatives of Ukrainian national identity, like the Cossack hetmans Bohdan Khmelnytsky and Ivan Mazepa, the spokesmen of the nascent Ukrainian literature Taras Shevchenko and Ivan Franko, and the founding father of Ukrainian historiography Mykhailo Hrushevsky, but those Ukrainians whose socialization and careers were set predominantly in the Russian or Soviet context, like Nikolai Gogol, who hailed from Mirgorod, and Anna Akhmatova-Gorenko, who was a native of Odessa. Its cast of characters would include Russians who were born in Ukraine or worked there, such as Ilya Repin, Sergei Prokofiev and Nikita Khrushchev, as well as prominent Jews who hailed from Ukraine, such as Leon Trotsky, Sholem Aleichem and Isaac Babel. Even Paul Celan, Rose Ausländer and Joseph Roth, Jewish authors born in Bukovina and Galicia who wrote in German, would be figures in a genuinely multi-ethnic history of Ukraine. This history would cover the ordeal of the Holodomor in the Ukrainian village, the anti-Jewish pogroms of the Civil War, and the extermination of Ukrainian Jewry at the hands of the German invaders and their accomplices; it would shine a light not only on the victims of the German and Soviet occupations, but on the collaborators and profiteers. Traces of the multiplicity of cultures are all over Ukraine. You can spot them especially on the local scale, in the places where the languages and cultures have overlapped, often clashing but sometimes begetting something unique and characteristic. The diversity of Ukrainian culture is legible in the textures and palimpsests of the country's cities and towns. Even after the violent ethnic and social 'purges' of the twentieth century – the murder of most of the country's Jewish population and the 'ethnic unmixing', whose victims included Poles, Crimean Tatars, Pontic Greeks, Black Sea Germans and other minorities – after the destruction or closure of churches, synagogues and mosques, after the effacement of names and toppling of monuments, the mélange of cultures is instantly recognizable today. Ukraine's landscapes as well as its urban centres reflect the full spectrum of this great European country.

The Boundary Experience and the Work on the Political Nation

The experience of boundaries external and internal is constitutive of Ukrainian life. In many ways, the country can be described as a 'frontier society'.

The frontier has spawned a growing body of historical scholarship ever since Frederick Jackson Turner's essay 'The Significance of the Frontier in American History' (1893), which profoundly influenced not only the historiography of the United States but, more generally, the understanding of America's emergence as a nation and its national mentality. Turner highlighted the settlers' steady advancement across the continent and the way the frontier informed the nascent American society and nation, rewarding boldness, initiative, individualism and self-reliance rather than dependence on, let alone submission to, the institutions of a central state. Many American virtues, Turner argued, that seemed to have withered in the settled and consolidated circumstances of life along the eastern seaboard and the routines and self-satisfaction they bred were continually born anew in the struggles of the pioneers cutting their way through the pathless wilderness.

Analogies can be blind alleys, but we can highlight several parallels between this society taking shape along the moving boundary of the American West and Ukraine. *Ukraina* – I have mentioned it – means 'borderland', and the characteristic experiences of life in borderlands are key to the gradual formation of the Ukrainian state and nation. Early on, there was the fundamental distinction between steppe and woodland, between the environments in which sedentary populations lived and those inhabited by nomads. The steppe, a natural and cultural region that stretches from the northern shores of the Black Sea across Central Asia to Mongolia, was always a space of transit, the domain and area of operations of nomadic peoples. Kievan Rus', which established itself in the ninth century along the Dnieper, the most important transport and trade route, had to repulse some of them. After its demise, the territories it had controlled came to be ruled by the Grand Duchy of Lithuania and then the Polish–Lithuanian Union. Still, large parts of today's Ukraine remained a borderland, now abutting the Crimean Khanate. It was along this boundary, in this intermediate space, that the first rudiments of a modern nation appeared around the turn from the sixteenth to the seventeenth century in the area of the Dnieper Cossacks and the hetmanate. Many of this society's practices, virtues and customs recall Turner's portrayal of the American settler: self-reliance, the basic democratic structure of the Cossack assembly, insubordination to authorities, a rather anarchical notion of freedom. These will later form the basis of a veritable myth of the Cossack (in sharp contrast with the negative myth painting him as an instigator of pogroms and stalwart pillar of Russian autocracy).

Ukrainians were not the only ones deprived for a long time of the right to an independent political structure of their own. After the Partitions of Poland in the eighteenth century, the Polish were likewise divided for more than a lifetime between very different religious, institutional and social environments, which set them on divergent linguistic, cultural and experiential trajectories. The rift between the contrary historical experiences of these communities had only begun to close when the wrenching upheavals of the twentieth century followed, and some of its traces are still in evidence. Ukrainians have been vouchsafed very few and very brief moments of opportunity to constitute their state as a self-determined and sovereign political subject: the short interval of 1917–20, and the quarter-century since the dissolution of the Soviet Union, which released them into a new existence as an independent nation.

Outside Threats as Catalysts of Nation Formation

The recent foreign military interventions have abetted secessionists and led to the drawing of new boundaries that now separate Crimea and the para-states in the occupied territories in eastern Ukraine from the rest of the country, but they have also had a second, paradoxical consequence. The Ukrainian sociologist Tatiana Zhurzhenko argues:

> At the same time, the Russian aggression has done what previous Ukrainian presidents from Kravchuk to Yanukovych had failed to achieve – catalyse the creation of a political nation. Ukrainian identity, which for so long had been associated with ethnicity, language and historical memory, suddenly has become territorial and political and thus inclusive for Russian speakers and Russians, as well as for Ukrainian citizens with other ethnic origins. A good example are the Crimean Tatars, who remained largely loyal to Kiev after the Russian occupation of Crimea and are now perceived and celebrated as 'true' Ukrainians.

The Lviv-based historian Vasyl Rasevych similarly believes that the pressure exerted by a foreign power may smelt down antagonistic memories and self-images, writing that 'the Revolution of Dignity and the war for a sovereign independent Ukraine – this is already common Ukrainian history, the history of an emerging political nation, the history of the victory of Ukrainian civil society.'

But might one not also assert the opposite: that Maidan has widened and deepened the rifts; that it has shattered the inclusiveness born of indifference, the laissez-faire attitude that stood the country in good stead for more than twenty years, obviating any militant, let alone military, engagements; that it has exacerbated Ukraine's internal division and perhaps made it irreversible? How can the country mitigate the sharp antagonisms fomented from outside, how can it bring about a rapprochement and eventual reconciliation of the different factions? How can it assemble a shared conception of history out of the glorification of the anti-Soviet underground, which to many is synonymous with Bandera and collaboration with the Nazis, and the iconic image of the Ukrainian Red Army soldier whose fight for his country took him all the way to Berlin? How can one square the memory of the heroic achievements of Soviet modernity – the DNEPROGES dam, the Kharkov Tractor Plant – with that of the mass death of the Holodomor that afflicted the country at the same time? How can the old and new national celebrations be harmonized with the cherished habits of Soviet-era public holidays without stirring up fresh bad blood? Who might credibly rise above the fray to symbolize the integration of all the different parties?

Such reconciliation will not be possible without disarmament of the politics of history and a frank and thorough discussion of the darkest hours of Ukrainian history – collaboration on both sides, betrayal on both sides. It will not be possible without pluralization of the interpretations and narratives. And there are encouraging examples to suggest that this process has begun; see the conferences held inside the country in the past several years on the most controversial issues in Ukrainian history. But the key medium that might become a catalyst for the dismantlement of the antagonistic narratives will be the political movement filling the space with life in which the nation can come to a shared understanding of itself, unhampered by pressure or interventions from outside parties, whoever they may be.

Phenomenology of Revolution and the Birth of the Political Nation

What Maidan was is a question future historians will study. What is indisputable is that it was difficult for us to understand. There must be a reason when the elementary reflexes – in this instance, solidarity with the victim of an attack – fail. Václav Havel once said that the stance of the Western left towards the civil rights movement in Eastern Europe was characterized by an 'anatomy of reticence'. Still, there can be no doubt that the event, however colourful the details – flash mobs, Cossack tents, field kitchens, barricade fighting, homemade projectiles, improvised universities and clinics – merits a chapter in the history of Europe's revolutions. Maidan as a popular movement stunned us, whose ideas were shaped by Hannah Arendt's *On Revolution*; we had grown up with Walter Benjamin's image of the revolutionaries shooting at church clocks to stop time and leap into a new age: revolution as disruption, discontinuity, caesura, sea change or point of no return.

The qualitative innovation of 1989, we kept emphasizing in retrospect, was non-violence: Jadwiga Staniszkis's 'self-limiting revolution' and the practice of the 'round table', which made it possible to send the toppled dictators into exile or retirement rather than to the gallows.

Revolution, we argued, was generous, not vengeful; it needed no barricade fighting or martyrs; it demanded no choice between stark alternatives, between life and death, but emphasized arbitration and compromise. Negotiation was the magic word, as befits a time that thought of itself as post-heroic. A new paradigm of profound change had been established, the peaceful revolution, the one true achievement at the end of a blood-drenched century full of civil wars.

And then came Maidan, the popular uprising, and shattered the image that had been virtually enshrined as the ideal. The timeline of the events from 21 November 2013, when around 1,000 people assembled shortly after 10 p.m. to protest the government's withdrawal from the Ukraine–European Union Association Agreement, to the marches drawing a million people, from the barricade fighting to the abscondence of the president on 22 February 2014, is documented in great detail, allowing us to glimpse the 'face of revolution'. Between these milestones, the country underwent not only all possible stages of acceleration, confusion and radicalization, but the intermittent easing of tensions and growing hopes for a peaceful conclusion.

I did not trust my eyes; I was wary of the revolutionary pathos and cast my lot with the champions of the 'self-limiting revolution' model; I did not arrive on the scene – a monumental landscape of scorched asphalt, fire-blackened facades, improvised memorials to the heroes of the 'Nebesna Sotnia' or 'Heaven's Hundred' – until after everything

Euromaidan anniversary, Kiev, 20 February 2017.

had been decided. I came too late and ultimately cannot speak to what was a matter of life or death for those who lived through it. So all I can do is point to the pictures, even though it has become fashionable to claim that pictures are the most inconclusive evidence. But no, evidence exists, and it is plain to they eye: the students – mobilized via Facebook by the brilliant Afghan-born Ukrainian journalist Mustafa Nayyem – being clobbered by Berkut men who were perplexed that there were people who would not submit to them; the growing and converging crowds who could not have been paid, certainly not by the CIA; the faces of citizens who joined the protests simply because they wanted to be left in peace, who were stunned that their government ordered its security forces to beat them up and even open fire on them. Here are pictures that show a society of average people, without poses, without heroic gestures. Here are pictures of a city that would no longer put up with everything, and the manifestation, the 'city within the city', the citizens persevering on the central square, guarding it and bringing supplies. Here are pictures of protesters standing sentry and sleeping in shifts while the exhausted and injured were being taken to St Michael's Monastery to be fed and treated.

I contend that these pictures disprove the lie that 'fascism took hold in the centre of Kiev'. Just take a look at the hundreds of thousands who came on New Year's Eve to listen to the band Okean Elzy perform. Only broad-based and confident movements have the strength to establish an 'open university' and set up and staff clinics that treat thousands of injured mid-battle, to organize concerts and push a piano between the frontlines on which the so-called 'terrorist pianist' played Chopin. The mask was his defensive cover, not an attacker's gear.

The violence, too, has a face, and I would argue that we can recognize it. Here are the robots in black armed to their teeth, the snipers, the thugs dragging injured protesters out of the hospitals in order to torture and kill them: see, this is what we will do to you. And here are the targeted shots fired at those who have already taken a bullet and lie on the pavement on Instytutska and Hrushevsky Streets, and the next shots that hit the aid workers rushing to assist them. We can now read up on all of this and see it for ourselves in numerous documentaries.

We have few images to draw on as we try to identify a precedent for what happened between November and March (there was a time when events of this kind were not captured in pictures): the Paris Commune and, yes, the revolutions in Russia; the uprisings in Berlin in 1953, in

Poznań and Budapest in 1956, in Prague in 1968. The question is why a generation that vividly remembers the Paris May Days remained largely silent on Kiev, why it found no words for basic facts such as moral courage, pluck, the bravery it took to stand up to the violence of a corrupt regime, why even the scant expressions of sympathy were muffled by reflexive inhibitions, qualifications and reservations. We are aware of what Victoria Nuland, then the u.s. Assistant Secretary of State for European and Eurasian Affairs, said about arms shipments into Ukraine, of the billions the United States supposedly poured into building up NGOs, of the Bandera posters right next to the Maidan stage, and much more. But all these – whether rumours or based in reality – do not unmake the pictures of the 'Revolution of Dignity'.

More than a year has passed, but it is not too late to revisit Maidan and, more saliently, reconsider the view we took of it. My purpose is not to romanticize it or spin a theory of revolution to glorify it. It is to get a grasp of a contemporary reality that ambushed us.

War: Violence Erupts, Discourses Cease

What blindsided us even more was the return of violence, the onset of a period of war. We cannot yet tell: is this a belated rearguard action of – or the beginning of a slide back into – the forty-year Cold War? Is it even the dawn of a new pre-war era of disintegrating hegemony and global disarray? After the Second World War, a long period of peace shielded by the deterrence capabilities of the superpowers had habituated Europeans to the thought that borders were sacrosanct, that all sides, whatever their differences, agreed on their inviolability. The forcible annexation of Crimea was an infraction against this rule that, if others were to follow the precedent it set, would overthrow the whole international order. The reasoning offered in its defence reads like a how-to guide to the destruction of the European post-war order. Using Putin's ethno-nationalist argument and historical justification of his demands as a template, any given border may be called into question. The seizure of land by military means was without precedent in post-1945 Europe. The breach of the rules shattered an entire world founded on negotiation, diplomacy and a culture of discursive engagement.

Sober-minded and seasoned observers of the Yugoslav Wars have described the war against Ukraine as a kind of déjà vu, and there are indeed striking parallels. Still, a war against a European nation started by a highly armed nuclear power evinces a new or different quality. The resurgence of violence is dismaying not just because of the specifics – the snipers, the torture, the downing of a passenger aeroplane, the atrocities perpetrated by separatist irregulars and mercenaries – but because it is a vivid example of military escalation dominance: an evolving crisis that is controlled by the side that always has the last word – in this instance, military might, including the nuclear option.

And last but not least, we are dealing with an undeclared war, a war that officially does not exist. The aggression is perfectly obvious – Russian troops are on Ukrainian territory, not vice versa – and yet flatly denied. It is not those who ferry arms and instructors into the occupied parts of Ukraine that are the arsonists, we are told, but those who stand up to them. Self-defence is portrayed as provocation that occasions further escalation. Not only are the facts turned upside down, the very idea of fact is called into question. Even soldiers of whose existence we have incontrovertible documentary evidence are said to be not soldiers but inventions, projections or perhaps tourists who lost their bearings and inadvertently crossed the border. Soldiers killed in action are shipped back to Russia in sealed unmarked coffins, and their relatives must keep their names and cause of death a secret to receive the dependents' pension, making the dead disappear a second time. The instructors and choreographers behind the occupations of Simferopol, Slavyansk, Kramatorsk, Donetsk and Lugansk are so sure of the justness of their cause and by now also so voluble in their triumph that we know the specifics of operations that we were told a year ago were a figment of our imaginations. On the first anniversary of the occupation of Crimea, Putin himself could not help boasting about the details of his professionally conducted blitzkrieg.

This has long ceased to be about propaganda and counter-propaganda and has become a struggle over whether the distinction between reality and fiction still obtains. Facts are turned into a matter of interpretation, in keeping with the motto that everything is a lie and everything is equally true. Brazen lies are proffered at press conferences, and even in diplomacy, where a distinctive kind of discretion is supposed to be observed, a veteran professional like Russia's foreign minister Sergei Lavrov seems to have lost all scruples, serving up the demagogic rhetoric of a 'genocide of the Russian people' in Ukraine. On the talk shows, too, lies are bandied about without shame and often remain uncontradicted, either because none of the other guests are prepared to cut the liar off or because the moderators are under pressure to triangulate; the idea is that truth is always somewhere in the middle rather than something that can be determined. The talking goes on while the tanks roll. We have been overrun in an information war whose masterminds deftly employ the postmodernist rhetoric of the multiplicity of perspectives and the relativity of everything.

The military early warning systems have failed, and so, obviously, have the intellectual ones. We have virtually no adequate responses to the imperial-ethno-nationalist projects of the 'Russian World' (Russky Mir) and neo-Eurasianism; we have barely begun to mount anything like an organized defence against the armada of trolls and the targeted disinformation campaigns on social networks; we are largely oblivious of the virtuosic choreographies in which alliances are forged that span the spectrum from the far right to the far left, and oblivious also of how those alliances harness the internal contradictions that abound in a structure as complex as the European Union and may yet be its undoing.

Europe's Frontier

So this is not just about Crimea, or about the Donbass, or about Ukraine; it is about something more, and in that sense I would call Ukraine Europe's frontier. After 1989 many of us pondered a possible 'reconstitution of Europe'. I confess that the destruction of the Europe that had taken shape after 1945 was beyond my imagination. Now the threat is real: that Europe might fall apart, that it might not stand up to the extortionists, that the battlefield that eastern Ukraine became a year ago might expand westward and the instability into which Ukraine is to be pushed might seize – indeed, has already seized – Europe as a whole.

Whenever the European Union today discusses decisions to be taken, a kind of 'Stone Guest' has already taken a seat at the table: behind the flailing attempts to rescue Greece looms the fear that the country might take refuge in Putin's embrace and the arms of the Russian oligarchs – and Konstantin Malofeev, the Orthodox oligarch, friend of Alexander Dugin, and sponsor of undercover activities in Crimea and the Donbass, has long established his Greek connection. On the issue of Europe's energy supplies, the question of how the continent can ensure its independence and become immune to blackmail has finally been put on the agenda. Cities and countries that depend on tourism revenues – the 'Golden Mile' in Vienna's 1st district, Berlin's

Kurfürstendamm, the real estate industry in Barcelona – have started to think about how to win back their free-spending Russian clientele or make up for the slowdown in business in other ways. The editorial boards at newspapers and television stations zealously try to show no weakness and more vigilantly than ever maintain an equal distance from all sides so as to avoid the slightest suspicion of trafficking in 'anti-Russian stereotypes'.

Europeans were unprepared for this eventuality, and it took them some time to adjust to the new situation. The hybrid war, though undeclared, had begun, but they continued to have faith in the effectiveness of symmetrical deterrence. As Russian equipment and armed personnel were streaming across the Ukrainian border, the institutions tasked with gathering information were still incapable of producing evidence – or unwilling to do so for political reasons. The work of documenting, identifying and reconstructing arms shipments was left to reporters who often took extraordinary risks to follow leads, conduct interviews in embattled areas, and take photographs that removed all doubt concerning the aggressors' identities. Last year, intellectual and academic circles worked themselves into a criminological frenzy over minutiae in their efforts to reconstruct the outbreak of the First World War, while the military conflict incubating right before their eyes failed to catch their attention. They were more at home in a past that engaged their entire analytical acumen – 2014 was, above all, the anniversary of the outbreak of the First World War – than in the present. Who had any idea what 'Eurasianism' was? We knew that it had been the moniker of an intellectual circle in the 1920s, but that was of interest only to historians of ideas. Yet Dugin, the leading mind of the neo-Eurasian movement, is not just an exegete and interpreter of interesting texts, he has given public speeches and written blog posts in which he calls on his followers to form Freikorps-style volunteer battalions: 'Kill! Kill! Kill!' The concept of the 'Russian World' promulgated by Putin was, precisely, not just a programme for admirers of Russian literature and culture, it was a straightforward proclamation: Russia is wherever Russians are, wherever Russian is spoken. It reminded one of the slogan of the German Freikorps in the 1920s: Wherever we are is Germany. And Russians living outside the country's borders were suddenly assigned a position that resembled the one ethnic Germans living abroad had occupied in the interwar years: a readily deployable 'Fifth Column' for irredentist and revanchist movements – then it was the Sudeten Germans in Czechoslovakia, now it is the Russian-speaking populations in the Baltic countries and Ukraine.

The tragedy is not just that these groups are exploited for nakedly imperial policies; the nationalist and ethnocentric rhetoric strikes at the roots also of the Russian Federation itself. As the name – *Rossiyskaya Federatsiya* rather than *Russkaya Federatsiya* – indicates, Russia is not a Russian nation, not ethnically homogeneous, it is the federation of the Russian lands, the space of a multi-ethnic state. The 'Russian World' is also meant to be an alternative to our world: a place of immutable values closely bound up with the moral precepts and ideas of social order of the Russian Orthodoxy. The Russian media deride Europe as 'Gayropa', an object of contempt, although Russian oligarchs and officials still send their children to boarding schools in England and spend their vacations in villas on the Côte d'Azur. Not unlike fundamentalist Islam, a fundamentalist orthodoxy and an authoritarian regime can be profoundly alluring to disoriented young people. The ethnic German Russian citizens who enlisted with the pro-Russian separatist forces in the Donbass were surely not the last peculiar twist in this story.

The Russian Crisis behind the Ukraine Crisis

It must be said, and said clearly: the true cause behind the so-called Ukraine Crisis is a fundamental crisis of Russia. We can discuss the obvious weaknesses and grievances that have bedevilled Ukraine in the quarter-century of its independence, the cancerous structures, the dismal failure of its political elites, the mismanaged privatization that allowed a select few to become unimaginably wealthy overnight by embezzling the people's property (and stash it away abroad); we can discuss the production of nationalist myths, which was understandable after so many years of oppression but still unnecessarily provocative and divisive – a prudent effort which would have stood the country in better stead would have been to devise a historical narrative that integrated the experiences of all Ukrainians, including those in the Donbass. We can discuss the systemic and seemingly ineradicable corruption and the poverty into which large parts of the population have been plunged. But that is a discussion for Ukrainians themselves, and they, especially those stirred by Maidan, know more about it than outsiders. In the past twenty years, Ukraine, whatever its failings, has held substantially fair elections and managed non-violent transfers of power; it has a public sphere in which the nation's problems are debated and proposed solutions negotiated. Given the outside threat and the internal subversion, it is if anything a miracle that Ukraine has stood firm until now.

It is far more difficult to gain even a basic understanding of what is happening in Russia today. True, the post-Soviet Russian Federation faced enormous challenges. Yet there was a time when the demise of its empire was seen not only as a loss but as relief from a burden and an opportunity to direct all energies towards restoring and rebuilding a country that had been dealt terrible blows and bled dry in the twentieth century. For well over a decade, revenues from oil and natural gas were abundant, yet Putin temporized, gambling away the opportunity. Instead of bringing the country into the twenty-first century and unlocking its potentials, he redistributed the nation's wealth to a small kleptocratic clique and irreparably hollowed out the institutions that might have allowed Russians to take their collective fate into their own hands: the media, the parliament and the organizations of civil society. Faced with the crisis into which he had led his country, he chose the easy way out: waging this war and winning it would be less difficult than addressing the monumental task of modernizing Russia. It was the perfect way to deflect responsibility – the other side was to blame. Still, in the long run, no country, not even one so sorely tested by calamity as Russia, can be held together and governed by diktat. At some point the cohesion enforced by 'negative integration', as noted by Lev Gudkov, is bound to grow brittle. I mention Putin by name not because I feel the need to demonize or expose him but because the destruction of the country's institutions has massed all power in the hands of a single person – a calamitous development in any country and doubly so in Russia. He has done something that was unthinkable to Russians and so cannot exist officially and must be hushed up, a crime for which he will be called to account: he has instigated a war against the 'sister nation'. Despite his current standing in the opinion polls and popularity rankings, Putin shows all the hallmarks of a failing man.

Ukraine Will Make Its Way

The war against Ukraine continues. The ceasefire is observed or broken as needed. We do not know what will happen tomorrow and the day after. Escalation dominance is still the name of the game. Putin's choreography is being refined; competing and clashing factions within Europe and the West are being played off against each other with great skill. And yet his scheme has not (yet) come to fruition. He has won a battle but lost the war. He has taken Crimea in a *coup de main*, but Novorossiya and the secession of southeastern Ukraine have become stuck. Putin's colonial project, as Timothy Snyder has characterized it, has failed. The occupied areas around Donetsk and Lugansk are not viable as a regional unit, although they are enough to keep Ukraine permanently on edge. The damages the war – a war in Europe, not somewhere far off – has inflicted are monstrous: ravaged cities, over a million refugees, over 6,000 dead, an infrastructure in ruins. Still, Ukraine has not fallen to its knees. It has lost control of part of its territory, but the pushback against the aggression has propelled the genesis of a political nation. So far, civil society has made the enormous sacrifices; volunteers, ordinary citizens, have stepped in where a weak state proved incapable of functions as elementary as mounting an adequate defence. In short, the outside threat has certainly not derailed the process of nation building.

Historians cannot prescribe how to resolve the problems of the present, but that does not mean that they view current developments with unconcern. The future of Ukraine must be charted by the Ukrainians themselves. They will surely accept advice and material support from outside when they are helpful. Everything must be done to contain the conflict – but that is a commonplace. Ukraine's friends must find ways to become less susceptible to extortion – but that is more easily said than done. For lack of other responses, sanctions have been imposed, now they must be enforced – but how, if such decisions require the unanimous agreement of all European Union member countries? All diplomatic means must be exhausted – but what if the other side offers assurances only to break them? The West must stand up to Russia – but how do you stop an aggression that cannot be quelled with talks?

The attack on Ukraine is an attack not only on Ukraine. At stake is Europe, the West or whichever label we choose: a way of life that Putin and his ilk perceive as a threat. War has returned to Europe. The emergency for which Europeans, despite the Yugoslav experience, were no longer prepared after 1989 is here. They must bid farewell to the illusion that conflicts can be checked through diplomacy alone. We need not trot out the analogy with Munich 1938 to see that. It is enough to call things as they are. Yet it seems that that is infinitely difficult, because it has consequences – one way or another. We must insist on the distinction between the aggressor and the victim of his attack. A war is being waged, even if it is undeclared. Ukraine's self-defence is not only legitimate, but deserving of our support – which form that support should take is a question solely of political-military expediency. These things go without saying, or they should, and so they bear repeating. In an age of purposeful conceptual confusion, as Russian aggression wraps itself in the mantle of antifascism and a 'Revolution of Dignity' is branded as a 'fascist coup d'état', everything has become possible. We should look the emergency that has erupted in our lifetimes squarely in the face. It remains to be seen which practical conclusions we – our societies, and perhaps each of us individually – will draw. But we must not surrender the distinction between fact and fiction, between truth and lie. That is the least we can do to avoid repeating the *trahison des clercs*, the 'treason of the intellectuals', that Julien Benda lamented in the interwar period. The work to be done begins with looking around and seeing for ourselves so that we can begin to assess the gravity of the situation and grasp the distress, but also the strength, of a country that is standing its ground.

FOUR

KIEV, METROPOLIS

Only a poet of Osip Mandelstam's calibre could begin an essay on Kiev, penned in 1926, with these words:

> The oldest, most indomitable city in the Ukraine. Chestnut trees clothed in shining candles, comfits draped with pink and yellow plumes. Young ladies in contraband silk jackets. The down of the lindens, reminders of pogroms in the neurotic May air. Wide-eyed, large-mouthed children. An itinerant cobbler at work under the lindens, rhythmically exuding the joy of life.

Mandelstam continues to pile up the details: in the centre, the 'Kievan mansion is a storm-tossed ark, creaking but enamoured of life'. He peers into the apartments, each 'a tight little world of its own, torn by hatred, jealousy and intrigue'. On the city's largest boulevard, the Khreshchatyk, the Hotel Continental, a palatial structure from pre-revolutionary days, shines like new. 'At each window there is a Negro jazz musician.' Everyone who is anyone in the world of Soviet theatre and circus arts of the 1920s comes to visit: the Jewish Chamber Theatre from Moscow, the legendary animal trainer Durov, the avant-garde director Meyerhold. 'The city,' Mandelstam affirms, 'has a splendid and indomitable soul. This Ukrainian-Jewish-Russian city breathes a triple breath.'

The poet jotted these observations down only a few years after the end of the civil war in which the old Kiev had perished. The city's residents were gingerly returning to a kind of normal life. But who was to say whether this was a genuine recovery or merely a feverish yet specious and short-lived florescence?

Between Yesterday and Tomorrow

A visitor arriving today, after the Maidan revolution, would have to have Mandelstam's gift for recording all that is happening at once in this big city, for finding a form in which to capture the peculiar twofold state of affairs in which everything is both real and precarious, open to challenge. It would let him render the suspended state of uncertainty: despite incontrovertible evidence that the city stands intrepid, that business as usual continues apace, one senses that it would take no more than an incident, the paradoxical concurrence of a few contingencies, a misguided gesture or a precisely placed provocation, to explode the serenity that is the hallmark of urban life's routines.

Kiev in the spring of 2015. The book fair – it is held only for the fifth time – has just opened in the halls of the Arsenal, a giant nineteenth-century munitions factory that has been converted into an exhibition centre. Publishers from all over Ukraine have come; there are discussion events and readings around the theme of 'war and language'; a vast number of works in translation is on display; the exponents of the new, the young Ukrainian literature, polyglot and worldly, bask in the admiration of their readers and fans, an audience not unlike those one might encounter in Frankfurt or Gothenburg. Despite the large crowds, everyone is friendly and relaxed. From the outdoor café, the visitor looks over the walls towards the golden domes of the Monastery of the Caves, and a short walk brings him to the parks that take up the entire high bank above the Dnieper, from one end of the city to the other. He strolls down well-tended paths, past fountains and kiosks, and takes in the incomparable vista of the wide river, the islands, the new neighbourhoods on the left bank extending to the horizon. In the distance he sees the first bathers unpack their swimwear; he hears the muffled whoosh of traffic. Kiev's drivers like to go fast, their pursuit of speed records checked only by the rugged relief – the city is furrowed by ravines – and the cobblestoned streets that can still be found in the centre. Kiev is luminous: neon signs dot the night sky, spotlights pick out monuments and facades, squares are awash in light. The central district around the Khreshchatyk and Maidan is closed to cars on weekends, when Kievans amble amid shops, cafés, break dance ensembles and bandurists. Visitors from out of town marvel at their majestic and vibrant capital; foreigners have come to see with their own eyes the scenes they know from television. Little more than a year ago, humans were killed where traffic now flows again and people saunter. After the end of the fighting, a year ago, the sidewalks were still pitted with craters; vestiges of the barricades were embedded in the asphalt that melted when they were set on fire; tyres, cobblestones and sandbags were heaped up in mounds. On Hrushevsky Street, drivers still needed to navigate a slalom course between the barricades, almost as though in honour of the protesters who died here. For weeks after the fighting ceased, the smell of burnt tyres lingered over the square; graffiti with the slogans of the Maidan activists were emblazoned on doors and facades; the sidewalks on Instytutska Street were covered with makeshift memorials to the dead, with candles, paper flowers, objects from the victims' belongings, portrait photographs sheathed in plastic on which someone had noted their names, places of birth, occupations and ages. Approaching along Instytutska from the metro exit above the square or from the Hotel Ukraine, the visitor overlooked an almost sublime scenery where everyone seemed to lower their voices and tread gently, pausing before the memorials or studying the posters put up by people looking for missing relatives and friends. The tents and encampments still stood, guarded by sentinels, with all sorts of folk, some in exotic attire, milling about, apparently reluctant to return to the normalcy of urban life. Now, one year later, Kiev appears to have devised more permanent forms for what were initially spontaneous and improvised acts of homage – portrait galleries, preserved barricade fragments, inscriptions – and integrated commemoration of the events into everyday life. Traffic is flowing again, most of the pavements have been repaired, the windows have been reglazed, and the entrance to FC Dynamo Kiev's stadium has been painted an almost tauntingly bright white. Only the union hall on the corner that was gutted by fire is still covered with tarps and awaits rebuilding. Glory to the Heroes! Glory to the Heavenly Hundred! the posters read.

Meanwhile, signs of a new struggle already overshadow this scene of remembrance. Since the Russian aggression against Ukraine began, first in Crimea, then in the eastern part of the country, thousands – citizens in the occupied territories, volunteers, Ukrainian army soldiers – have fallen victim to a fresh wave of violence.

One year after the brutal clashes on Maidan, the war makes itself felt wherever one goes. It greets the visitor arriving at Boryspil International Airport in the form of breaking news from the front on the television screens mounted in the waiting halls. Fighting has erupted again

Anti-government riot in Kiev: the anti-government protest on Mykhailo Hrushevsky Street after news emerged about police shooting and killing two protesters with live ammunition, 22 January 2014.

where the ceasefire had brought an end to earlier battles. Next to the monument to the 'Heavenly Hundred', who died on Maidan, freshly printed posters show the dead in the most recent rounds of fighting. 'Heroes Never Die', the banners in the display cases proclaim. The war is there at the hotel's reception desk, where a donation box for the army has been set up; at the railway ticket counter and the supermarket checkout, where volunteers solicit money for food to be sent to the frontlines; inside the museum, where the commemoration of the victorious 'Great Patriotic War' seven decades ago is complemented by tributes to the dead of today's war. Although Kiev can seem far removed from developments on the front – in Donetsk, Shyrokyne and Mariupol – everyone constantly checks the news to stay current on the evolving situation because almost everyone is directly concerned. On television, families bid their fathers or sons a final farewell; volunteers report the positive response to their donation drives; entrepreneurs and businessmen give advice on how to contribute to better equipment for the army. Like other cities, Kiev has taken in tens of thousands of refugees from the areas around Donetsk and Lugansk, recognizable by the registration numbers of their cars. On Sunday mornings, groups of young and not quite so young men in camouflage uniforms board the metro to Darnytsia. They are obviously coming from home, the backpacks and sports bags they usually take to the office or the gym stuffed with extra provisions, their laptops and fresh underwear. Most other passengers exit at the Hydropark station to go to the beach, but they continue to the assembly point from which they will be ferried to the front. In the blink of an eye, they step outside the routines of daily life in a major European city and into a theatre of war. Everything changes: a mere metro ride takes them from peace to war.

Kievan Panorama, Kievan Relief

The point of view that has come to define how we think of Kiev was that of the cameras installed atop the Hotel Ukraine high above Maidan. Far below, the city had converged on the square. It felt as though we were peering down on an arena and watching the drama unfold. This was where the resistance congregated, the logistical centre, the platform for public appearances and speeches to the nation and the world, the place to relax in the lulls between rounds of street fighting, the stage for readings and religious services, the sheltered space to which the wounded were taken, the meeting place where the activists who had rushed to the scene from all parts of the country – from Chernihiv, Odessa, Lviv, Poltava and Vinnytsia – coordinated the resistance.

On older maps, today's Maidan Nezalezhnosti or Independence Square bears other names: in the Soviet era, it was called Soviet Square, then Kalinin Square for the Union's head of state; under German occupation, it was 19 September Square, after the day the city was conquered by the Wehrmacht; later it became the Square of the October Revolution. Before that revolution, it had been known as Dumskaya Ploshchad, or Council Square, after the City Duma building; after Pyotr Stolypin, the great reformer, was assassinated at the Kiev Opera House in 1911, his monument was erected here. With Khreshchatyk Street, which bisects it, the square had emerged as the centre of the up-and-coming capital of the Russian Empire's southwestern reaches. It was where the city's upper classes came to mingle, and so today's bustling Maidan – characteristically, the word, designating an urban open space, is ultimately a loan from Arabic – also signals the renascence of the city's erstwhile hub, the node where everything came together. The Khreshchatyk has been compared to the Champs-Élysées, although it is not even a mile long. Lined up along it are the most important offices, banks, department stores and hotels. It runs from today's European Square, where the Kiev Philharmonic has its home, to the Besarabsky

Market. In his memoirs, Ilya Ehrenburg recalled the Khreshchatyk of the belle époque he saw as a child:

> A stationery store sold exercise books in gleaming colourful covers that made even a percentage calculation a cheerful affair. One confectionery offered a dry jam the confectioner had named Balabukha after his family, with a bonbon in the box that resembled a rose and was fragrant like perfume. In Kiev I ate cherry pastries and garlic pies. Pedestrians smiled. In the summer, patrons in the cafés on Khreshchatyk sat out on the sidewalk, drinking coffee or eating ice cream. I regarded them with a mixture of envy and rapture.

From Maidan and the Khreshchatyk, the ground rises in terraces towards the hills, on one side towards the high bank of the Dnieper crowned by the Monastery of the Caves compound and the genteel residential neighbourhoods of Lypky and Pechersk; on the other, towards the Upper Town with St Sophia's Cathedral and St Michael's Golden-domed Monastery, remnants of the historic centre of Kievan Rus'. Also part of the 'Kiev Kremlin' were the city's oldest stone church, the Church of the Tithes, which was ruined during the Mongol invasion in 1240, and the imposing Golden Gate, which survived in fragments – tourists can now visit a sumptuous 'reconstruction'. In the nineteenth century, the area on this side of the Khreshchatyk was taken up by the rapidly growing new town, with the major public buildings arrayed along its main thoroughfares, Vladimir and Bibikov boulevards: the Kiev Opera, St Vladimir University, the Polytechnic Institute, secondary schools and museums. Pechersk and Lypky, meanwhile, boast the most luxurious villas and apartment buildings from the pre-revolutionary boom years, post-war residential complexes and apartment towers erected after the dissolution of the Soviet Union. They were also home to the highest ranks of the government and political apparatus.

Further north, separated by a steep slope from the Upper Town as well as the high bank of the Dnieper, down by the river, lies the third urban nucleus, Podil, the town of artisans, traders, petits bourgeois, of the market and the National University of Kyiv-Mohyla Academy. A stronghold of humanism and enlightenment in the golden age of the Cossack Hetmanate, it became the centre of Kiev's Jewish life in the nineteenth century; poor and middle-class Jews, in particular, moved to the area.

Cathedral of the Dormition, Pechersk Lavra, Kiev,
c. 1902.

Yet there is another spot from which to look down on Kiev for a
very different view: the high ridge above the Dnieper. The panorama
of the wide river, and the lowlands on the far side, is breathtaking.
'Sublime' is a word one should use sparingly, but here it fits; here the
city says: I was, I am, I shall be. The visitor vividly senses the vastness
of the plains extending east of the Dnieper and basks in the beauty of
the parks that take up the hills, with the gold of church domes and
bell towers rising from the verdant greenery, a scene that, as the exiled
Russian philosopher Georgy Fedotov noted, left even the 'poet from
the North' – he meant Alexander Pushkin – lost for words. The vista
from the hills explains why Kiev, in no small part because of its particular situation, has a firm place in visual culture far beyond Ukraine's
boundaries: it is famed not only as one of Europe's most beautiful
urban centres, but as the 'mother of Russian cities'.

The privileged location was recognized and prized throughout history: by the monks who, in the eleventh century, founded the Monastery of the Caves, which would grow into a veritable 'Vatican of Orthodoxy'; by the hetmans who fostered Kiev's return to its erstwhile glory in the seventeenth century; by the tsars of Russia who erected residences including Mariinsky Palace, armouries such as the Arsenal, and numerous government and administrative buildings. In the nineteenth century, merchants financed the creation of the parks, an Arcadia right in the city; by contrast, most of the twentieth century's contributions to the sights arrayed on the hills along the Dnieper are monuments to the cataclysms suffered by city and country: the steel Mother Motherland statue – the overall structure stands 102 m (335 ft) tall – completed in 1981 to commemorate the Great Patriotic War; the crypt-like Holodomor monument, built by the newly independent Ukraine, with a tower in the shape of a stylized candle; the Park of Eternal Glory for the soldiers who died in the battle for Kiev with its laconic obelisk at the centre. A 30-m- (100-ft-) wide steel arch on a platform high above Podil commemorates the 1654 Treaty of Pereyaslav and the 'everlasting friendship between Russia and Ukraine', surrounded by a cluster of hotels, cultural institutions and Pioneer Palaces, a landscape of recreation, reflection and amusement.

Kiev's relief is in constant motion. The city has steeply pitched streets; the visitor is baffled by how long the trips on the metro stations' escalators take and how deep they convey him into the underground. A funicular from the early twentieth century covers the considerable elevation difference between the upper and lower towns on a precipitous track. 'One passes through mazes of cobblestoned courtyards, through empty lots and swathes cut right through the stone,' Mandelstam noted, succinctly capturing Kiev's character: 'Piled up in terraces rises the great city on the Dnieper that has survived all adversity.' The sudden ups and downs, the abrupt changes of perspective, will remind some visitors of Lisbon or San Francisco. The proximity of the wide river and the deeply gouged terrain of the high bank produce forever new vistas. This kind of relief has no room for oversized parade grounds. Kiev's appearance is dominated by nature, which reaches into the heart of the city in the large parks and along wide boulevards. The relief forces architects to make economic use of space and encourages picturesque solutions. Kiev is by nature incapable of magisterial perspectives and grand *prospekty*. Hence its lack of imperial potency; where other cities are infatuated with geometry, Kiev's is a quieter love for the contours and gradients of its ridges. Its people would rather go to a café than watch a display of military prowess.

'Vatican of Orthodoxy': Monastery of the Caves, Pechersk

The hills high above the Dnieper are the seat of the 'Vatican of Orthodoxy'. The temple precinct, a town unto itself hemmed by a wall and paths, by stately gates in the 'Cossack Baroque' of the seventeenth and eighteenth centuries, occupies the ridge and the slopes facing the river, with cathedrals, a refectory, a library, a bell tower, a printing shop, outbuildings, living quarters and lodging houses for pilgrims. Miles of tunnels have been hewn into the bedrock in which the monastery has buried its monks for a millennium. This is the spiritual centre, the birthplace of the *Tale of Past Years*, known as Nestor's Chronicle, our most important source of knowledge about the Kievan Rus'. In Soviet times, the monastery was converted into a museum intended to demonstrate the absurdity of the veneration of relics, of obscurantism and the belief in miracles. Now the monks and pilgrims have returned to the monastery; small groups of tourists, candles in hand, wander through the corridors, reverently eyeing the mummified corpses of monks. An entire cavalcade of black jeeps, Humvees and luxury limousines stands at attention in one courtyard, an unmistakable sign that the church hierarchy, once marginalized, has resumed its place at the centre of society – or more precisely, by the side of the powerful – and embraces the modern world when it comes to displaying its grandeur. A photography gallery on the Pechersk Lavra's grounds documents the history of the complex after its conversion into a museum in 1926. The bell tower looking out over the Dnieper survived the German occupation unscathed. By contrast, the Cathedral of the Dormition, a splendid Baroque structure, was destroyed by an explosion on 3 November 1941; most probably, Soviet specialists had planted charges in the building and detonated them using wireless controls. The young Anatoly Kuznetsov saw the Monastery of the Caves in flames: 'It was burning. The Lavra's main belfry shone with a bright orange light, as if it were illuminated, yet there was little smoke. There was no more Cathedral of the Dormition – there was nothing but a heap of stones, with the remains of frescoed walls protruding from it. All the museums and the entire walled town

Pechersk Lavra (Monastery of the Caves), Kiev.

St Sophia's Cathedral, Kiev, *c.* 1890–1900.

were burning.' After the reconstruction programme of 1998–2000, the ensemble now appears as if nothing had happened: at great expense and with much artistic expertise, the cathedral was rebuilt in record time, as were other 'cultic objects' in a city that, before the wave of demolitions of the 1930s and the war, counted almost 160 churches and monasteries.

Looking across the Dnieper towards the east, the visitor senses that he stands on an ancient outpost of the Eastern Church, an *antemurale Christianitatis*; the baptism of the Rus' in 988 is commemorated by the nineteenth-century monument to St Vladimir.

The verticals of the belfries and golden domes visible from afar define Kiev's silhouette in the Upper Town as well: St Sophia's Cathedral, St Vladimir's Cathedral, St Michael's Monastery. The exteriors of the gates, bell-towers and cupolas of St Sophia's may be examples of the colourful Cossack Baroque, but once the visitor enters, he feels transported to Byzantium. If he has seen similar frescoes and mosaics before, it was in Constantinople or Ravenna. The play with the vertical is carried to extremes in Francesco Bartolomeo Rastrelli's lavishly ornamented blue-and-white St Andrew's Church atop Andriivsky Descent, which leads down to Podil. The edifice soars from the rampant greenery of the park along the Dnieper like a Baroque sculpture. Each renaissance of religious feeling – the current one no less than the one around 1900 – prompts a wave of church-building, adding new golden domes to the city's crown. The sight is most imposing when the visitor, coming from the airport, reaches one of the bridges across the Dnieper and looks up towards the Monastery of the Caves. Already marred by the late Soviet monumental sculpture of Mother Motherland, the silhouette is in even greater danger now that post-Soviet architects seem intent on emulating postmodernism and disfiguring the heights with their ungainly creations.

Podil: Town on the River, Magdeburg Rights, Mohyla Academy

Well into the nineteenth century, Kiev was really three towns – Pechersk with the Monastery of the Caves, the Upper Town of St Vladimir, and Podil down by the river. They stood for ecclesiastical power, secular rule, and the trades, transport and commerce, respectively. Kiev's growth is inconceivable without the river. Podil was most likely the site of the first human settlement in the area. The river and its tributaries facilitated the exploration and development of the vast land. Rising – like the Volga and Daugava rivers, which flow in very different directions – in the Valdai Hills in central Russia, the 2,200-km (1,370-mile) Dnieper is an ancient trade route connecting the Baltic and Black Seas, Scandinavia to the Mediterranean and the Orient. It was down the Dnieper that the Varangians arrived in the ninth century; they played a key role in the consolidation of the Old Rus', the greatest medieval polity of the Eastern Slavic tribes. And down the Dnieper – known as Borysthenes to the Greeks, Slavutych to the Slavs and Danapris to the Scythians – they travelled to the Black Sea and Byzantium. Where trade between the Baltic and Black Seas intersected with the network of the Silk Road, which connected China and Central Asia, the Orient, to Western Europe, a city arose; shortly before the Mongol destruction in 1240, it was said to have 50,000 inhabitants, making it one of Europe's largest at a time when Paris numbered 5,000 and London 30,000 residents. Coins found where the Lybid and Pochaina rivers enter the Dnieper show that Podil remained a major trading centre after the fall of Kiev. In 1494 the Grand Duchy of Lithuania, which had gained control of the area in 1362, awarded Podil Magdeburg rights – the privilege to have its own judiciary, administrative autonomy and the right to elect a mayor – which it retained until 1834, a crucial factor in the city's development that is memorialized by a column down by the river. After the merger of Lithuania and Poland in the Union of Lublin in 1569, Podil continued to thrive, not only as a commercial hub – the annual market on Kontraktova Square was one of the most important trade fairs – but as an intellectual centre of the first rank. Growing Polish and Catholic influence led to the establishment of the Kiev Collegium in Podil in 1632; under its founding director, Petro Mohyla, it was a vital gateway for the ideas of Humanism and the Renaissance that transmitted modernizing impulses into the Muscovite Tsardom long before Peter the Great. Merchants from all nations met in Podil: Greeks, Armenians, Italians, Jews, Germans and Slavs. In 1690 the town had a magistrates' building and thirteen Orthodox and three Catholic churches. After the eighteenth-century Partitions of Poland and the subsequent influx of Jews, the neighbourhood would become Kiev's most Jewish borough, with numerous synagogues and houses of prayer.

The treaty between the hetmanate under Bohdan Khmelnytsky and Moscow in 1654 opened the door to steadily growing Russian influence, and the focus of urban development shifted yet again. In 1706 Peter the Great visited and decided to fortify Kiev as a bulwark against Poland, Sweden, and the Ottoman Empire and its allies, the Crimean Tatars. Catherine II stopped here in 1787 during her voyage to Crimea and was perplexed to find nothing but battlements and ruins. She issued an order to draw up a new general plan for Kiev. By 1800 the city's integration into the Russian Empire was virtually complete.

Yet it was above all the fast-paced development of the nineteenth century – industrialization, modernization and urbanization – that forced Kiev to overcome the sectionalism of its semi-independent constituent towns and fuse them, within no more than a few decades, into a European metropolis.

Boomtown, Belle Époque

The centre of this new Kiev was neither the Monastery of the Caves in Pechersk nor St Sophia's Cathedral in the town of St Vladimir nor the Lower Town in Podil, but a new place: the Khreshchatyk. Its addresses and facades were an open book that spelled out to the attentive passerby the interlocking structures of economic and political power, of urban society and culture, that made Kiev the 'third city' of the Russian Empire. Khreshchatyk is not easy to find today because the urban space that bears its name is a remake, a reconstruction of enormous dimensions: days after German troops took the city on 19 September 1941, a series of huge explosions reduced large parts of the old Khreshchatyk to rubble, and the entire city suffered heavy damage throughout the war. What the visitor now sees is the boulevard as it was recreated after the war, with the telegraph and post office, department stores, restaurants, cafés and apartments. It is an almost perfect planned urban core, far grander in its dimensions than the pre-war Khreshchatyk, on whose design and proportions, with wide pavements, stairs, archways and forecourts, it is nonetheless recognizably modelled: a spacious but by no means intimidating urban ensemble. Of the major urban-planning inventions of the post-war years – Stalingrad, Minsk, central Warsaw, East Berlin's Stalinallee – Kiev's may well be the most compelling solution. Framed by the symmetrically arranged volumes of buildings rising to up to ten storeys, the Khreshchatyk's width is made less monotonous by stairs, fountains and monuments. Almost all the major international brands have representations on the street and in the adjoining arcades, and the familiar prestigious limousines speed down the broad avenue (unless traffic is congested, which it often is). Still, on the whole the avenue is a space in which the city can stroll and experience itself, despite the abundant red granite, the ground storeys clad in black rock, and the oak-wood window frames (the characteristic building materials of power). Soviet urban planners and the Kievans who returned after the war or moved here from elsewhere in the Union have achieved something admirable: the operation of implanting a new and vigorous heart in the city was successful.

A few surviving fragments give an intimation of what the Khreshchatyk was before the devastations of war and the rebuilding programme: the 1882 Merchants' House, now home to the National Philharmonic, Fyodor Lidval's Russian Bank at 13 Khreshchatyk, Leonty Benois' Volga-Kama Bank at number 8, the Constructivist central Univermag on the corner of Bohdan Khmelnytsky Street, and the audacious roof construction of the Besarabsky Market (1908–12).

It is no coincidence that the Kiev of the belle époque is being rediscovered now that the city is gearing up for a new era. A slew of coffee-table books and collections of historic postcards feeds the understandable nostalgia. A city of no more than 20,000 inhabitants around 1800, Kiev grew rapidly throughout the nineteenth century; the 1913 census counted 594,400 residents. With its bridges across the Dnieper, it became a major railway hub; prominent educational institutions – secondary schools, the Technological Institute, St Vladimir University, whose bright red main building is still a sight to behold – were established. But the primary source of the city's wealth was agribusiness: grain export, the sugar industry and the flour mills. The urban landscape was defined less by the tsardom's public buildings than by the representative mansions of its industrialists, merchants, ship owners, railway entrepreneurs and sugar barons. Situated at the heart of a region known in St Petersburg as Little Russia, this Kiev had all the hallmarks of a major city in a multi-ethnic empire. Its mayors had names such as Gustav Eisman (a brickworks owner descended from Baltic Germans), Ivan Tolli (whose ancestors were Odessan Greeks), and Józef Zawadzki, an ethnic Pole. By 1900 a majority of Kievans spoke Russian; Ukrainian literature was banned and the use of the Ukrainian language was prohibited at the universities. The Polish community was comparatively small but still influential. The Ukrainian middle class was rising, represented, for example, by the Tereshchenkos, a family of industrialists. With legal restrictions relaxed, Jews from the Pale of Settlement moved to the city in large numbers: a community of no more than five hundred souls in 1862 grew to almost 90,000, or 15 per cent of the total population, by 1917. In 1911, 17 per cent of Kiev's university students and 44 per cent of the members of its merchants' association were of Jewish descent. The Brodskys, Halperins and Zaitsevs own the largest sugar plants, mills and breweries, while

40 per cent of the Jewish population in Podil are dependent on the charity of Jewish philanthropists and patrons.

The infrastructures that turned Kiev into a modern big city were realized in rapid succession: the Kiev-Balta-Odessa railway, in 1863–8; the municipal water supply, in 1870; the telephone network, in 1888; a horse tramway, in 1891, and then the electric tram, Russia's first, in 1892; the municipal sewer system and a power station, in the 1890s. Industrialization begins with construction of the grand complex of the Arsenal, followed by machine engineering plants and working-class housing estates. The cogwheel railway between the Upper and Lower Towns is taken into service in 1905. Kiev has the allure of a city where life is good, with seemingly innumerable places of amusement, smart hotels and fine restaurants (the Baedeker highlights luxury hotels such as the Continental and the Leipzig). Many of the parks along the ridge high above the Dnieper, with music pavilions and a legendary Château de fleurs, were financed by the city's merchants (one that was named in their honour was later renamed Pioneers Park). Ilya Ehrenburg, born in Kiev in 1891 as the son of a director of Brodsky's brewery, would later recall:

House with Chimaeras, Kiev, 2005.

Kiev had enormous gardens in which chestnut trees grew. For a boy from Moscow they were no less exotic than palm trees. In the spring the blossoms gleamed amid the foliage like candelabras, and in the autumn I collected the burnished chestnuts. There were gardens everywhere: on Institutskaya Street, on Mariinsko-Blagoveshchenskaya Street, on Zhitomirskaya, on Aleksandrovskaya . . . Later, whenever I returned to Kiev, I was fascinated by the ease, cordiality and vitality of its people. It appears that each country has its own South and North.

Along the streets criss-crossing the steep slopes of Lypky – the neighbourhood begins right behind the Hotel Ukraine – the villas of magnates were crowded out by stately apartment buildings: space was tight, buildings grew higher and higher, and the area was the site of Kiev's first 'skyscraper', the Ginzburg House.

Building activity was feverish from the 1890s until the outbreak of the Great War, and virtually every architect trained at the Academy in St Petersburg contributed designs. After the classicism that had effectively been the empire's signature style since the early nineteenth century, Kiev now produced an excessive eclecticism and Art Nouveau. Particularly splendid specimens include the Karaite Kenesa, a synagogue in the Moorish style, on Yaroslaviv Val Street (now the Ukrainian House of Actors); the Brodsky Choral Synagogue near the Besarabsky Market (used as a puppet theatre in Soviet times); and many apartment blocks in Lypky, which come in a plethora of styles: Romanesque Revival, Gothic Revival, an especially sumptuous neo-Baroque. Among the many architects – their renown was not necessarily confined to the empire – one stands out: Vladyslav Horodetsky, often dubbed 'Kiev's Antonio Gaudí', a passionate big-game hunter and writer when he was not working on his designs, whose villa on Bankova Street has been praised as one of Kiev's miracles. The so-called House with Chimaeras is Art Nouveau cast in concrete, a cement-grey phantasmagoria with animals, from frogs to rhinoceroses, crowding the roof and facades. Now a residence of the Ukrainian president, the building and a generous security perimeter are closed to the public. Some of the villas in the area survived the expropriation of privately owned homes as office buildings or shared residences and are now open to visitors who wish to study the interiors of pre-revolutionary Kiev: see, for instance, the lumber magnate Mohylevtsev's 'Chocolate House', with Moorish rooms and some original furniture. After decades of neglect, many of these structures are currently being renovated. The gallery commissioned by Bogdan and Varvara Khanenko in the 1890s has become a public museum; so has the residence of the Tereshchenkos. As elsewhere in the Russian Empire, wealthy private individuals made up for the failings of the public authorities, and the need for such private initiative was the greater in a city far removed from the centres of power. These benefactors and philanthropists were ill repaid for their generosity by the Soviet authorities. Many were forced into exile: the Tereshchenkos left for France (one returned to Ukraine a few years ago and took Ukrainian citizenship); Horodetsky died in Iran; when Lazar Brodsky, to whom the city owes the establishment of numerous scientific institutes, a lung clinic, the synagogue named after him, and the Besarabsky Market, died, in Basel, in 1904, his body was brought back home by train and received at the station by a large procession – the Soviet Union largely effaced his name from the official historical record. It was not until after the downfall of communism that these representatives of bourgeois Kiev were remembered and honoured with exhibitions and public dedications.

Frenzied economic development and fevered agitation, competition and hatred went hand in hand. Late imperial Kiev exemplified both. In 1913 the city hosted the All-Russian Industrial and Art Exhibition, a triumph for the 'third capital'. But 1913 was also the year it made headlines around the world with the trial for ritual murder against the Jewish factory superintendent Mendel Beilis and the sensational acquittal his attorneys gained against the court's predisposition and the anti-Semitic sentiment fomented by the country's highest authorities.

Mikhail Bulgakov: The Master and the City

For Kiev, as for Ukraine as a whole, the Great War was both a godsend and a disaster. The revolution it sparked toppled the last of the distant rulers who had for centuries resisted and repressed the emergence of a Ukrainian nation and its quest for political self-determination. The disintegration of the Russian Empire paved the way first for autonomy – proclaimed 'to the entire Ukrainian people' in the summer of 1917 in the First Universal of the Tsentralna Rada, the Ukrainian provisional government – and then independence: in January 1918 the Fourth

Universal declared that 'from this day forth, the Ukrainian People's Republic becomes independent, subject to no one, a free, sovereign state of the Ukrainian people.'

But only days later Bolshevik troops occupied Kiev, soon to be ousted by the Central Powers. The champions of independence had sought to end forever the second-class status of the 'Little Russians' (or 'Ruthenians', as they had been called in the Habsburg Empire) and the suppression of the Ukrainian language and literature as well as the discrimination against the Jews confined to the Pale of Settlement until 1915. Yet the downfall of the empire also meant the end of the public order that had propelled and sustained the city's rise as an economic powerhouse in the decades since the great reforms. The struggle for national self-determination, the uprising against the old elites, peasants' revolts, counter-revolutionary armies, anti-Jewish pogroms – over the years that followed, these interlocking forces and conflicts turned Kiev into the scene of an unending and dizzying string of skirmishes that concluded not with the consolidation of a Ukrainian People's Republic but with the victory of the Bolsheviks and the country's reincorporation into the empire reborn under the acronym USSR. Kharkov was chosen as the new Ukraine's first capital.

The succession of competing powers and intersecting frontlines in Kiev between 1917 and 1921 is hard to disentangle. An inevitably incomplete enumeration of the major events and actors might look as follows: the proclamation of the Ukrainian People's Republic, the brief reign of the Bolsheviks, the arrival of imperial German troops after the Treaty of Brest-Litovsk and the installation of the puppet government under Pavlo Skoropadskyi, a former general in the tsar's army, as hetman of Ukraine; the short-lived regime of the leftist nationalist Directory under Symon Petliura; the arrival of White troops under General Denikin, fighting, with French and British support, for the restoration of a 'one and indivisible Russia'; and, lest we forget, the *coup de main* in which Józef Piłsudski's Polish troops took Kiev in 1920, only to destroy the bridge across the Dnieper, Europe's longest, before retreating. The victory of the Red Army eventually ended this 'time of troubles'. Amid rapidly moving frontlines and under alternating rulers, there were armies, refugees, marauders and wartime profiteers of all stripes passing through Kiev. Ilya Ehrenburg later recalled the German officers with Kaiser-Wilhelm-style moustaches strolling up and down the Khreshchatyk and gorging themselves on Viennese schnitzel, Berliner pastries, shashlik and sour cream. For a while, the city was one great waiting hall and transit point:

> Kiev resembled an overcrowded mid-size spa town. The locals were outnumbered by the mass of refugees from the north. The Khreshchatyk was the first stop on the Russian emigrants' journey, before the quay in Odessa, before the Turkish islands, before the boarding houses of Berlin and the mansard apartments of Paris. How many future Paris taxi drivers you might have met on the Khreshchatyk in those days! There were high officials from Petersburg and nimble journalists, music-hall singers and landlords, as well as plenty of ordinary philistines, all scattered by the northern wind like dry leaves.

Gambling houses, cabarets and the black market were booming. Kiev became the fallen empire's grand bazaar:

> Countless consignment shops popped up. That was new and baffling. They sold furs, pectoral crosses, icons, silverware, earrings, Scottish plaids, lace, in short: everything that people had been able to take with them from Moscow and Petersburg. Several currencies circulated: the tsar's money, Kerensky's scrip, Ukrainian tender; no one knew which of them was the worst. Outside City Hall, speculators offered German marks, Austrian crowns, English pounds and American dollars. When a German defeat in France was reported, the mark fell and the pound rose. Dollars were especially in demand.

Like the money, officers and soldiers came in all varieties: Denikin's and Krasnov's followers, erstwhile defenders of the Kuban People's Republic and members of the Astrakhan Host, anti-Bolsheviks, and anti-Semites intoning 'Smash the Jews! Save Russia!' 'The newspapers changed names. Yellow–blue flags fluttered in the streets. The banknotes bore a trident. Companies were ordered to change their signs: wherever you went there were painters' apprentices atop ladders replacing the Russian letter "i" with the Ukrainian one.' Every armed contingent that passed through destroyed a piece of the city. Munitions depots blew up, leaving thousands dead or homeless. Those who were able to find shelter in the countryside fled the city, hoping to survive the imminent famine. 'I sometimes felt,' Ehrenburg writes, 'like I was sitting in a movie theatre, watching a wild chase.'

The years of turmoil laid waste to the orderly world of the bourgeoisie. The epic of its downfall is narrated by Mikhail Bulgakov, born in Kiev in 1891 as the son of a professor of theology. He painted the violent dawn of a new era and the demise of the old world in *The White Guard* (1924) and the play *Days of the Turbins*, whose coldly analytical account of the ruin of the bourgeoisie endeared it to Stalin; another play, *Flight*, about the journey into exile, draws on the same experiences. Kievan scenes are everywhere in Bulgakov's texts, and it might be said that all his milieus and personages were inspired by the city of his childhood and youth. Not everyone goes so far as the Kiev-based literary scholar Myron Petrovsky, who, in the brilliant study *Master i gorod* (The Master and the City, 2001), has argued that even *The Master and Margarita*, Bulgakov's 'novel of a century', is ultimately rooted in the primal experience of the fall of bourgeois Kiev. Revolution and civil war are depicted as apocalypse, the novel's Moscow and Jerusalem decoded as Kiev – or as Bulgakov himself suggested with the title of a 1927 essay: 'Kiev – The City', the paradigmatic city, the city as such. As Petrovsky puts it, Kiev became the railway carriage from which the writer gazed upon the world on his journey through time. So many motifs that appeared in the *faits divers* sections or among the theatrical reviews in Kiev's newspapers resurface in Bulgakov's texts: the production of the mystery play *King of the Jews* in 1917; Kiev as a bastion of operetta culture; the site of the assassination of the German General von Eichhorn; the First Kiev Gymnasium on today's Taras Shevchenko Boulevard, where Bulgakov went to school; the Pedagogical Museum; Madame Anjou's Salon in the house on the corner behind the opera; the square outside St Sophia's Cathedral. For connoisseurs, *The White Guard* is a virtual guidebook to Kiev's topography, and first and foremost to the house on Andreevsky Spusk, now Andriivsky Uzviz. A bourgeois residence on perhaps the most beautiful and steepest of the streets leading down from the Upper Town to Podil, just a stone's throw from Rastrelli's soaring St Andrew's Church, the building in which the Soviet intelligentsia's 'cult author' had lived between 1906 and 1919 had become a kind of pilgrimage destination already in Soviet times. At some point a commemorative plaque was installed, and in 1989 a museum opened its doors, with everything a reconstruction of an exemplary intelligentsia household required. A recent redesign was even more ambitious: the museum now stages a kind of 'magical realism', with some of the furniture – the metal bed, the sideboard, family photographs, issues of the journal *Niva* – presented in the original condition while other elements are painted all white to give the visitors a sense of moving between reality and phantasmagoria. After the revolution, the Bulgakov family's refined home, like most bourgeois residences, was divided up into separate lodgings, which allowed the building to survive the Soviet Union. Looking out the window at 13 Andriivsky Uzviz, the visitor today enjoys a fine view of Podil and the crowds of tourists making their way past the kiosks of memorabilia vendors towards the Upper Town.

The fates of houses and mansions: another theme that might be used to narrate the history of Kiev. Mariinsky Palace was taken over by the Council of People's Commissars in 1919. The new rulers commandeered numerous villas. The home of Countess Uvarova at 16 Ekaterininskaya Street, today's Lypska Street, became the headquarters of the All-Ukrainian Extraordinary Commission, also known as Cheka. The Governorate Cheka took up quarters in the former residence of the Governor-General at 40 Instytutska Street, and the same agency, later so notorious, requisitioned one of Brodsky's villas.

The ruin of bourgeois Kiev was the apocalyptic core that inspired a masterpiece. Bulgakov not only observed it in his own home, he saw the houses set on fire by the various parties in the Civil War and, on later visits to his native city, the demolition of St Michael's Monastery to make room for the planned Soviet Square. The end of the city in which he had grown up was the end of his world.

Laboratory Kiev: Malevich Decorates the City

But this end of a world also allowed energies to break to the surface that had been stymied under the *ancien régime*. The crisis initiated a kind of nuclear fusion – all ingredients had been present in the city, and the flow of migrants and escapees during the civil war had further enriched and 'weaponized' them. Malevich's Suprematist compositions mounted on the facades along the Khreshchatyk for the celebrations of the revolution's anniversary may serve as a symbol of this sudden florescence.

Strolling around the city today and reading the plaques on buildings commemorating intellectual luminaries whose work was associated with it, the visitor begins to imagine the cultural laboratory that was

Kiev. The university honours not only the great names of Ukrainian literature and intellectual life – Taras Shevchenko, Nikolai Kostomarov, Mykhailo Hrushevsky – but the philosopher Lev Shestov, the writer Vasily Grossman, who studied here from 1921 until 1923, and the theatrical director Alexander Tairov. Writers including Isaac Babel and Konstantin Paustovsky published their earliest literary attempts in Kiev. The pianist Vladimir Horowitz gave his first recital at the Merchants' House, now the Philharmonic. The philosopher Nikolai Berdyaev, the scion of a Kievan noble family, attended the same lyceum as Dmytro Chyzhevsky, who later taught Russian intellectual and literary history in Halle and Heidelberg. Lev Kopelev was born here – the houses in which he was raised, on Reitarska Street and at 37 Dmytrivska Street, still stand. Anna Akhmatova lived for a few years in one of Lypky's finest Art Nouveau buildings, at 7 Zankovetska Street. Nadezhda Khazina, Osip Mandelstam's wife, who would save his work for posterity, grew up at 25 Reitarska Street and attended the private school at 36 Yaroslaviv Val Street. Arnold Margolin, who was one of Mendel Beilis's defence lawyers and later served as the Directory government's envoy for minority affairs, lived at 4 Velyka Zhytomyrska Street. The Soviet writers Ilya Ehrenburg, Viktor Nekrasov and Anatoly Kuznetsov were native sons of Kiev. A number of addresses that figure prominently in the history of Jewish Kiev are clustered around the Besarabsky Market. The house in which Sholem Aleichem, the author of the short story series featuring Tevye the Dairyman, lived during his time in Kiev stood at 5 Velyka Vasylkivska Street; Golda Meir, later prime minister of Israel, was born in Kiev and raised at 5a Baseina Street. Leon Trotsky worked as a foreign correspondent for the newspaper *Kievskaya Mysl*. Serge Lifar, the star dancer of the Saisons Russes, was a graduate of a school in the building in Lypky that is now the Ivan Franko Theatre – the costume he wore in *Apollon musagète* and his golden ballet shoes are on display in the National Museum of the History of Ukraine. Besides the secondary schools, the studio of Alexandra Exter at today's 1/27 Leontovych Street seems to have been a favourite stomping ground of the young Kiev avant-garde; Osip and Nadezhda Mandelstam were frequently among her guests. Visual artists from Kiev include the sculptor Alexander Archipenko and the painter Alexander Tyshler.

Alumni of the Kiev scene went on to brilliant careers or darker fates all over the world: Serge Lifar left for Paris and danced in *Prelude to the Afternoon of a Faun* at the Salle Pleyel; the architect Horodetsky emigrated to Tehran; the pioneering aeroplane and helicopter engineer Igor Sikorsky built a major business in the United States; Hetman Pavlo Skoropadsky, the figurehead of a puppet regime, lived out his last decades in Berlin and Potsdam; Nadezhda Khazina followed her husband into internal exile and preserved his work when he was shipped off to the camps and died. Mikhail Bulgakov, like many others, moved to Moscow, completing his novel *The Master and Margarita* as a Russian writer, whereas Golda Meir had left with her parents in the early years of the century and eventually settled in Palestine. Berdyaev and Kopelev died in exile, one in Paris, the other in Cologne. Ilya Ehrenburg, who had spent more time in Moscow and Paris than in his native city, was there for its liberation in 1943. Symon Petliura was assassinated in Warsaw in 1926; Mykhailo Hrushevsky, the first chairman of the independent Ukraine's Tsentralna Rada, found shelter at the Academy of Sciences, but his monumental study of Ukrainian history would not be published until after the end of the Soviet Union.

General Plan for the Capital of Soviet Ukraine

The 1920s left few traces in Kievan architecture and urban planning beyond the fire brigade's watchtower in the Shuliavka neighbourhood, a number of workingmen's clubhouses and culture houses near Pushkin Park, and Noi Trotsky's radically elegant 'October' movie hall in Podil – fine examples of the formal vocabulary of a pure Constructivism. All energy, all funding and all efforts to erect representative and symbolic edifices seem to have been absorbed by Kharkov, the first capital of Soviet Ukraine and centre of 'Red modernism'. This period of relative neglect ended when the republic's government moved to Kiev on 24 June 1934. People's commissariats, the Party, central institutions and, not least importantly, a nomenklatura expecting comfortable residences all required a great deal of space. Still, few buildings from the 1930s are examples of what has been called 'Stalinist architecture', which will not come to define the cityscape until the rebuilding and expansion after the war.

The power elite settled in, requisitioning prominent buildings of the old Kiev and making plans for new structures to suit its needs and tastes. The old governorate administration at 30 Volodymyrska Street, across the street from St Sophia's Cathedral, was taken over by the People's Commissariat for Internal Affairs, better known by the abbreviation NKVD, an empire that has many other addresses as well: several villas in Lypky and Vincent Beretti's classicist edifice high above Instytutska Street, where the service operated a prison and torture chamber in the 1930s, now commemorated by a small Monument to the Victims of the Repressions of 1937 by the side of the building. The NKVD's power was cast in grand demonstrative form in the monumental structure on Hrushevsky Street that Ivan Fomin, the doyen of the Petersburg Academy of Arts, designed in 1935. A massive eight-storey building with a characteristic elliptical concave facade, it was completed with incredible speed between 1936 and 1938. Today it accommodates the government of Ukraine, and lined up outside its portal are the idling black luxury cars, with chauffeurs waiting behind the wheel, that are everywhere the insignia of political might. Diagonally across the street sits the building of the Verkhovna Rada, a Neoclassical palace, white with yellow details, the signature colours of the Bolshevik empire, built in 1936–9 for the Supreme Soviet of Ukraine. The glass dome providing the parliament with natural lighting distantly recalls the Tauride Palace in St Petersburg, or perhaps a palm house in a botanical garden.

Only a portion was realized of the largest project of the 1930s that would have completed Kiev's urbanistic and architectonic transformation into a capital. But even a passing glance at what the Leningrad architect Langbard proposed in 1936 – I happened to spot the design in a glass case in a museum – reveals what Kiev was spared: the creation of the world's largest parade ground in the city's most historically prominent spot. The square Langbard envisioned would have stretched from the gate and belfry of St Sophia's Cathedral to St Michael's Monastery, most of which was demolished to make room for the planned construction in 1936. The terrain between these two architectural cornerstones of the old Kiev was to be levelled into a large plateau bordered, towards the Dnieper, by a semicircular pair of matching buildings on symmetrical footprints framing a monumental statue of Lenin. The square would have extended to the edge of the Upper Town, overlooking Podil and the Dnieper. The realized fragment that lets the visitor imagine what the completed ensemble would have looked like is one of the two wing structures, a colossus with a large forecourt built in 1936–9 based on Langbard's designs. Originally occupied by the Central Committee of the Ukrainian Communist Party, it now houses the Ministry of Foreign Affairs. Another building that grew out of the same plans is today's National History Museum, which is worth seeing, not only for its attempt to devise a new narrative of Ukrainian history, but for the gorgeous views of Podil and the river from its windows. The visitor realizes at once that the new rulers recognized the *spiritus loci* of the elevated spot and resolved to put their stamp on it. The creation of the enormous square would effectively have shifted the city's centre yet again: away from Podil, the middle-class town of merchants and trades-men, which had held Magdeburg rights for almost four centuries, but away also from the Khreshchatyk, a quintessential urban core moulded by capitalism and a bourgeois public. Paradoxically, this scheme to raze the old Kiev was foiled by the outbreak of the Second World War.

It is probably not a coincidence that the most massive buildings from the 1930s and the first ones to be completed were designed for use by the People's Commissariat for Internal Affairs, the NKVD. But to find traces of the hurricane of violence unleashed by this apparatus, the visitor must go on excursions. One takes him to the high bank above the river, where a monument and museum commemorate the Holodomor; the other, out beyond the city boundary, to Bykivnia, where the victims of Stalin's terror are buried and remembered.

The monument to the victims of the Holodomor and the museum documenting the history of the catastrophic famine were inaugurated in 2008, under President Viktor Yushchenko. The ensemble was inserted between the Park of Eternal Glory with the obelisk above the Tomb of the Unknown Soldier and the Monastery of the Caves com-plex. Sunken into the slope facing the Dnieper, the museum suggests a crypt, with a candle-shaped tower above it that is illuminated at night. Emblazoned on the tower are four falcons – or so I was told; to my eyes they looked more like rising cranes with broken wings. The stairs leading down towards the plaza in front of the museum entrance are flanked by stone slabs with engraved quotations from writers and his-torians, including Robert Conquest, Andrea Graziosi, Alain Besançon, Malcolm Muggeridge and Vasily Grossman, who made important contributions to the scholarly study of the Holodomor, the killing by starvation of the Ukrainian peasantry. Millstones set up in the sur-rounding park are apparently meant to symbolize the Ukrainian village, and a row of black flagstones is inscribed with the names of thou-sands of villages that were afflicted by the famine; the museum shop sells a map of the 'landscape of the Holodomor' dotted with villages whose populations were almost entirely wiped out. Most of the quotes from Soviet leaders illustrating their enmity towards the peasantry and especially the so-called kulaks are from Lenin ('Victory over the smallholder will not be won in a year'), others from Trotsky. The tenor is that everything may be taken away from farmers and everything may and indeed must be done to them to shore up the embattled Soviet power. The map notes the areas that were particularly hard-hit by the famine: Poltava, Zinovyevsk (now Kropyvnytsky), Dnepropetrovsk, Nikolaev, the Don basin, the countryside around Zaporozhye, Kherson and Odessa, and Kharkov, Kiev and Chernihiv.

Inside the museum, documentary footage and the definition of genocide proposed by Raphael Lemkin in 1948 are projected on a wall. On display in the permanent exhibition are agricultural implements, carts, millstones, grain sacks, resettlement ordinances, and a letter to Stalin in which a low-ranking functionary reports what is happening in the villages and what he has seen. Also on view are photographs that I had not been familiar with by the Austrian engineer Alexander Wienerberger documenting the 'dekulakization' campaign; he included them in his – tendentious and anti-Semitic – book *Hart auf Hart: 15 Jahre Ingenieur in Sowjetrussland. Ein Tatsachenbericht*, which was based on his experiences working in the Soviet Union for fifteen years and published by Anton Pustet in Salzburg in 1939. There is a small catalogue, but it is not for sale. Everything has been selected and staged with evident passion but, unfortunately, not always with commensurate taste and skill. Most arresting are the 'books of victims' listing those who died due to deportation, violence and starvation; visitors are invited to browse the pages, an unending litany of villagers' names, occupations, dates and causes of death – the work of gathering them was begun under President Yushchenko and is far from complete. Who compiled all this data? The statistical offices? The staff of the NKVD? The department of epidemics control? Relatives? The books document the extinction of entire extended families. It is almost a relief to see that the millions of dead who had vanished from the historical record, their facelessness and namelessness a kind of second death, have left a trace after all, a name, dates, perhaps a face or a gaze to meet ours.

The other destination is a bit out of the way, but it helps the visitor grasp the magnitude of the terror much better than the monument outside October Palace, the former Institute for Noble Maidens and sometime NKVD prison in the city centre. To reach it, one takes the underground bound for the Lisova stop on Brovarsky Prospect. As the train emerges from the tunnel on the right bank of the Dnieper and crosses the river on the Metro Bridge, the gorgeous silhouette of Kiev comes into view, then recedes. The tracks traverse the massif of prefabricated housing estates toward Darnytsia, where the Germans held hundreds of thousands of Soviet prisoners of war in camps after the Battle of Kiev; thousands upon thousands were murdered or died abjectly of starvation or illness. Brovarsky Prospect today is a corridor lined with supermarkets, kiosks, coffee shops, car repair shops and petrol stations. From the underground terminus, it is a short trip by bus in the direction of the suburb of Brovary, through a sparse pine forest with youth camps and playgrounds. The bus stops by the entrance to the memorial complex, which was set up in 1994 after decades of silence. A geomorphological map is inscribed: 'Victims of political repression lie buried here in sector 19 of the Bykivnia forest.' There are crosses on which someone has hung shirts with blue embroidery – burial shrouds? Further to the left stands a statue representing a camp inmate; the year '1937' is carved into a rock. The map marks the site of a museum complex to be built in the future, a knoll covered with pine trees with portraits of victims and the most basic biographical data pinned to them, and the monument to the Polish officers who were murdered here.

Visitors not familiar with the site cannot tell quite where in the 14,865-square-metre (160,000-square-foot) tract archaeologists have found the mass graves. Estimates of the number of people who were killed here range from several tens of thousands to well over 100,000. One must venture deep into the pine forest; in the spring, the scent of resin and lilies of the valley is powerful. A diesel-powered cargo tramway bearing the number 23 stands by the wayside; it shuttled between Kiev and Brovary and was used to cart the prisoners who had been brought to Kiev from all over Ukraine to this remote site, fodder for the NKVD's firing squads. The path is lined with rocks engraved with crosses. One reads: 'We paid for your freedom with our lives'; another, 'Everlasting remembrance of thousands of innocent victims.' Relatives have pinned commemorative notes to the trees: Petro Parkhomenko, agronomist, shot on 25 April 1938; Gavrilo Matsiuk, shot on 13 April 1938; Maksym Btyokha, shot on 22 December 1937; Kindrat Sidoruk, 1989–1937, with a photograph; Iosif Tkach, 1881–1937; Ivan Kharchenko, 1903–1938. Most of them were killed in the prime of their lives. They came from all parts of the Ukrainian Soviet Republic, from all religious groups and nationalities. They were priests, members of the Ukrainian Guard from the days of the Ukrainian People's Republic, and school directors. Some of the notes mention the date of their rehabilitation – 1959 or, in some instances, not until after 1991. The American historian Hiroaki Kuromiya has written a study on the history of the site and the veil of silence that was drawn for decades over the 'mass operations' against so-called kulaks, anti-Soviet elements and alleged spies for the foreign enemy in 1937–8.

Deeper into the forest, the visitor encounters a clearing surrounded by a marble wall on which the names of thousands of Polish officers are engraved, from Kazimierz Abczyński to Aleksy Żełnoruk; room has been left on some of the slabs for victims who have not yet been identified: 3,435 of them were murdered here. The portal leading to the site bears the inscription: 'Monument to the Poles who were arrested by the NKVD after 17 September 1939.' White-and-red ribbons have been tied around the trees, and two flagpoles flying the Polish and Ukrainian flags signal that the memorial was jointly established by the two nations.

Few people come out here to wander among the religious symbols that are everywhere – the portal, the altar and the altar wall; the Orthodox cross, but also, less pervasively, the Star of David, the crescent, the cross of the Greek Catholics. Shared grief over a past of suffering is a powerful bond.

Kiev under German Rule

The destruction of Kiev at the hands of the Germans ended where it began: on the Khreshchatyk. Anatoly Kuznetsov watched the German troops enter the city:

> On 19 September 1941, the Germans marched into the Khreshchatyk from two sides. One column came from Podol. They were the soldiers we had met in Kurenyovka: strapping cheerful lads in cars. The other column moved in from the opposite end, past Besarabka. These Germans came straight from the battlefield on motorcycles and were covered in soot. They drew near like a dark cloud, flooding the pavements, filling the entire Khreshchatyk with the noise and fumes of their engines.

Two years later, after the liberation of Kiev on 6 November 1943, gallows were set up on Kostelna Street, between today's Maidan

Nezalezhnosti and European Square, and the sentences handed down against Germans in a war crimes trial were carried out amid the loud applause of the bystanders. A photograph shows an endless file of 40,000 German soldiers, miserable wretches, being marched off into captivity, a spectacle observed by Kievans standing atop the mountains of rubble.

The First Battle of Kiev ended on 19 September 1941; the city was in German hands. By 7 November 1943, in time for the anniversary of the October Revolution, the Red Army had recaptured the Ukrainian capital. The history of the battle on the Dnieper and the occupation regime, of the history of Kiev's liberation and reconstruction, is told in great detail – especially when it comes to the military operations – in the Museum of the Great Patriotic War, which occupies the base of the monumental Mother Motherland statue, as well as the City Museum. Of around 900,000 residents Kiev had before the 778 days of German occupation, no more than 180,000 remained in the liberated city; 240,000 people died in Kiev and the immediate periphery. Almost 250,000 were deported to Germany as forced labourers. The centre lay in ruins, the towering steel-and-concrete shell of the legendary Ginzburg House was etched into the sky like a sepulchral monument. The bridges across the Dnieper and the railway tracks had been destroyed by blasts. Kiev's Jews, save for the few who had been evacuated or had fought in the ranks of the Red Army, had been exterminated. The violence inflicted on the city itself is recorded in the aerial photographs of the German reconnaissance, whose focus was on infrastructure; in the pictures soldiers took of themselves and posted home (others were found on the bodies of the dead); and in the recorded recollections of Kievans. Written sources include Anatoly Kuznetsov's documentary novel *Babi Yar*, which could not be published in unabridged form in the Soviet Union – in 1966 *Yunost* ran a censored version – as well as the testimony of one Valentin Terno, a boy from Leningrad who had come to Kiev to spend the summer holidays with his grandparents just three days before the Germans attacked the Soviet Union.

Scattered across the cityscape are the marks of the fighting, of slaughter and death. Virtually every city park contains a small monument commemorating the soldiers who died in the vicinity; virtually every institution, museum and factory honours the staff members who fought on the front line and perished: an interminable list of names that stretches from the Tomb of the Unknown Soldier in the Park of Eternal Glory up on the hill to the monument to General Vatutin, commander of the First Ukrainian Front and liberator of Kiev, outside Mariinsky Palace and on to the foyer of Taras Shevchenko University's main building and the lobby of the theatre.

Kiev after 778 days of German rule: a landscape of battle, scorched earth, the scene of the population's struggle for naked survival and of mass death in the concentration and prisoner-of-war camps, of deportation into forced labour. It is also the city whose name will forever be associated with Babi Yar, a ravine then still just outside its gates.

Of all cities the Germans occupied, Kiev had the densest network of internment, concentration and extermination camps. Executions of hostages, partisans or victims of random arrests were routine. Hundreds of thousands of war prisoners passed through the camps in Darnytsia, on the left bank of the Dnieper, and Syrets. More than 600,000 Red Army soldiers had been taken captive in the Battle of Kiev, and thousands died of starvation and disease in captivity; Jews and commissars were selected for targeted killing. At one point or another, almost 300,000 of them were in the camp in the Darnytsia forest, where 70,000 of them died or were killed. In August 1943, when the occupiers sought to erase all traces of the mass murder in Babi Yar, Soviet prisoners of war from the Syrets camp were brought to the scene to exhume and cremate the bodies.

The new rulers put their stamp on the city from day one. The Germans had chosen Rovno (Rivne) as the capital of their Reichskommissariat, but of course they also took over the central buildings and institutions of power in Kiev. The headquarters of the German city commandant, Major General Kurt Eberhard, was set up in the 'World of the Child' on the corner of Prorizna and Khreshchatyk Streets, and it was there that, on 21 September, Kievans had to queue up and surrender their radio sets. The commandant's ordinances – some are on view behind glass in the museums – were issued in three languages: Ukrainian, Russian and, in fine print, German. Ukrainian newspapers, produced by emigrants who had returned with the German troops or locals for whom collaboration with the occupiers was the smaller of two evils and who, for a brief moment, thought that Ukrainian independence was within reach, translated German policies into Kiev's daily life. Squares and streets were given new names: the Khreshchatyk became Eichhorn Street (after the German commander who was assassinated by a leftist revolutionary in Kiev in 1918); Katerynynska Street (today's Lypska Street), German Street; Pushkinska Street, Street of the Goths. There was a Bahnhofstrasse and a Horst-Wessel-Strasse; Bankova Street, where the presidential administration is now located, became Bismarckstrasse. Cars made by Horch, Mercedes and Opel started to appear on Kiev's streets. The occupiers made themselves at home. They commandeered the best apartments in Lypky and the hotels on Volodymyrska Street, but they also set up latrines in the botanical garden they then used in full view of the public and captured in snapshots. They turned the Polytechnic Institute into a military hospital, looted the museums (a catalogue available in the Khanenko Museum near Shevchenko Park lists 2,000 works of art that are missing from its own collections alone) and transferred animals from the Kiev Zoo to the one in Königsberg – now Kaliningrad – where they would later die. The 'House of the Physician' became the 'House of the German Officer'. An 'employment agency' opened in the building of the Art Institute (now at 20 Smyrnov-Lastochkin Street) – built in the late nineteenth century as a seminary, it had housed an art school starting in 1925, a hotbed of Ukrainian modernism where Kazimir Malevich, Vladimir Tatlin and others had met. Now the swastika flew on the facade, and Ukrainians, men and women, were enticed with fantastic promises to enlist as labourers in the Reich – or simply rounded up in raids like cattle. Kiev Central Station, a Constructivist edifice erected between 1927 and 1932, which played an important part in their fate, is an especially remarkable address. Numerous photographs show the large sign in Roman letters: 'Kiew Hbf'. The journeys of hundreds of thousands of forced labourers – 2.3 million, out of a total 3 million, came from Ukraine – began here, on the same platforms where German soldiers on their way to the frontlines or on leave and heading back home stopped off; their paths, their gazes, must have crossed. Travellers arriving today are welcomed by a newly built Orthodox church and a McDonald's branch. The Gestapo and the Sicherheitsdienst moved into the NKVD's buildings at 33 Volodymyrska and on Instytutska. The Academy of Sciences became the police headquarters. The occupying forces buried their dead at military cemeteries that they set up in the parks and other green spaces, including in Pushkin Park and vis-à-vis Mariinsky Palace; after the war, German soldiers taken captive were interred at more than seventy sites within Kiev alone.

The city offered a broad range of entertainments and amusements; there were cafés 'for Germans only', a diverse movie programme, and designated places for fraternization, collaboration and prostitution. Civilian and military personnel and ethnic Germans shopped in privileged stores while ration cards were introduced for the general population and more and more Kievans went hungry. One central location where the remaining residents of the occupied city could try to barter for urgently needed goods was the 'Yevbaz', the 'Jewish bazaar' – though there were no more Jews – on Galicia Square (which has since been completely redesigned and renamed Victory Square). Germans came, too, and purchased whatever caught their fancy – antiques could be had for a song – or loaded up on victuals. Dozens of cinemas in central Kiev operated under new names: the 'Communards' at 95 Lvivska was now the 'Lux', the 'Avantgarde' at 31 Moskovska was the 'Metropol', and the 'October' in Podil, the finest of the new movie halls from the 1920s, became the 'Gloria'. The film selection was the same as back in the Reich: *Der Tiger von Eschnapur*, *Das Indische Grabmal* and *Hochzeitsnacht zu dritt*, complemented by newsreels reporting the victories on the front and rabidly anti-Semitic propaganda pieces such as *Der letzte Schlag* (The Final Strike), which drew on documentary footage to impress upon Ukrainian viewers the horrors of collectivization and Stalin's purges in Ukraine. The opera served up a conventional repertoire: *Madama Butterfly*, *The Queen of Spades*, *Faust*, *Coppélia*. One highlight that became a myth after liberation was the 'Death Match' that pitted members of Dynamo Kiev's football team, brought in for this purpose from the prisoner-of-war camp in Boiarka, against a selection from the German Luftwaffe. Several of the Ukrainian players who vanquished the 'Flakelf' then disappeared into the Syrets camp and were later shot.

In the first weeks of German rule over Kiev, between 24 and 28 September, a series of devastating explosions that started near the corner of Khreshchatyk and Prorizna Streets rocked the city. Remotely set off by Soviet agents, they reduced the 'World of the Child', two renowned hotels, the Spartak and the Continental, and several other buildings on both sides of the Khreshchatyk to rubble and ignited fires that raged for days; the whole centre including the old City Hall, more recently the headquarters of the Communist Party – all in all, more than twenty blocks – was ablaze, lighting up the night sky. Walls collapsed, attempts to put out the fires were in vain and the panicked population fled into the parks above the Dnieper. 'It seemed like the entire city was exploding,' Anatoly Kuznetsov noted: 'The detonation and incineration of the Khreshchatyk, which have not been described by anyone anywhere, must to my mind be regarded as a key event in the history of the war.' For a comparable destruction of another city, he wrote, one would have to imagine detonations flattening Moscow within the Boulevard Ring, St Petersburg's Nevsky Prospect or all of downtown Paris. The demolition of an urban core was different from that of a bridge. As Kuznetsov saw it, the remote-controlled explosions were the first manifestations of a genuine patriotism; no other city, he argued, had prepared such a welcome for the Germans. 'Yes, they had marched into this city, which lay open before them as the capitals of Western Europe had. They were getting ready for their victory meal, but instead they got their faces smashed in so hard that the ground beneath their feet started to burn.' On 3 November 1941, Kuznetsov also watched as Dormition Cathedral in the Monastery of the Caves went up in flames and collapsed.

The traces of the German–Soviet war are everywhere – and inter-mingled among them are now the fresh marks of the new and very different war Russia wages on Ukraine, which claims more victims almost every week. In the weeks leading up to the seventieth anniver-sary of the victory over Hitler's Germany, an installation of uniforms and personal possessions of soldiers – volunteers as well as members of the armed forces – who died in the Donbass was on display in the foyer of the Museum of the Great Patriotic War. The present war eclipses the earlier one, which had become a kind of foundational myth of the Soviet Union and which is now remembered very differently in Russia and Ukraine.

Finding Babi Yar with Anatoly Kuznetsov

In 1963 Evgeny Evtushenko opened his poem with the line: 'No monu-ment stands over Babi Yar.' That has changed, but it is still not easy to find one's bearings in the area, which extends on both sides of Melnykova Street in northwestern Kiev. The city has provided land for a museum of the history of Kiev's Jewry, but to date there is no institution that would walk the visitor through the complete history of Jews in Kiev from their first mention in 1018 to the extermination of the community in Babi Yar and the recent revival of Jewish life. So the

Babi Yar Monument, Kiev.

best guide is still Anatoly Kuznetsov's report, unless the visitor is lucky and Rabbi Alexander Dukhovny, who knows the area's topography and history better than perhaps anyone else, has time to accompany him. Getting off the undergound at Dorohozhychi station, the visitor emerges onto a major intersection, from which paths lead to several monuments. There is the monument where, on 29 September 1961, Kievans congregated to commemorate the twentieth anniversary of the massacre, the first such public remembrance. A little farther down stands the monument erected in 1976, under Brezhnev: a towering sculpture shows a group of figures, heroic entwined bodies – a Red Army soldier, a seaman, a woman and child. The inscription is in three languages – Ukrainian, Russian and Hebrew – but neither the iconography nor the official name of the memorial indicates with any specificity that, on 29–30 September, 33,771 Jews were murdered here in an organized mass operation. Only the inscription beneath a menorah-shaped monument that was added much later on the grounds of the old Jewish cemetery explicitly commemorates them as the victims of the massacre against Jews.

Additional monuments are dedicated to the tens of thousands of other victims who were killed in Babi Yar besides Kiev's Jews: Soviet prisoners of war, 'gypsies', children, mental patients from nearby hospitals, partisans, representatives of the Ukrainian intelligentsia and the underground national movement. The ravine on the edge of the city became a mass grave in which, all told, around 100,000 human beings lay. The sharp-edged gully, its bottom as far as 10 metres (33 ft) below the surrounding terrain, which was known before the war as an excursion destination and for the loam that was quarried here for the nearby brickworks, is virtually unrecognizable today. 'It was a huge ravine, positively majestic, deep and wide as a mountain valley. If you called out on one side, someone standing on the other side barely heard you,' Anatoly Kuznetsov, who was twelve at the time of the events, recalled. Of the structures that stood in the area back then only the administrative building of the nearby Jewish cemetery remains. For the rest it is an ordinary park, with paths, benches, playgrounds; joggers pass the visitor. But then Rabbi Dukhovny leads him to a place where the ground has not been levelled, the edge of a ravine. And it is here, above a steep slope exposing the clayey soil, that the visitor begins to recognize the Babi Yar he knows from the photograph of the massacre that was held up as evidence in Nuremberg.

Kuznetsov, who watched it happen, resolved early on that he would write down what he saw. He quotes the poster that went up after the explosions in the city and announced the immediate reprisal – the suggestion that the Jews would be resettled still served as cover for their extermination: 'All Jews of the city of Kiev and its vicinity are to arrive by 8 o'clock on the morning of Monday, 29 September 1941, to the corner of Melnykova and Dokhturovska streets (near the cemeteries). They are to take with them documents, money, valuables, as well as warm clothes, underwear, etc. Any Jew who, in contravention of this ordinance, is found elsewhere will be shot. Any citizen entering an abandoned Jewish dwelling and stealing property will be shot.' He watches the procession moving up the hill:

Here came the entire Jewish Podol. Ah, Podol! That most heart-wrenching neighbourhood of Kiev was recognizable by its heavy air, a blend of rot, cheap fat, and dry laundry. Since time immemorial it had been home to the Jewish poor, the poorest of the poor: shoemakers, tailors, charcoal burners, plumbers, packers, upholsterers, fences, thieves, courtyards without any green, fetid refuse pits, crooked barns full of giant fat rats, cesspits over which swarms of flies hovered, dusty dirty alleys, half-dilapidated houses and damp basements: that was noisy, fertile, desperately unhappy Podol.

They were herded into the ravine. They heard the gunfire: so they were not being taken to the nearby freight yard in Syrets for deportation; they were being shot. One of the very few who saved themselves in those days was Dina Mironovna Pronicheva, a mother of two children and actress at the Kiev Puppet Theatre. Having seen it all, she testified in the trial in Kiev in 1946, relating the unimaginable: the killing of more than 30,000 people in three days by an Einsatzgruppe of just over 1,200, assisted by Ukrainian volunteers.

In August 1943, as the Red Army was pressing towards Kiev, the Germans ordered Soviet prisoners of war from Syrets to exhume the bodies in Babi Yar, pile them up on fire grates made of railway ties, pour kerosene over them and incinerate them; what was left was ground up by a cyclopean bone mill that is now on display in the Museum of the Great Patriotic War. Around 330 of the prisoners recruited for this horrendous labour staged a revolt, and fifteen escaped – they would be important witnesses in the trials and later gathered every 29 September.

In September 1943 the forcible evacuation of Kiev commenced. The order was to deport the entire population to Germany. The city would cease to exist. Another trek of miserable wretches, a procession of tramway cars, people with bundled possessions carrying the ill and children on their backs; thousands upon thousands on the roads until the refugee flows dissipated somewhere along the way to Poland, some returning, others fleeing further west with the Germans.

Yet that is not the end of the history of Babi Yar. The ravine was filled in, but on 13 March 1961, a dam broke that had been built to impound water while the sludge containing ashes and bone fragments would settle. Early in the morning, as people were going to work, a 9-metre (30-ft) wave of muddy water raced through a neighbourhood of post-war blocks of flats, sweeping trams, cars and entire buildings along. 'Babi Yar's vengeance,' people whispered.

The third attempt to make Babi Yar disappear began in 1962. The mud was dried and carted back to the ravine. A block of flats was built on the area of the Syrets concentration camp, atop the bones of the victims that the ground kept spitting up. The Jewish cemetery, too, was cleared; only a few headstones were preserved. The site is now taken up by a television centre and broadcasting tower.

Then, on 29 September 1966, a demonstration was held in Babi Yar, attended by the survivor Dina Pronicheva, the Marxist dissident

Ivan Dziuba and the Kievan-born Russian writer Viktor Nekrasov, who later went into exile. The succession of monuments that have been erected since would seem to vindicate Kuznetsov's confidence: 'One can burn something, scatter it into the winds, bury it, trample it down, but human recollection remains.' Kuznetsov did not live to see the day when the complete and uncensored text of his *Babi Yar* was finally published in his native country, nor the day when a monument in his honour was erected. He died, an exile in London, on 13 June 1979.

Kiev: The Third Place

The most recent past feels immediately familiar, yet in a sense it is the history we know least about. From the ridge above the Dnieper, the visitor looks out towards the new neighbourhoods built on the left bank of the river after the war, a landscape like a mountain range. Each of these boroughs is a major city unto itself, with its own vital structures. Their existence is living proof of Kiev's rebirth and resurgence. Yet we circle as though spellbound around the microscopically small but crystal-hard core of the thousand-year-old city with all its nicks, scars and wounds. The metropolis, roaring with life, is all around us, yet we understand little of what is going on in this jungle, of the energies that drive it, of the passions and machinations that pervade it and hold it together. Why do we know so little – is it, in my case, a kind of *déformation professionnelle* that afflicts the German historian? Is he numbed by a surfeit of history? Or is it because he would rather leave the recent past and the present to the observers and commentators who are experts on current affairs?

Kiev's renascence after the war, like that of so many other devastated European cities – Warsaw, Minsk, Stalingrad, Kaliningrad, even Berlin – is in a sense baffling. There are, of course, many factors that help explain it: the ineradicable desire of humans to rebuild their wrecked homes and lives, to defy the attempt to displace them; ambitious plans drawn up by the authorities and large public investments; the physical resistance to evanescence that flickers even in ruins; the hope that the old magic can be conjured afresh of what were, despite everything, communities in which lives, and good lives, were shared; and the stark destitution that forced some to settle on scorched earth. Whatever it was that made people spin again the thread of life in the ravaged and utterly exhausted wastelands the war had made of these cities, there remains, to my mind, something miraculous about it, something that ultimately defies explanation. And such a miracle happened in Kiev.

Visiting today, you would hardly know what the city has been through. It pulses with life, it is vibrant, even feverish. It has begun a second life, or even – if we think of Batu Khan's devastating campaigns in the thirteenth century – the latest of many lives.

More than half a century has passed since the work of removing the traces of destruction and exhaustion began. In a decades-long strenuous effort, the city is back in shape and has grown beyond its erstwhile dimensions. Now that it is the capital no longer merely of a Soviet republic but of an independent and sovereign European nation, everything has changed yet again: a new confidence, a new openness to the world are palpable, the transformation into an international city precipitated by novel forms of communication and transportation and new media. Kiev has shaken off the provincial drowsiness that was its lot in the imperial periphery. The visitor feels that a new Kiev has emerged, one that will never again be the administrative centre of a province dependent on Moscow's good graces. Too many of its young people have seen the world and are determined to make something of their lives. Kiev is a destination on the international airlines' route maps; the names of its leading politicians are familiar to attentive audiences beyond Ukraine's borders; it is on television and in the papers, although the country would surely benefit if it stopped producing breaking news and everyone were free to focus on solving its internal problems. Many traits of the Soviet way of life persist, but Kiev has indisputably entered a new era. Maidan was a watershed moment, one that has acquired the symbolic function of holding together, and indeed uniting on a new basis, a country a foreign aggressor seeks to force to its knees.

There are many places where the visitor begins to appreciate the magnitude and complexity of the task at hand. The National Museum of the History of Ukraine, for example, ventures to chart a narrative for a polyglot, religiously diverse, multi-ethnic and socially fractured society embroiled in the process of constituting itself as a political nation. In that process, the country's elites as well as the general population face enormous and infinitely varied challenges.

Somehow Kiev has always been thought to possess a particular capacity for integration, even by those who found it difficult to imagine a post-imperial Russia. In an essay on 'Three Capitals', Georgy Fedotov, a Russian philosopher who lived in exile, singled out Kiev as the city that, unlike 'Westernizing Saint Petersburg' and unlike Moscow, whose eyes were turned towards Asia, might become the birthplace of a non-imperial Russian culture. The view from the high bank of the Dnieper, he argued, was a panorama comprising all points of the compass and all landscapes for which the city might be the unifying pole, for which it might find an adequate language: Kiev, he believed, was not only a sacred place, not only the most beautiful of Russian cities, it was a beacon from which the gaze ranged across the steppes stretching eastward – but also towards the Carpathian Mountains and Poland, towards the Black Sea and, especially, towards Greece; the Cathedral of St Sophia, he thought, was the spirit of Hellas hewn into stone.

Kiev was the paradoxical anchor for a reflection on fundamental questions also for Prince Nikolai Trubetzkoy, another exiled thinker who yearned for the recreation of the Russian Empire but, unlike Fedotov, envisioned it in a Eurasianist perspective. Despairing over the loss of the empire after the Bolshevik revolution, he argued that Kiev's Petro Mohyla Academy, by channelling Western influence, had allowed for the modernization of Muscovy long before Peter the Great: Kievan ideas, he thought, had been instrumental in turning a regional into a major and eventually an all-Russian power. An independent Ukraine outside the empire was unthinkable to Trubetzkoy – it would be doomed, he believed, to provinciality and second-class status – but he highlighted the paramount civilizatory influence of the 'Western Russian–Ukrainian' spirit of sixteenth- to eighteenth-century Kiev. So both Fedotov and Trubetzkoy identified it as the third metropolis, the symbolic locus of a position astride the opposition of West and East, Europe and Asia, rationalism and irrationality, modernity and tradition, enlightenment and Orthodoxy for which 'Petersburg' and 'Moscow' have long stood as shorthand, an opposition that has always informed and indeed transfixed and blinkered the Western perspective on Russia.

So it is not only the Western world and Western intellectuals who may in Kiev encounter a history of which they knew little or nothing. The city may come to be the site of a reflection on the fate of Russian culture as long as that culture's freedom is suppressed in Moscow and St Petersburg. Russian is widely spoken and universally understood in Kiev; there are Russian newspapers, publishing houses and television stations; the city is home to a small but growing community of Russian intellectuals who can no longer stand the situation in Moscow or St Petersburg but would prefer to live in a culturally and linguistically familiar environment, which is difficult to do in Berlin, Vienna or Paris: in short, Kiev has become the hub of a contemporary diaspora. The Russian intelligentsia hardly shares the vulgar prejudices that underlie the mutual stereotypes of the *khokhly* on the one hand and the *katsapy* or *moskaly* on the other: the Ukrainians as coarse shaven-headed or ponytailed Cossacks, the Russians as goateed Muscovites. Still, despite the extended families that straddle the border and the thousands who have paid visits to the other side, a certain tenacious discordance is palpable. With mild resignation, the keen-eyed Russian observer Sergei Medvedev noted in an essay on 'Russian Resentment' in the journal *Otechestvennye zapiski* (2014, no. 6) that, while the Moscow intelligentsia had quickly adjusted to the independence of Georgia or Belarus or, certainly, of the Baltic states, it was still not reconciled to Ukraine's, which was felt to be abnormal, even hubristic. Within ten years, Ukrainians rebelled not once but twice against their 'older brother', but, Medvedev wrote, Russians still perceived Ukrainian insistence on self-determination as treason. Despite the 23 years that had passed, the country's independence was regarded as a kind of mis-understanding, a mere anecdote, and even large parts of the educated classes viewed their neighbour to the southwest with the indulgence reserved for a 'kid brother' or perhaps a banana republic that should not be taken altogether seriously. That this view is not universally shared is hardly reassuring, but it is at least cause for cautious hope that things will not remain as they are.

In 2014 President Putin remarked that, if only he wanted, his troops would easily reach Kiev, and points further west, within mere hours. He miscalculated. Kiev is about to become what it was before, and was for a long time: the third place, where the old game of East and West is obsolete and something new begins.

(2015)

FIVE

AH, ODESSA: A CITY IN AN ERA
OF GREAT EXPECTATIONS

L ITTLE MORE THAN a year ago, it was inconceivable that the war might come to Odessa. By and large, that was still so in April 2014, when I arrived from Donetsk via Mariupol. True, there had been demonstrations, pro-Maidan and anti-Maidan, there had been clashes, and some had called for a referendum like the one that had been held in Crimea. Trains were still running, though buses already had to pass improvised checkpoints. But everything was quiet on Prymorsky Boulevard and the plaza from which you look down Eisenstein's stairs towards the harbour. Passengers fresh off the cruise ships slogged up into the city high above the sea. Souvenir vendors and inline skaters seemed to embody the relaxed atmosphere for which Odessa has long been acclaimed. But the calm was deceptive. Tensions exploded on 2 May 2014, when a brawl between local football fans and the supporters of a team from Kharkov turned into a bloody encounter between pro-Maidan and anti-Maidan activists. Eventually a trade union building in which some participants in the fighting, mostly from the pro-Russian side, had sought refuge was set on fire. Forty-eight people died of asphyxiation or leaped to their deaths from the windows of the upper storeys. Hundreds were wounded in the brutal clashes on Kulikove Pole Square and throughout the city. Although Molotov cocktails were thrown and targeted shots were fired, the police did not intervene, and fire trucks were very slow to arrive on the scene of the conflagration. It remains unclear to this day what led to the disaster – and worse, no one believes that the authorities are willing or capable of identifying and punishing those responsible.

Ever since that day, the city has lived in fear that fresh violence might break out at any moment and escalate into a general destabilization of the situation. A community that was famous and notorious for its levity, its sense of humour, its stubborn insistence on its own ways, is under permanent stress. A city that had grown large and wealthy in the liberal air of the free port, that had mostly lived by the conviction that trading partners do not shoot at each other – or in contemporary parlance, that it is better to go to the beach than to wage war – is suddenly confronted with an utterly new situation, the fate that might befall it on display not far away: in Donetsk, which was flourishing and functioning only months ago and now lies in ruins. If one city might be made the capital of a 'New Russia', then it is Odessa, founded in 1794; if one city might arouse the neo-imperial appetite of Putin's Russia, it is this one, located a few hours' drive from Russian-occupied Crimea and less than an hour by car from Russia's client, the para-state of Transnistria.

The following portrait of Odessa, written in 2000, does not gloss over the darkest hours in its history: the pogroms, the civil war or the violent reign of German and Romanian occupying troops during the Second World War. But more than anything else it is a tribute to the enormous vitality and productive energy of this central node in the web of European history and culture. Odessa has survived the age of extremes with its lethal simplifications, its radicalizations and polarizations, and there is reason to hope that it will stand firm this time, too.

(2015)

✛

A SINGLE STRUCTURE is the undisputed centrepiece of the public imagination of Odessa: the grand staircase featured in Sergei Eisenstein's motion picture *Battleship Potemkin* (1925). It is the setting for one of the most sublime scenes in movie history. A baby's pram rolls down the steps, pitching and tossing. The mother watches, her eyes wide with terror, her mouth frozen in a silent scream. Soldiers march down the stairs like automata, their bayonets pointing towards the shore. They will put down the revolt of the workers who have rushed to the quay to support the mutiny on the warship. The infant in the pram stands no chance. The sequence is a primal scene of human impuissance and panic-stricken fear. But with its 192 steps and ten landings, the staircase, designed by the architect F. K. Boffo and constructed between 1837 and 1841, is a masterwork in itself. The steps grow wider towards the bottom, producing an optical illusion that heightens the effect. From

Richelieu Stairs, Odessa, *c.* 1890–1900.

the outset, this structure was more than merely a connection between port and city. It was the vantage point from which one took in the view of the amphitheatre formed by the bay and harbour. The visitor who had ascended the top landing reached a wide boulevard with the statue of the Duc de Richelieu, an important early governor of Odessa, at its centre and the mercantile exchange building and the governor general's mansion at the far end. The staircase is the grand entrance into a city that became the stage for one of the most magnificent episodes in the great theatre of the world. It was where a city produced itself that basked in the aura of nicknames such as 'Second Saint Petersburg', 'Southern Palmyra', 'Queen of the Black Sea' and 'Little Paris'. And it was where the curtain went down that, for several generations, hid the metropolis from the eyes of Europeans.

Auspicious Beginnings

When Mark Twain arrived in Odessa in the mid-1860s, he immediately felt at home. 'Look up the street or down the street, this way or that way, we saw only America!' A German traveller likewise noted: 'The outward impression Odessa gives is that of a beautiful, modern, elegant city; to appreciate its prominence as the metropolis of trade on the Black Sea, the visitor must see the port, the scenes of unceasing movement and business, of a perpetual ebb and flow, of surging and pressing throngs of thousands of people and unending processions of cargo vessels.' When these lines were written, Odessa, which celebrated its bicentennial in 1994, was still a young city.

Its history begins with an edict issued on 27 May 1794 in which Catherine the Great ordered the founding of Odessa in the place of a Turkish-Tatar stronghold called Hacıbey. The empire had gained possession of the Black Sea coast in the recent Russian–Turkish War and incorporated it as the Province of New Russia. Odessa was to be its capital; its port, the empire's gateway to the south. The name was derived from that of an ancient Greek colony, Odessos, which was believed to have been located in the vicinity. The day that soldiers under the command of Vice Admiral Joseph de Ribas started construction for the town and port, 22 August 1794, is regarded as Odessa's official birthday. It marked the beginning of the meteoric ascent of a city that, within a century, would become the empire's fourth-largest, after St Petersburg, Moscow and Warsaw. The newly founded town had just under 2,500 inhabitants; twenty years later, in 1815, it counted 35,000 residents, and by the early 1860s, their number had grown to 116,000. The abolition of serfdom, the arrival of the railway and the onset of industrialization triggered another major leap forward. On the eve of the First World War, Odessa's population numbered 630,000, more than twice what it had been only 25 years earlier. But it was not just the city's quantitative growth that amazed contemporary observers. Odessa was a multi-ethnic community, the heterogeneity of its populace virtually unrivalled on the continent. 'There can be no other city whose citizenry is as mixed, as composed of all nations of Europe and Asia, as Odessa's,' a German traveller wrote. 'A truly Babylonian confusion of languages fills the streets; one hears Italian, English, German, Greek, Turkish, Persian, Tatar, Serbian, Polish, Russian, and a host of other far-flung idioms.' Several factors combined to make Odessa a workshop of human diversity: Catherine's plan to populate New Russia, cast into policy by the governors general she appointed; the plentiful jobs provided primarily by the grain trade; and finally, the mass influx of migrants for whom Odessa was the Promised Land. From day one, the leaders of the new municipality sought to bring in construction workers, craftsmen, merchants, teachers and experts in all branches of industry and business. The promises of the recruiters drew Greek and

German colonists, and over the next few decades, Odessa became a centre of thriving Black Sea German and Black Sea Greek communities. British, Dutch and even Swiss expatriates settled here. One group that would play a prominent role in Odessa's economic and cultural life were Italians from Genoa, Livorno and Venice. Polish land barons built city mansions, and numerous Armenian and Syrian merchants made the city their home. The population was swelled by runaway serfs, Cossacks and farmers from the borderlands of the empire, and by Ukrainian and Moldavian day labourers. Yet the city's single largest and most compact ethnic group were the Jews. Just after its foundation, Odessa is said to have had six Jewish residents; in 1855 there were 17,000, or 22 per cent of the overall population; and the 1897 general census reported that almost 140,000 Jews lived in Odessa: just over one in three Odessans was Jewish. They usually came from Volhynia, Podolia and Lithuania, but also from Austrian Galicia and even from Germany. The city's largest synagogue in Odessa was called Brodsky Synagogue, because of the large contingent of arrivals from the Galician town of Brody. After Russian, Yiddish was the second most-spoken language.

Odessa's founders and early leaders embodied its international flair. Admiral de Ribas, who was tasked with laying the first stone, was a Spanish-Irish soldier of fortune from Naples. The city's premier boulevard, Odessa's Champs-Élysées or Kurfürstendamm, is named after him: De Ribas Street or Deribasovskaya (now, in Ukrainian, Deribasivska). French names such as Richelieu and Langeron are everywhere. The plan for the geometric street grid was drawn up by an engineer called de Voland. The two mayors under whom Odessa took shape were a French emigrant and a Russian aristocrat trained in England. The Duc de Richelieu – Odessans still call him, simply, 'Duc' – strikes a rigid Roman-classicist pose in his statue, and he, too, has a major thoroughfare named after him. A native of Paris, he had enlisted in Russian services after the French Revolution, and from 1803 until 1814 he led the efforts to enlarge and populate Odessa; founded in 1817, the Lycée Richelieu named in his honour still exists. His work done, the 'Duc' returned to France. Prince Mikhail Vorontsov, who steered the city's fortunes from 1823 until 1844, had been trained in Cambridge; the Tudor Renaissance palace he built himself in Alupka, Crimea, served to accommodate the British delegation during the Yalta Conference. Odessa had been declared a free port in 1819 and quickly became the main port of export for Russian grain. The firm and capable rule of these early leaders paved the way for Odessa's rise. Their imprint is still visible in the cityscape today: the mercantile exchange and the governor's mansion are the most representative early buildings. Odessa being a young city, classicism and the Empire style are the oldest strata. Many facilities and amenities required for effective urban life and the welfare of the citizenry date from this period: granite-paved streets lined by locust and lime trees in whose shadows pedestrians can stay cool on the hottest summer days; recreational beaches and parks along the shore; hundreds of cisterns and fountains (the question of water supply, an urgent problem early on, has still not been satisfactorily resolved); and the large and well-laid-out harbour, the economic heart of the new city on the Black Sea.

The Good Life: Odessa between 1870 and 1930

From 1861 until 1914, a period bookended by the great liberal reforms and the outbreak of the First World War, Odessa's population grew five-fold. Railways reached the city, pumping wheat and people into the port metropolis, which burst at the seams. Odessa was now a major hub for the flows of commodities and capital and part of the Mediterranean–Levantine world, a space extending from Constantinople to Port Said, from Smyrna to Marseille. When Victor Hugo's characters dream of quick and boundless riches, their dreams are set in Odessa. The city becomes the capital of a colourfully diverse bourgeoisie and one of the destinations to which the miserable and burdened masses of Eastern Europe hope to escape. The new Odessa outgrows the classicist facades of its early years. The mercantile exchange moves from its first home, which is repurposed as the Hôtel de Ville, to a new building in the Florentine style decorated with the insignia of Mercury. Hotels, banks, restaurants, a skating rink and tearooms crop up along Deribasovskaya and Rishelyevskaya Streets, including illustrious establishments such as Robinat's and Fanconi's coffee houses. The old aristocratic mansions are edged out by palatial apartment buildings, which take up entire city blocks and, despite their splendour, lack the charm of the Palais Royal from the 1830s with its intimate sculpture garden. The city zealously embraces everything neo: neo-Renaissance, neo-Romanesque, neo-Gothic. The hotels have the same names as elsewhere in Europe: the Londres, the Bristol, the Bolshaya Moskovskaya, the Hôtel du Nord. Atlases, caryatids, Medusa's heads, grates and lift doors with Art

Postcard of Richelieu Street in Odessa, *c.* 1890–1905.

Nouveau ornaments identify Odessa as a capital of the belle époque. It is eerie and touching today to find that door handles and mirrors with flower garlands have survived the devastations of the twentieth century. The rapidly expanding city builds itself a grand domed central station, which will more than once be a fiercely contested prize in the coming revolutions and wars; it modernizes the port and erects state-of-the-art hospitals and clinics that still serve their purpose today, as well as schools, water towers and the large prison by the old municipal cemetery. Tracks are laid for horse-drawn trams, soon replaced by a Belgian-made steam-powered tramway. Stores of a new kind, known as arcades, open. An aqueduct carries water from the Dniester across a distance of more than 32 km (20 miles) to relieve the vexing drinking water shortage. Electric lights are installed along the boulevards. New factories go up in the periphery: Brodsky's large sugar mill, the Bellino-Fendrich engineering works, a cluster of grain elevators that is almost a town unto itself. Renowned architects from the capital such as Schröter and Bernardazzi design buildings in Odessa. Movie palaces open along the major boulevards: the Beaumonde, the Odeon, the Paris, the Urania and the Elefant. A prosperous city of Odessa's stature cannot be without a stage that will draw international stars, and so, in the 1880s, it raises one of the most sumptuous and elegant opera houses in Europe, a Palais Garnier overlooking the sea, designed by Fellner & Helmer architects, Vienna, who build these palaces of culture throughout the Austro-Hungarian Empire and beyond. The city undergoes cell division. As Isaac Babel, who would have known, reported, Odessa had 'a very poor, densely populated, suffering Jewish ghetto, a very self-satisfied bourgeoisie, and an arch-reactionary city duma'. Immigrants from the shtetl and from the villages of Ukraine and Bessarabia crowd their respective neighbourhoods. Moldavanka is the stronghold of the Jewish petty bourgeoisie as well as the city's tricksters and thugs, the territory of Benya Krik, known as 'the king', from Isaac Babel's *Odessa Tales*. In Peresyp, working-class slums surround the new factories. And the slopes down towards the sea, along French Boulevard, in Lanzheron, Novaya Arkadiya, and the Little and Big Fontanka, fill up with villas and weekend homes: the white architecture of the seaside resort, with glazed verandas and the amenities the leisure class covets. The uniformity of the cityscape is broken up by fresh accents, and different materials complement the friable shell limestone of which Odessa was built. The formal vocabulary of the new buildings bespeaks the melting pot; a city of many nations, languages and religious denominations wears more styles than others. The gold on the belfry and onion domes of the Russian Orthodox Cathedral contrasts with the red brick of the Lutheran church; the bright blue of a Catholic house of worship in the style of the Italian Baroque harmonizes with the Romanesque-revival contours of the synagogue; the mosque's green-and-white cupola rises next to the colourful brick facade of the Karaite prayer house. The city is dotted with picturesque markets; handsome monuments embellish the parks. Many of them will be taken down or destroyed in the following decades.

If many of these sights survive at least in pictures, it is much harder to get a good sense of the intellectual world of the Odessa of those decades. We must reconstruct it from concert and theatre programmes, from literary histories and memoirs, from war diaries and notes from the underground. Many such sources can be found among the ample holdings of Odessa's museums. Dozens of newspapers were published in the city, in numerous languages; some, such as the Odesski Listok and the major Russian-language Jewish paper *Rassvet*, were also widely read outside Odessa. Franz Liszt, Feodor Chaliapin and Anna Pavlova graced its stages. A motley company of Greek, Italian, Jewish and Russian grain brokers, stock exchange speculators and merchants met at the English Club, while the professors of the Imperial University of New Russia, founded in 1865, preferred the various learned societies. A distinctive kind of society – an urban citizenry, or as Tsar Nicholas I called it, a 'nest of conspiracy' – formed. Odessa was one of the most important bases of the Hellenic freedom fighters of the 1820s; the Decembrists had co-conspirators here; it was here that, in the 1870s, the South Russian Workers' Federation launched its activities. And Odessa became a hotbed of the struggle for emancipation of Russia's and Eastern Europe's Jewry, almost all of whose leading thinkers lived here at one time or another: Chaim Bialik at 9 Mala Arnautska; Simon Dubnow at 12 Bazarna; Leon Pinsker, the author of Auto-Emancipation, at 40 Rishelievska; Meir Dizengoff, later the first mayor of Tel Aviv, at 30 Osypova, and Sholem Aleichem at 26 Kanatna. On the other hand, Odessa was also a major gateway for the flow of Jewish emigrants bound for the New World and Eretz Israel – especially after the pogroms of 1881 and 1905.

Odessa may not have produced philosophers, notes Evgeny Golubovsky, vice president of the World Wide Club of Odessites, but the number of writers and musicians among its sons is legion. 'Everything came together so felicitously in Odessa,' Konstantin Paustovsky writes, 'to raise a crop of energetic, talented and educated people, a pleiad of writers, poets, painters, politicians, musicians, scholars and mariners.' The city supplied the entire world with prodigies and geniuses. Graduates of its conservatories such as Nathan Milstein and David Oistrakh went on to international careers. Yet Odessa was also where the father of Sviatoslav Richter, organist at the German Lutheran church, was executed by the NKVD in 1941. Its urban folklore spawned a rhythm and wit that infiltrated and subverted the entire Soviet Union: in the sentimental romantic ditties and chansons of Pyotr Leshchenko as well as the nervously ironic jazz of Leonid Utyosov, which took Moscow by storm in 1937, of all years. Utyosov's sound may be Odessa's secret triumph, the victory of the periphery of the centre, comparable only to the later success of another Odessan, the comedian Mikhail Zhvanetsky. If the city's population can seem like a nation unto itself, its unique mixture, born of over a hundred ethnic groups living together in close quarters, appears to have given rise also to a singular idiom. Vlas Doroshevich, one of the doyens of cultural criticism during Russia's Silver Age, once described the language of Odessans as the 'eighth wonder of the world'. Literary historians are familiar with the labels 'Odessan' or 'southern Russian school', introduced by Viktor Shklovsky to designate a distinctive new tone that blended extraordinary terseness and irony, sorrow and an unsparing gaze upon reality. Also members of the Odessan pleiad were Isaac Babel and Konstantin Paustovsky, the writers' duo Ilf and Petrov, and the poets Eduard Bagritsky and Vera Inber. Civil War-era Odessa was their university. Babel left the comforts of his parents' middle-class home for an abode in Moldavanka to study the world of criminals and drifters up close. Only in Odessa could Ilf and Petrov have discovered the ingenious con artist Ostap Bender and followed him on his wanderings through Soviet everyday life. One of the Twelve Chairs stands as a monument in the City Garden on Deribasivska Street, and the Museum of Literature presents a reconstruction of the bureaucratic interiors in which Bender and his associates played their tricks. Paustovsky chose Odessa as the backdrop for his unsurpassed epic account of life during the Revolution and Civil War. His memoirs guide us on a voyage back in time to the 'era of great expectations'. So brightly do the lights of this 'Odessan pleiad' shine that we might almost forget the other eminent creative minds who found inspiration in Odessa: Alexander Pushkin and Adam Mickiewicz, for example, who spent part of their years in internal exile in Odessa.

Blockade, Closed City

Odessa's golden era ended in a series of violent upheavals: the Great War, revolution and civil war, the repressions of the 1930s, the terror regime of the German and Romanian occupiers during the Second World War, and the long decades during which the city's gates were shut to the wider world. It is a history of decline, depopulation and mass death, followed by the city's almost inconceivable rebirth. A piece of Odessa perished in each new storm. It might be easier to enumerate the powers that did *not* try to lay claim to it in the turmoil of war and civil war: Germany, Romania, the Reds, the Whites, the Italians, the Greeks, Great Britain and France all sought to capture and hold it. Odessa between 1918 and 1920 was a landscape of forever moving frontlines and utter confusion. Paustovsky recalled that the city

> was filled with an amazing mixture of people that year. Small local gamblers and speculators could not meet the competition of the cruel and brazen types who were pouring into the city

from the Soviet-controlled part of the country . . . They flashed diamonds, which always came from the tsar's crown, of course, they handled brand-new pound sterling and franc notes, and the rarest furs from the shoulders of famous Petrograd beauties passed into the hands of Greek traders in the city . . . Any evening along Deribasovskaya Street you could see a great many famous people around the flower stalls. Most of them, it is true, were out at the elbows, and in a violent temper over the crazy rumours which spread like fever. Odessa easily outstripped all the cities of the south in rumours.

Surveying the bay from the famous staircase, he observed:

Ships loaded with fugitives were leaving for Constantinople . . . All the roads leading down to the port were jammed with people. It looked as if the fences and the houses were bending under their pressure and would soon collapse . . . Bulging suitcases, packages and baskets slithered along under the legs of the people like some horrible living creatures. Their contents poured out of them, getting tangled in people's legs, and men dragged along with them women's chemises, lace, children's

Red Infantry on the move during the autumn manoeuvre of troops of the Kiev military district in the Odessa region of the Ukranian Soviet Socialist Republic, September 1936.

garments and long ribbons. These peaceful-looking objects made still more tragic the total picture of this frenzied flight . . . We could see men on the ships chopping through the mooring lines, and the ships pulled away from the docks without even raising their gangplanks. These broke away under the strain and slipped down into the sea with the people who were on them.

The city was dying a slow death. The 'wild houses', which stood empty because their owners had vanished, numbered in the thousands. 'Odessa was deserted. Many workers had left with the first Red Army units – supply divisions and sailors' detachments – before the arrival of Denikin and the Interventionists . . . For months the sea lay flat and lifeless, without a trace of smoke from a ship's funnel. At the same time, blocked railways, blown-up bridges, bandit gangs and the "wild lands" which knew no law, cut Odessa off from the north.' There was no electricity. Vera Inber remembered using a precious Art Nouveau vase to carry water, and dark-stained oak furniture was chopped up for firewood in the courtyards.

Once the civil war was over, the city rallied quite quickly, despite the decimation of its population and especially its middle class. Regular steamship service to Constantinople was resumed, with two ships leaving every week. Odessa's polyglot culture even thrived; there was a Yiddish and a German theatre. On the eve of the Second World War, the population had rebounded to 600,000. What had changed was the character of a community that had been cosmopolitan from its founding. Intercourse with the wider world had been the basis of its existence. Ze'ev Jabotinsky, another native son of Odessa, once argued: 'Who was the true creator of these extraordinarily beautiful cities, ports, railways, streets, the granaries and ships, the theatres and hospitals and universities? It was the merchant.' Stalin's Soviet Union, however, had no need for a city of trade. It needed a city of industry, and heavy industry if possible. The dictator abhorred the cosmopolitanism of seaports. The Odessa of old was an alien element in the body of the workers' and peasants' state. A city of businessmen and merchants was to be transformed into a stronghold of the proletariat. Richelieu Street was renamed Lenin Street; Catherine Street became Karl Marx Street; Trade Street was now Street of the Red Guard; French Boulevard turned into Proletarian Boulevard. The Bristol Hotel reopened as the Red Hotel. These were the more harmless and easily reversible among the changes the Soviets wrought, and in recent years they have indeed been reversed. More difficult to undo have been the clearing of cemeteries where famous Odessans such as the film star Vera Kholodnaya lay buried, the demolition of the Transfiguration Cathedral in 1936, the conversion of synagogues into gymnasia, and the removal of the monument to Catherine the Great. The large mercantile exchange building sat useless and was repurposed as a concert hall. Paustovsky described how the new bureaucracy started to proliferate and how an organization called 'Oprodkomgub' set up shop in plywood cubicles inside an old hotel on Deribasivska. Odessa, the shimmering 'Pearl of the Black Sea', was to become just another grey Soviet provincial town.

A second immensely destructive blow was the occupation by German and Romanian troops during the Second World War. The war wrought havoc on physical structures such as the railway station and the port facilities. It depopulated Odessa, as 300,000 people and some of the city's industrial installations were evacuated ahead of the enemy's arrival. Above all, it annihilated Jewish Odessa. The Germans ruled for 907 days. The resistance withdrew into the catacombs, a system that extended for hundreds of miles; bits of it are now open to tourists. The 100,000 Odessan Jews who remained in the city were left without a way out. They were penned up in Moldavanka and Slobodka, herded together on Khvorostin Square, and sent on death marches to camps in Transnistria, where tens of thousands were murdered and many more died of epidemics. A city map on display in the municipal museum, drawn up in 1944 by the Prague Military Cartography and Land Surveying Office and marked 'for official use only', shows the topography of German Odessa. The German writer Anna Seghers set an episode in her novel *The Dead Stay Young* (1949) in the occupied city. A Wehrmacht soldier reaches the top of the famous staircase:

> They marched into Odessa. Once before in his life – long, long ago – Hans had felt as if he stood on those harbour steps, and giant boots had trampled him . . . Perhaps many of the boys who were now tramping down the harbour as victors had sat before the same film, *Battleship Potemkin*. If one's memory of one's own experience is frail, the memory of the picture of some other person's experience is as faint as a breath. But not so with Hans. He felt as if he were doubly present; the boots

The 62nd Stalingrad Army marching on the streets of Odessa.

were his own boots, tramping down those steps, and at the same time he could feel the pressure of those devilish boots trampling him till his bones cracked.

Also among the museum's exhibits are announcements of concerts by the unfortunate Pyotr Leshchenko and his wife at the Odessa Opera.

Odessa quickly recovered from the outward damages of the war. Architects carefully patched up the urban fabric, with new constructions blending now more, now less fully into the extant building stock. The decor of the late Stalin years is not in fact a bad fit for the architecture of the city's boom years. The evacuated population returned and the city grew rapidly, the number of residents almost doubling in the post-war decades so that Greater Odessa now has 1.2 million inhabitants. A visitor today might not realize that the city has recently undergone such considerable expansion because the historic core has remained virtually unchanged. The new boroughs, the dormitory suburbs, stretch out towards the hinterland and along the bay shore. From elevated vantage points one can see the housing blocks looming in the distance like mountain ranges.

And yet many feel that the time may have come for them to say farewell to Odessa. The Jewish emigration of the 1970s through to the 1990s was a bloodletting that Perestroika and the dissolution of the Soviet Union did little to staunch. Odessans now live all over the world – in Tel Aviv, Brighton Beach, Berlin. Those who knew the Odessa of decades ago lament an increasingly provincial atmosphere and the growing dominance of Ukrainians in what was once a transnational city. Yet they also know that 'Odessa Mama', as her people almost tenderly call her, raises her children to be devoted to her. It does not take two generations to turn non-natives, be they Ukrainians, Moldovans, Russians or Jews, into Odessans.

A City in an 'Era of Great Expectations'

Now that the borders are open again, Odessa has been trying to grow back into the role it played before the Revolution: a city of trade and transport, of culture, recreation and amusement. It dreams the dream of the free port and hopes to become once again a gateway to the world. All the myths of the Odessa of yore are mobilized to help the new Odessa get on its feet. Such optimism may seem misplaced considering that the city contends with problems that had been resolved by the early twentieth century: there are scheduled power and water outages. Visions of a bright future might be a futile luxury given an average monthly per capita income of u.s.$40. Major industries are depressed and the port is operating well below capacity. Statistics circulate and horror scenarios are bandied about: narcotics use and HIV infection rates are rising; the city is a trans-shipment point for drugs between the Orient and Europe. And yet the transformation Odessa has undergone over the past decade is impossible to miss and certainly impressive. Far from relying on its legend, the city is putting forth a vigorous effort. Once again a major change of decorations is underway. The boutiques and cafés now often bear French names: Champs-Élysées, Le Cardinal, Madame de Gaulle. Lenin Street has been renamed back to Rishelievska. Tourists and expatriates travel back and forth from Brooklyn, Tel Aviv and Berlin. Standing on the square outside the central station during the tourist season, one might think that all of northeastern Europe is converging on Odessa, as trains from St Petersburg, Kiev, Lviv and Warsaw, plus through carriages from Berlin, the Donbass and the Urals, disgorge an endless stream of holidaymakers onto the platforms, to be instantaneously and effortlessly absorbed by the city. Odessa is a fast-paced place, a city of beaches, hotels and sanatoria. Factories sit idle, but the markets are bustling as though the entire city were out and about. The throngs are densest where, twelve years ago, enterprising seamen started selling imported merchandise. What began as a bootstrap operation of questionable legality has grown into Ukraine's largest market. The location, 7.2 km (4½ miles) outside the centre, in a commercial area, on the premises of a waste disposal plant, has given the bazaar its name: Sedmoi Kilometr, or seventh kilometre. Rush hours are early in the morning and again in the afternoon. The arcades, built from shipping containers stacked atop each other, stretch for miles. Vendors sell everything from wedding dresses to church bells, from bathtubs to condoms, from living rooms to perfumes. The city's biggest source of employment after the port, the market straddles the intersection of trade routes between Dnepropetrovsk and Istanbul, between the United Arab Emirates and Kiev, between Poland and the Caucasus. Lately there has been an influx of merchandise from India. On a typical day, almost 100,000 people come here to shop; buses arrive from all over Ukraine, and there are connections to Warsaw and Łódź. The bazaar has its own telephone switchboard, restaurant, police station and first-aid facility. It is divided into sections; one of them is solely devoted to used cars of all types and makes (there is also a separate second-hand car market further out in Kuialnyk). What is playing out here day after day is the market as the nucleus of urbanization, the ongoing refounding of the city. It is only a matter of time until this city outside the city's gates will return into the centre of Odessa, into the arcade on Deribasivska and the shops by the Palais Royal from which it was ousted decades ago. Sooner or later the improvised city will shed its latency and reveal itself.

In fact, one can already glimpse the Odessa of the future – on summer evenings, for example, when Odessans parade up and down Prymorsky Boulevard, enjoying the cool breeze and taking in the view of the moon's glittering reflection on the wide sea. Or in the cafés on Deribasivska, where locals and tourists alike chat until well after midnight. Gleaming luxury cars roll up to the casinos. Fast-talking *biznesmeny*, forever on their mobile phones, stand outside the coffee shops. The music of countless bands fills the air. One hears a lot of Arabic: students from Damascus, tourists from Lebanon or the Gulf. Odessa is what it was: a Levantine city. For incontrovertible evidence, take a nocturnal excursion to the beaches of Lanzheron and Novaya Arkadiya, jokingly called Las Vegas by the locals. The streets are crowded until the wee hours. Laser beams slice the night sky, and the thudding of music can be heard from discotheques such as the 'Ithaca', a Doric temple on a platform jutting out over the sea. There are none of the drunks that were a common sight in Soviet culture and recreation parks. Everyone is young and beautiful, like Greek deities or the runners on the beach in Santa Monica. They are having a fun night out and know that everything has its price. Needless to say, few of them have watched Eisenstein's movie – there are more interesting things to see and do. The Potemkin Stairs are not an icon for the twenty-first century. The stage on which Odessa is preparing for its comeback is merely one tourist attraction among others, and in urgent need of repair.

(Summer 2000)

SIX

PROMENADE IN YALTA

I N FEBRUARY AND MARCH 2014, Russia, in an operation executed with
surgical precision, annexed Crimea. After Viktor Yanukovych was
toppled and fled Ukraine, protests against the new government in
Kiev broke out in Simferopol, the capital of Crimea, on 23 February
2014, and the mayor was ousted. On 27 February unidentified soldiers
occupied the regional parliament and several government buildings. An
election held behind closed doors installed a new pro-Russian leadership, which promised a referendum on Crimea's independence. Over
the following days, 'polite little green men' – around 20,000 soldiers
without badges of rank or national insignia who had entered from
Russia and the Russian naval base in Sevastopol – took control of
strategic points throughout the peninsula. On 1 March, the newly
appointed governor Sergei Aksyonov called on Russia to 'protect the
Russian-speaking population of Crimea'. On 6 March, his government
announced that a referendum would be held on Crimea's accession
to the Russian Federation, and ten days later, 96.8 per cent of voters
– a number the Russian Human Rights Council called fraudulent –
approved 'reunification with Russia'. The Republic of Crimea requested
to be admitted to Russia on 17 March, and the Treaty of Accession
of Crimea and the City of Sevastopol to the Russian Federation was
signed the next day. The annexation of Crimea, a brutal contravention of international law, was complete. One year later, many of those
involved in the operation have described their machinations in great
detail; on the first anniversary, Putin himself boasted of its efficiency.

For Crimea, this 'Russian Spring' marks a new chapter in its history – and the end of a history I had sketched in 2000 under the title
'Promenade in Yalta'. 'Promenade' was written in the wake of the

empire's decline. The cultural imprint, the physical and mental legacy, of Russian and Soviet imperial rule were omnipresent, and there was no sign of discord between Ukrainians, Russians, Crimean Tatars and the other ethnicities that make up the peninsula's population. Not even Yury Luzhkov, the mayor of Moscow, whose rhetoric had frequently veered into strident nationalism, had gone so far as to claim that the Russians in Crimea were victims of persecution, threatened by 'annihilation'. The focus of my trip in 2000 was a very different one: how would a post-Soviet Ukrainian Crimea 'reinvent' and 'reposition' itself? How was it managing the transition from 'Red Riviera' to European holiday destination? How might the all-Union sanatorium and recreation combine with other European holiday regions without blighting its distinctive magic, the unique density of its cultural and historic heritage? The shift from a communist to a consumerist economy, from Yalta to Mallorca, presented daunting challenges. As state-organized tourism dwindled, would Crimea's paradisiacal landscapes be privatized, the pieces snapped up by oligarchs who would grab whatever they wanted – Chekhov's villa, Prince Vorontsov's castle? Would one of Europe's most charming coastlines be sold off to the highest bidders? And what about the rights of the Crimean Tatars, who had been forcibly deported from their native land? Putin's Russia has robbed Crimea and all its people of the chance to nurture this paradise to a new bloom. The 'Russian Spring' he proclaimed began with queues, out-of-service cash dispensers, rising prices and empty beaches. The appetite of the new rulers is considerable: the mercenaries and privateers who took Crimea by force of arms will now have their share of the booty. Other people's property – beachfront plots, sanatoria, hotels, villas, dachas – is being redistributed. The 'volunteers' who fought in Chechnya and then participated in the 'liberation' of Crimea now hang out on the promenade in Yalta, unless they have moved on to the Donbass. The Russian brass eye the Black Sea coast as the ideal place to retire to. The new Moscow aristocracy of high-ranking intelligence officers and oligarchs have long identified the coves that will make for the most exclusive private pleasure grounds. Having only just begun to open up to the wider world after the end of the Soviet Union, the peninsula is reverting to a restricted military area. The Lenin monument in Simferopol has already been refurbished. What could be a holidaymakers' paradise is turning into a missile base, with military parades instead of bathers.

But as Neal Ascherson, the Black Sea's biographer, knows, the last word has not yet been spoken:

> Crimea's contemporary significance lies in its beauty and its history. The monuments, palaces, graves, and ruins of almost three millennia lie scattered across an extraordinary landscape whose character varies from the summits of the coastal range to the greyish-green plains of the inland steppe and the forests around the former residence of the khans in Bakhchisarai. Throughout the ages, invading nomads, travelling merchants, and visiting rulers have aspired to possession of this land, this great brown diamond jutting out into the Black Sea. But Crimea is a place of arrivals and departures; it has seen many settlers come and, sometimes centuries later, go. Crimea, where everyone is in some way an immigrant, can never truly be anyone's possession.

(2015)

✛

RUSSIA, LIKE GERMANY, has its 'land where the lemon-trees blossom'. A tourist drifting southward from Russia through Ukraine will eventually reach the Isthmus of Perekop. Before him lies a dream destination for an entire erstwhile empire. The peninsula has been part of Ukraine since 1954, and Ukraine has been independent since 1991, but dream landscapes are more stable than nation states, and the maps in people's heads remain unchanged long after new boundaries have been drawn. Trains from all over the former Soviet Union pull into Simferopol, the Crimean capital, as though the empire had never fallen: from Riga and Minsk, from St Petersburg and Moscow, from Murmansk and Vorkuta, even from Tyumen in Siberia, a five-day journey. Simferopol is, in modern parlance, the hub, where holidaymakers are put on transportation to their various destinations and where they converge again to board the trains back home. Anyone bound for the towns, coves, sanatoria and beaches on Crimea's coast and anyone heading back home to their ordinary lives in the north must pass through Simferopol.

Most of the trains arrive around dawn. The early light grazes the station building. The air is crisp, with a hint of the scent of flowers, a pleasant surprise after the stale atmosphere of the compartments in which the travellers have been stuck for the last few days. Some cafés are

From the Gurzuf Road, Yalta, *c.* 1890–1900 – in my mind,
this is the best view of Yalta.

already open, and taxi drivers promise a quick and affordable transfer to
the coast beyond the mountains, less than an hour's drive. We cannot
for a moment be in doubt as to where we are. The Soviet architects who
rebuilt the cities after the war had all studied the squares and edifices of
Piacenza, Florence and Siena at university. The columns and arcades,
the large courtyard and the campanile are suffused with a glossy sheen;
it must be white marble from Inkerman. The station itself is a tribute
to Italy. But Simferopol is only the gateway. Everyone wants to be on
their way, to the shore that was once the 'Russian Riviera'.

As we reach the pass and begin to descend the 'lilac-blue escarp-
ment', the Black Sea comes into view. Making our way down through
a series of switchbacks and then along the coast on a wide and well-
maintained road, we might almost think that we are in Liguria or on
the Côte d'Azur. The Crimean Mountains fall off precipitously towards
the sea. Clouds hover over the ridge like a veil. The slopes – verdant
green rather than sun-baked brown – are home to rare plants and
trees, including cedars, though much of the land is covered by spruce
forests: the quintessential northern tree on a southerly shore. A new
cove opens behind every promontory, and the names of the towns

and villages we pass through have a magical ring for any citizen of the former Soviet Union, be it because they are familiar from poetry or because they invoke memories of the happiest moments in life. They are arrayed like a string of pearls: Alushta, Gurzuf, Yalta, Foros, Sevastopol and Evpatoriya in the west, Sudak, Koktebel, Feodosiya and Kerch in the east of the trapezoidal peninsula, which is not much smaller than Belgium. The narrow strip of land between the sea and the mountains is built up with hotel towers, every balcony turned towards the sun and the sea. The towns straggle up the terraced hillsides. White porticos and the facades of expansive palaces surrounded by lush green parks can be glimpsed through the gates in tall walls. A scent familiar from the shores of the Mediterranean Sea fills the air: oleander, azaleas, lavender and pines.

The Promenade in Yalta

After years of decline it seems that things are now looking up. When the Soviet Union collapsed, Crimea was sometimes difficult to get to for its regular visitors, especially from Moscow. The sanatoria and hotels sat empty, while the organizations that had operated them unravelled. Many holidaymakers preferred Antalya, Cyprus, Eilat or the Costa Brava, destinations that were cheaper and beckoned with something they looked for in vain in the Soviet–post-Soviet world: friendly service. In Crimea, the infrastructure was crumbling; water and power were turned off for hours at a time. There were reports of Cholera infections. Two million people from all over the Soviet Union had come to the circa 140 recreation centres along the coast; that number now shrank to around 300,000. Hotel construction projects were left unfinished, their dilapidated shells dotting the hillsides around Yalta like the dinosaurs of a distant era. A wild privatization commenced. Campers pitched their tents on the beaches and in the mountains. That seems to be a thing of the past.

In the morning, the promenade in Yalta lies quiet. People are out on the beach. The waiters have time to tidy up. The air is cool. Workers hose down the streets. Spa guests sit in the shadows of the firs and palm trees and read. Many will go on a tour of the wine cellars of Massandra or Nicholas I's summer palace in Livadia, where the Yalta Conference was held in February of 1945, while others are setting out for the market – it is still not uncommon for thrifty holidaymakers to prepare their own meals. The port lies idle; the suspension of ferry service to Sevastopol, Istanbul and Odessa is the most visible effect of the crisis. The atmosphere is sedate. The more striking is what happens once the sun sets and the bay shines like an enormous luminous arc. As the city sinks into darkness, a city of lights emerges. Night after night, the promenade is transformed into a blend of funfair and catwalk, of theatrical stage and pageant. People venture out of their lodgings and take in the spectacle of the jostling crowd. A fantastically illuminated landscape unfurls before the visitor: a gambling den in the shape of the Pyramids of Giza; a restaurant inside the mythical Argo hovering high above the heads of the strollers; a dance floor projecting over the sea. A big wheel scintillates, seconded by the moon. The evening's entertainments conclude with a nightly fireworks display, its cascades momentarily bathing the bay in gaudy lights. The restaurants and cafés are packed, and stores are open until after midnight. The smallest bit of free room is put to one use or another. A band performs on every landing of the hillside city's numerous staircases, making nocturnal Yalta a maze of musical terraces: gypsy orchestra; jazz from Riga, Odessa or Moscow; a crooner accompanied by an orchestra belting out Frank Sinatra's 'New York, New York' over the bay; and, audible from afar, the panpipes of 'El cóndor pasa', the unmistakable signature ditty of cultural globalization. A combo from St Petersburg plays Viennese waltzes and Handel. But wait, there is more: the costume stock of a Russian theatre has been spread out at a photo booth. Just now a couple has slipped into ermine furs, red velvet, berets and white blouses to pose as Henry VIII and Anne Boleyn – before the Black Sea. The walls are covered with posters advertising performances by stars such as Bella Akhmadulina, Larisa Dolina and Anzhelika Varum. The city organizes cultural programmes at palatial indoor venues and beneath the palm trees of the parks for classical music, opera, singers and choirs, and folklore. Other posters promote massage therapists, dog trainers and manicurists. The statue of Gorky at the entrance to the park looks lonely. Men demonstrate imperturbable cool as they step out of their luxury Benzes with Russian, Moldavian and Ukrainian registration numbers. Many people, absorbed in conversation on their mobile phones, ignore the throngs. The spectacle is the same evening after evening during the season.

Like other cities and towns along the southern shore of Crimea, Yalta was first settled by Greeks (the name, formerly 'Yalita', is probably of Greek origin). Few traces remain today of Yalta's time as a Genoese trading post and stronghold of the khanate. The history of modern Yalta begins with the conquest of Crimea by Catherine II, who made presents to various high imperial officials of the land along the coast. The port was enlarged in 1837. An early plan for the redevelopment of the town was drawn up by the Swiss architect Karl Aeschlimann, who had been trained in Prague and Berne. Yalta as it appears today takes shape in the late nineteenth century, when it becomes the 'seaside resort of elegant society', as the 1893 Baedeker notes. Anton Chekhov observes that 'there are stores along the embankment that would not embarrass Paris.' Around this time, Yalta acquires the characteristic institutions and amenities that identify it as a rising city in the Russian Empire: electric street lights, lyceums for boys and girls, an Alexander Nevsky Cathedral, and a new central neighbourhood built from scratch with hotels, port buildings, sanatoria and villas. It replaces Biarritz and Ostend as the favourite summer haunt of the distant capital's elite. Much of that Yalta is extant today: the Hotel Rossiya, where Chekhov and Modest Mussorgsky resided, the Hotel Marino, the Catholic church, Chekhov's 'white dacha', the mansion of the emir of Bukhara and the numerous palaces in the surrounding countryside. The white facades with oriels and parapets in a hotchpotch of styles – from neo-Russian to Art Nouveau, from Tudor to classicism – is this period's characteristic legacy.

The revolution is the end of the clientele that had put Yalta on the map. The streets fall silent, the villas are subdivided into small apartments. The era of organized spa and holiday tourism is decades away. The earliest new buildings date from the 1930s: a few sanatoria and a new terminal building by the port. Here as elsewhere, the Second World War causes physical damage. But what changes the face of Yalta and the region is the expansive construction activity of the 1960s through to the 1980s: prefabricated housing blocks of the 464-AS series sprout up, along with new cinemas, athletic facilities and gigantic hotels – the Hotel Yalta, with its 2,700 beds, juts out into the bay like a promontory – and, further inland, a large motorway junction.

The Myth of Crimea

Yalta is more than a seaside resort, and Crimea is more than scenic beauty. It is a Europe in miniature, a microcosm of world history. It lies where the sea laps up against the steppes, where caravans traversing the waters encounter those criss-crossing the vast inland plains. The civilizations that Crimea has seen come and go! Greek antiquity, the Roman world, the steppe peoples of Eurasia, Byzantium, the Italian naval republics and the Ottoman Empire all left their imprints on it. Dreams and nightmares were never far apart. The dark side of the Russian colonization drive beginning in the early nineteenth century was the mass emigration of over 300,000 Crimean Tatars, most of whom left for the Ottoman Empire. The Germans played no small part in Crimea's traumatic history. The peninsula became a focus of Nazi Germany's plans for the translocation of populations and the creation of a future German-dominated Europe. In July 1941 Hitler announced that he would remove the entire population 'to make room for our own settlers' and establish a 'German Gibraltar to rule over the Black Sea'. Crimea would become a 'great German health resort' and the terminus of a four-lane Autobahn on which 'Strength through Joy' tourists from Berlin would reach the shores of 'Tauria' in two days. ss genealogists scoured the peninsula, whose projected official name was Gotenland; new names had already been chosen for Simferopol and Sevastopol, too: Gotenburg and Theoderichshafen. Crimea was a 'land where milk and honey flowed' and eminently suitable for the 'replanting' of the South Tyrolese expelled from their homeland, as the Austrian-born Gauleiter Alfred Frauenfeld opined, but it would first need to be 'cleared'. Roughly one in ten Crimeans lost their lives under the German occupation. Otto Ohlendorf's Einsatzgruppe D murdered the peninsula's 65,000 Jewish residents under the eyes of Erich von Manstein's 11th Army. By the end of 1941, Crimea was 'free of Jews'. The Red Army drove out the occupiers, but the ethnic 'unmixing' continued apace. The German colonists, who had been a sizable minority before the war, left with the Wehrmacht. Stalin indiscriminately accused the Crimean Tatars, around one-quarter of the pre-war population, of collaboration with the Germans, and in a secret operation on 17–18 May, the NKVD deported all of them to Central Asia, mainly to Uzbekistan. Tens of thousands did not survive the transports and perished wretchedly. The Black Sea Greeks, who had been an economically and culturally influential ethnic group in Crimea for centuries, fared not much better. The Crimean Tatars have been rehabilitated, and tens of thousands have returned to their home-land from Central Asia – 40,000 of them made the journey in 1991 alone. The community now numbers around 250,000, or roughly 10 per cent of the peninsula's total population, although the autonomous Tatar republic of the pre-war period has not been re-established. As one drives through the mountains and the steppes further north, their settlements are easy to spot. They were never asked what they thought, not by Khrushchev, who gave Crimea to Ukraine as a 'gift' in 1954, and not by the government of Ukraine, which had no right to accept this 'gift'.

Crimea was part of the ancient world, as the names of cities such as Feodosiya and Evpatoriya indicate. The peninsula is a paradise for archaeologists, no matter which era they specialize in. Their colleagues have excavated Panticapaeum and the temple of Apollo in Kerch and the remnants of the town in which Vladimir the Great from Kiev is said to have received baptism in Chersonesus near Sevastopol. The storms of the Great Migrations reduced the high culture that had formed along the northern Black Sea to ruins and distant memories. Crimea was variously ruled by Byzantium and the Khazars, later by the Golden Horde and the Genoese, whose forts can still be seen in Sudak, Feodosiya, Balaclava and elsewhere. From the early fifteenth until the late eighteenth centuries, Crimea was the seat of the Tatar Khanate, which presided over a new cultural florescence and exercised considerable influence over the powers further north – the Grand Duchy of Lithuania, the Polish crown, Muscovy and the Cossacks. Crimea paid tribute to the Sublime Porte and took inspiration from the art and culture of the Ottoman Empire. Extant traces of this period include toponyms such as Koktebel and the minarets of Simferopol and Bakhchisarai, where the khans of Crimea resided between 1422 and 1783. For Russians, the latter town, with its palace, mosques, madrasa, harem and the famous Fountain of Tears – immortalized by Pushkin's poem – came to epitomize the Orient.

The Crimea that is a familiar cultural trope – the peninsula as it appears to the visitor today – is a product of imperial history. But the contributions of tsarist Russia and the Soviet Union cannot be written off as colonialism and projections of Russian orientalism. Pushkin wrote his 'Farewell to the Sea', an ode to liberty, while staying with the Raevskys in Gurzuf in 1820. Crimea was everything that Russia was not: the South, freedom, a distant shore within the empire's bounds. And its magic enchanted them all: the Russian intelligentsia making pilgrimage to Maximilian Voloshin's house in Koktebel and Chekhov's refuge in

Yalta; the Soviet workers for whom the trade union had finally secured a spot in the 'Donbass' sanatorium; the hippies of the late Soviet era for whom Crimea had to stand in for California. There are probably few landscapes in the world so thoroughly, and so sumptuously, fashioned by art – an entire coast as a large park dotted with villas.

Crimea's transformation into the Russian Empire's own Cockaigne, the luxurious playground of its high aristocracy, is the fruit of over a century of hard work and a happy marriage of charming sceneries, boundless wealth, and, in many instances, exquisite taste. It started when Catherine the Great, who had personally visited Crimea in 1787, carved some of it up into generous gifts to her close associates: the Duc de Richelieu received land in Gurzuf; Prince Vorontsov, in Alupka and Massandra; Count Potocki, in Livadiya; Prince Golitsyn, in Koreiz and Gaspra. Over time, the peninsula's southern coast turned into a continuous man-made landscape, the 'Russian Riviera'. The ruins of a castle built for Grand Duke Konstantin can be seen in Oreanda; Grand Duke Peter Nikolaevich had Dulber Palace erected in Koreiz; Prince Dolgorukov's mansion stands in Miskhor; Prince Yusupov's in Koreiz and Count Panin's neo-Gothic pile in Gaspra. Vorontsov Palace,

The Gothic castle Swallow's Nest on a rock above the Black Sea.

in Alupka, was designed by an English architect and blends Gothic Revival architecture with orientalist motifs. Only years before the Great War, Tsar Nicholas II commissioned a summer residence in the style of the Italian Renaissance in Livadia. The 'Swallow's Nest', Baron Steingel's extravaganza, perches atop a bizarre rock spur. Members of the Academy of Sciences, landscape gardeners and aristocratic amateurs planted wonderful gardens such as the Vorontsovs' park in Alupka or the Nikitsky Botanical Garden near Yalta that charm visitors with the abundant diversity of their flora: cedars, giant sequoias, pines, oleanders, magnolias, palm trees, lemon trees, sugarcane, papyrus, cherry laurels, Persian silk trees, bamboo and Japanese date palms. The courtly clientele drew eminent St Petersburg architects such as Ippolit Monighetti, Auguste de Montferrand and Andrei Stackenschneider to Crimea. Leading Russian balneologists and physicians set up shop. These experts in their métiers helped turn the coast into a scenery of well-being, health and luxury. Industrialists, merchants and the owners of publishing houses followed suit. The last coterie to make itself at home in Crimea, at least for the season, were the intellectuals. Very few writers, composers and painters of the Russian Silver Age did not at some point sojourn in Koktebel, Gurzuf or Yalta. The peninsula was the palm-tree-lined terrace of the Russian belle époque. And then, in 1914, it was all over. The sanatoria were converted into military hospitals. After the collapse of the monarchy, Russians and Austrians moved into the villas for a while, joined, a little later, by British and French troops fighting on the side of the Whites. In the autumn of 1920, they, and tens of thousands of refugees, embarked for Constantinople.

The 'Red Riviera'

On 21 December 1920, Lenin signed a degree 'On the Use of Crimea for the Recreation of the Working People'. The document basically sanctioned the expropriations and unauthorized use of properties by revolutionaries and squatters during the civil war. The summer residences of yesteryear were repurposed as museums or sanatoria. The 58 rooms of Livadia Palace, completed only in 1911, were opened to the public, which was invited to inspect 'the last tsar's way of life in all its petit-bourgeois manifestations. Upstairs are the tsar's seven private chambers, furnished in the most tasteless fashion. The walls are panelled with rare woods and hung with an enormous number of cheap drawings, religious depictions, and icons,' as a 1928 guidebook puts it. The tsar's very own summer residence is also where the first sanatorium for peasants was established in 1923. Oreanda became the recreation home of the Moscow Printers' Association. The Central Executive Committee installed itself inside Erlanger Park. From the People's Commissariat for Posts and Telegraphs to the NKVD – each organization had its own piece of seaside real estate. The Ukrainian Council of People's Commissars had snaffled the 'Swallow's Nest', while the Mamluk-inspired Dulber Palace and Prince Dolgorukov's mansion were now sanatoria called 'Red Banner' (for political workers) and 'Red Dawn', respectively. When members of the Academy of Sciences needed to recover, they were sent to the palatial compound in Gaspra, while Prince Yusupov's property in Koreiz served as the summer residence of the GPU (State Political Administration) and its ailing director Feliks Dzerzhinsky. Milyutin's mansion in Miskhor became the GPU's tuberculosis sanatorium 'Mountain Sun'. Where aristocratic families ruled, trade unions and factory directors now called the shots. The Monastery of Saints Cosmas and Damian was turned into a labour and reformatory colony. White-collar workers were placed in the Hotel Mauritania in Feodosiya.

The exercise of dictatorial authority is exhausting, and just like everyone else, the clerks who staffed the Soviet administration needed time off to recover every once in a while. Control over access to these havens would be one of the most important privileges and instruments of power in the Soviet Union: those who wielded it were the gatekeepers of an earthly paradise. The landscapes of happiness became the people's property, and what was exclusive was now supposedly open to all. In reality, the playground of the Russian high aristocracy was taken over by the Comintern's VIPs. Yet despite the outward resemblance between the residences of old and the Stalin era's new sanatoria, there was a fundamental difference: the New Man has new needs. Holidays, to him, were not a luxury but recreation that served to restore and enhance his productivity. Well-being had turned into something that could be planned; happiness is quantifiable, measured in output rates. A scene of playful and dallying luxury was transformed into a health-and-recovery combo overseen by a central resort administration known by the abbreviation Kurupr. The sanatorium was Crimea's true *locus genii*. The holiday, formerly an individual experience, was now the purview of organizations that assigned the available slots and planned and arranged every aspect. In keeping with the Soviet penchant for acronyms, these organizations were known as Glavdortrans, Ukrastrakas, Narkomzdrav and so on. The names of the sanatoria – Donbass, Metallurg, Energetik, Rybak – indicated which corporations owned them. The organized recreation of hundreds of thousands of workers became the subject of a dedicated scientific discipline that synthesized all aspects of social reproduction: *kurortologiya* or 'spa studies'. Individual tourism virtually ceased to exist as holidaymakers – their personal preferences overruled by the solicitude of state or company administrators – were consigned to the care of professionals who prescribed their daily routines with a view to the rational use of time. Sanatoria engaged in socialist competition. A new kind of holiday took shape, the Soviet path to a place in the sun. Organization and collectivism are its defining features. The day began with mandatory morning exercises and concluded with an edifying popular-culture programme. Travelling in Crimea in the 1930s, the American journalist H. R. Knickerbocker was amused by these strenuous efforts to mass-manufacture felicity itself and the sun-and-light ideology of nude bathing; he found out soon enough that the recreational five-year plan was not working out any better than those in other sectors of industry. Still, Crimea was one of the few places of happiness that not even Stalin's Soviet Union could do without. Red Army soldiers seized the opportunity to take off their badges of rank; their wives, to put on their jewellery. And it is as a scene suffused with the golden glow of better days that Crimea was recorded in the family albums of generations of Soviet citizens: the beach in the background, the flight of white marble stairs lined with palm trees, the park in which peaches and oranges grew.

From Yalta to Mallorca

The 'Red Riviera' is no longer. It is perhaps not a coincidence that a key episode in the USSR's demise is associated with the Crimean coast: it was here, in the luxurious government dacha in Foros, that Mikhail Gorbachev was put under house arrest by the conspirators of the attempted coup d'état on 19 August 1991. Since then, the peninsula has rushed to catch up with a development that Western European holiday regions had decades to complete: a process lamented by the Russian intelligentsia that I would call Mallorcaization. Crimea has ceased to be a cultural signifier and become an advertising catchword. Today, the sanatoria are filled not with the working masses on reprieve from the toil of 'immediate production' but instead consumers who come with expectations. Animators have supplanted agitators; physical culture at daybreak has been replaced by gym classes. The patriotic songs have fallen silent, and everyone plays their own favourite music, usually at maximum volume. Formerly nationalized and union-operated facilities seek to lure individual tourists.

A new type has appeared on the promenade in Yalta. He has not been sent here – he has paid for himself and his statistically representative nuclear family. Russian, the old *lingua franca*, dominates in the street, but the anchor currency at the bureau de change is the u.s. dollar. The new type on the promenade is between 20 and 45; senior citizens are nowhere to be seen. He is fashionably attired and drinks juice rather than vodka. He knows he has earned this holiday. The younger children are still dressed up nicely, an echo of Soviet customs, but the teenagers tend to look like kids everywhere else. Where summer guests in Sochi display a lot of naked skin, in Yalta they undress just enough to let people know that they are in good shape. If you are one of them, you can afford to be here; that you are here is evidence that you are clued up, you can compare offers, you have travelled abroad for work and been to Antalya or Larnaca. There are many possible reasons why you chose Yalta. You have plans for yourself and the children. You are not one of the 'new Russians', nor a 'new Ukrainian', not a member of the *jeunesse dorée* that is in the papers all the time. You are a representative of a species about whom so little is known that some doubt whether it even exists. The sociologists who study the transition from the Soviet model of the mobilization society to a civil society in the Western mould have long expected its appearance. In their eyes, you embody the tendencies of an unstoppable modernity: privatization, individualization, differentiation. The species that has at long last begun to manifest itself on the promenade in Yalta, in Gurzuf, in Foros, Evpatoriya and Sevastopol, the species you exemplify, is the post-Soviet middle class. These *homines novi* had their fill of the 'earthly paradise' they were promised and enjoy the little piece of paradise they can afford by dint of their own hard work. It is a shift that is no less consequential than the end of the division of Europe that was sealed in Yalta many decades ago.

(Summer 2000)

SEVEN

LOOK UPON THIS CITY: KHARKOV, A CAPITAL OF THE TWENTIETH CENTURY

K HARKOV – in Ukrainian, Kharkiv – is Ukraine's second-largest city after Kiev, and one dares not imagine what would happen to it if it were drawn into the war that has already laid waste to Lugansk and Donetsk, a mere two hours away by train. In Kharkov in the summer of 2014, rocket fire, house-to-house fighting and ravaged infrastructure seem distant troubles. Travellers throng the square outside the railway station, and Sumska Street, the local Kurfürstendamm or Nevsky Prospect and artery connecting the old and new city centres, is clogged with traffic; the cafés that bear the same names as cafés all over the world are crowded in the evenings – many patrons stare into their tablet computers – and on the weekends the festively illuminated Maxim Gorky Central Park of Culture and Recreation, boasting the newest attractions from America, overflows with revellers old and young. And yet Donetsk looked just like this before Russian-controlled irregulars brought the city under their control. In the spring of 2014, Kharkov, too, saw attempts to topple the fragile balance. Interlopers from out of town tried to proclaim a 'Kharkov People's Republic', but thousands of demonstrators chased them away. There were blockades and gun battles downtown, and the Russian flag briefly flew over the regional state administration building. Supporters of Maidan were chased down a 'corridor of shame' and beaten up. Hennadii Kernes, the city's mayor, was severely injured in an attack whose perpetrators remain unidentified. More recently, pro-Ukrainian activists have toppled the Lenin monument in the city's centre, a symbol of its Soviet past in whose shadow rebellious poets had smoked their first joints. In the past few months, it had served as the rallying point for pro-Russian protesters, many of them embittered pensioners whipped into a frenzy by propaganda. Taking Lenin down was as unimaginative an insult as it was needless, but that has not stopped activists in other cities from following Kharkov's example. Once again it looks like a city's precarious equilibrium might be upset at any moment, transforming ordinary citizens into enemies ready to fire at each other. In May, on the day of the presidential elections, which took place for the most part in an atmosphere of tense calm, I chatted with someone about topics ranging from the strikingly relaxed mood in Kharkov to Constructivism. The conversation took a strange turn when my interlocutor confided to me that, although he was a piano tuner by training, he was also a sharpshooter with several decorations and a tour of duty in Afghanistan under his belt; he was prepared to leave his first for his second job at a moment's notice when the time came to face down the 'Kiev junta'. It does not take a great deal of imagination to envision what becomes of a city of a million and a half when piano tuners turn into snipers.

A Major European City Few Have Heard Of

We know little about Kharkov. In 2012 FC Metalist Kharkiv's stadium was one of the venues of the European football championship. Tens of thousands of fans, primarily from the Netherlands, flocked to the city 'on the edge of Europe', and some lasting effects of this push towards Europeanization are palpable even today. Notice, for example, the Ukrainian-and-English street signs and the worldly service at the hotel reception, utterly un-Soviet in its friendliness. More recently, reports about the downing of the Malaysia Airlines plane – the recovered bodies of the victims were temporarily held in refrigerator wagons on the grounds of the Malyshev factory – reminded the world of Kharkov's existence. A major city does not fall off the European radar just like that.

Kharkov is not only a city of a million and a half; it is a centre of science and culture with over 130,000 students, an industrial heavyweight with a long tradition in mechanical engineering, and a first-order transportation hub. In the late tsarist era, the city was the empire's eighth-largest, behind St Petersburg, Moscow, Warsaw, Odessa, Łódź, Riga and Kiev. From 1919 until 1934, it was the formal capital of Ukraine and a Mecca for the European avant-garde. Yet its annals also read as a digest of the tribulations and horrors that

Detail of the Gosprom complex in Kharkov.

afflicted Ukraine in the twentieth century: civil war, collectivization and Holodomor, Great Terror, German occupation and Holocaust.

Arriving in Kharkov, you know right away that you are in a city of the first rank. If the South Korean-built high-speed train that travels between Kiev and Kharkov, the country's first and second capitals, has not convinced you, the railway station and the square in front of it are unmistakably metropolitan: not, in this instance, a 'cathedral of the nineteenth century', but a palace in the Stalinist-empire style, with an enormous dome, ceiling paintings glorifying the Great Patriotic War and a sweeping flight of stairs down to the square. The complex stands as a monument to Kharkov's post-war reconstruction.

No expense was spared in the recent restoration of the model of Soviet Constructivist architecture along the square's northern edge, its gleaming white facade lined with Bauhaus-style ribbon windows. Across the square, occupying almost an entire street, is the building of the southern district railway administration from the 1890s, when the Russian Empire's industrial development took off and Kharkov became the central railway hub in the south. You need not go further than this square to encounter three distinct strata that will resurface throughout the city: the boomtown of the Russian fin-de-siècle, Soviet modernism on Ukrainian soil and the monumentalism of the late Stalin years. Yet everything thrums to the sound of a vibrant city of a million and a half that increasingly drapes itself – on posters, in shop windows and in the nocturnal illumination of its facades – in blue and yellow, the Ukrainian national colours.

Fin-de-siècle Kharkov

The town was a late foundation. The first settlers – Cossacks, farmers who had escaped serfdom – probably reached the area, then known as Slobodskaya Ukraina, or Free Ukraine, in 1653. Framed by the valleys of the Lopan and Kharkov Rivers and watched over by the bell tower of Dormition Cathedral, University Hill, with the university buildings and the representative ensemble around Constitution Square, is the heart of the old town. As in most capitals of the empire's governorates, the city's later expansion proceeded based on a geometric plan with major streets radiating from the centre. If you know about the terrible damage Kharkov suffered, first with the demolition of the central Cathedral of Saint Nicholas in the 1930s and then in the Second World War – when two-thirds of the building stock were destroyed and the population, which had swelled to a million and a half before the war, shrunk to 190,000 by the time the liberators arrived – you may be taken aback by how compact its architecture is. One reason is surely the solid quality of the structures that were erected in this major centre in the Russian Empire's south since the mid-nineteenth century, most of them in the historicist style, including the headquarters of the Volga-Kama and Azov-Don Banks, hotels such as the Astoria, the Rossiya Insurance complex, the theatre, and the building that is now home to the philharmonic orchestra. Most of the stars on St Petersburg's architectural scene at the time – Thon, Stackenschneider, Pretro, Veryovkin,

Lidval – built something here. When the Bolsheviks came to power, they inherited and renamed these edifices: the Noblemen's Assembly became the All-Ukrainian Central Executive Committee building and, later, the Pioneers' Palace; the consistory was converted into a state archive and the city's duma became its soviet. Strikingly large ensembles along commercial streets and in residential neighbourhoods have survived. Walk along Darwin Street, for example, to study Art Nouveau architecture in all the diverse variants that proliferated in Europe: English country cottage, German half-timber Romanticism and Moorish Revival orientalism – and, interspersed between them like meteorite impact craters, buildings that display the distinctive clear lines of Soviet Constructivism. The Byzantine-inspired Annunciation Cathedral, the neo-Gothic brick structure of the Catholic church on Gogol Street, and the Choral Synagogue on Pushkin Street all bear witness to the mix of ethnic and religious groups who lived together in Kharkov. The city's main street, the road towards Sumy (for a while it was named after Karl Liebknecht, and the square where it begins is still called Rosa Luxemburg Square), is an encyclopaedia of Kharkov's evolution. It witnessed each successive step in the emergence of a modern city: a horse tramway, electrification and street lighting; the construction of the sewer system, arcades and entertainment venues; the rise of luxurious housing complexes featuring lifts and telephones. Municipal parks were laid out; a hippodrome – which would later become the scene of mass political rallies – was built; a zoo was established. Indoor markets, schools, department stores and hotels sprang up. The names of Kharkov's major enterprises suggest the city's international flair: the Novaya Bavariya brewery, George Borman's confectionery (later renamed 'October'), the Dietmar iron foundry (later 'Mineworker's Light'), Helfreich and Sade's agricultural machinery factory. The old Kharkov with its merchants, entrepreneurs and bourgeois intelligentsia perished in the revolution and the civil war that swept through the city several times. Yet even after the occupation by German troops in 1918 and the conquest by the Red Army and Soviet power in 1919, Kharkov remained the city of modernity, unlike Kiev, which, with the Monastery of the Caves and St Sophia's Cathedral, stood for the venerable tradition of the old Rus', for the lands along the Dnieper and the hetmanate. A certain logic, and not just the calculus of power in faraway Moscow, suggested that Kharkov should be the capital of Soviet Ukraine.

Capital, Red Modernism, Red Downtown

Evidence of what Kharkov was in the period that followed – between 1919 and 1934 – is still abundant in the cityscape today. In retrospect, it is easy to see why it was once a pilgrimage destination for many who sought a glimpse of the world of tomorrow. Notorious champions of the Soviet Union such as Henri Barbusse and Theodore Dreiser came to visit, as did politicians including Édouard Herriot and Edvard Beneš, who claimed to have seen no sign of the terrible famine afflicting Ukraine. The city also attracted artists, architects, engineers, physicists and, later, emigrants from European countries threatened by Hitler's designs. For one decade, Kharkov became the powerhouse of an increasingly confident Ukrainian modernism spearheaded by figures – Alexandra Exter, the Burliuk brothers – that still occupy a prominent place in the annals of the inter- and transnational 'Soviet avant-garde'. For one decade, Kharkov was the crucible of a grand experiment in which social revolution and post-imperial emancipation were manifestly wedded to each other in a flourishing of Ukrainian culture. A young Ukrainian writer, Serhiy Zhadan, found nothing in it beyond the 'medieval sun city', a 'Red downtown', 'Valhalla's entrance hall', but in reality the buildings of the New Kharkov and Red modernism were linchpins in the European debate over architecture and urban design, expressions of the vigorous effort to build a rational world, imposing gestures that remind one of New York's Rockefeller Center, which, it should be noted, they pre-date by a decade. The Red modernism on display in Kharkov includes not only the splendid general post office next to the railway station (designed by A. Mordvinov in 1927), but the spectacular rail union hall by A. Dmitriev, 1929; social centres and libraries; factory canteens; public pools; and stadiums (such as Metalist, opened in 1926); the 'Gigant' student hall; the central telephone office on Ivanov Street, and of course the new factories designed to rival those built by Henry Ford in America. For mile upon mile the complexes of the farm tractor and turbine plants stretch out along today's Moskovsky Prospect; on the other side of the highway lie the working-class housing developments of the New Kharkov as well as schools, swimming baths and athletic facilities. To stand outside these plain yet aesthetically compelling structures today is to sense some of the fascination they exerted on contemporaries – and the provocation to the 'ancient and holy Russia' they embodied. Not for nothing did Sergei Eisenstein set his

The courthouse building of Kharkov in which Syenko, the so-called Gorilla of the Reds, dispensed quick justice, 1919.

movie *Bezhin Meadow* (1937) – a story of collectivization, the peasantry's resistance and how it was crushed – before Kharkov's Constructivist gleaming-white architecture and an armada of tractors fresh off the assembly line. At the entrance to the factory's administrative building, a statue commemorates Sergo Ordzhonikidze (1886–1937), the manager of Stalin's industrialization programme (with other monuments to Soviet grandees, it will be removed in April 2015); memorial plaques laud Red directors and Best Workers. One assures us that 'the heroic deeds of the workers of the tractor plant, which was built by their hands in 1930–1931, will live forever.' Another is dedicated to the eternal memory of the plant's workers who were killed in the Great Patriotic War. The inventory of models produced at the factory reads like an abridged sketch of the history of industrialization and motorization in the Soviet Union. The plaques on both sides of the main gate list the major dates: the first tractor, dubbed SKHTZ-15/30, equipped with a 30-horsepower engine, left the assembly line on 1 October 1931. In 1941 the plant was evacuated to Rubtsovsk at the foot of the Altai Mountains, where production resumed in August 1942 as the complex in Kharkov lay in ruins. Reconstruction began in November 1943, and only a year later the first post-war tractor was delivered. The transition to a market economy after 1991 left its mark as well – in the shift from production for kolkhozes to the needs of family operations and small farms.

But the heart of the New Kharkov happens to be the square where, in the fall of 2014, Lenin was toppled off his pedestal: the erstwhile Dzerzhinsky Square, now Freedom Square, one of the largest urban plazas in the world. To get an impression of the ensemble as a whole, you should survey it from above, from a bird's-eye perspective. At the western end, nine large buildings are grouped around a semicircular piazza: the six blocks of the Gosprom or State Industry Building, the National University and the Military College. The competition was announced in 1925, and the winning design by the Leningrad-based architects S. Serafimov, S. Kravets and M. Felger was realized within three years. The reinforced-concrete-and-glass buildings of the Gosprom complex were intended to house all ministries of the Ukrainian Soviet Republic, with thousands of offices, two conference halls seating audiences of 1,000 and 250, respectively, a large technical library, a radio station, restaurants, a cafeteria, and a post and telegraph office. Aligned with axes radiating outward from the square's centre, the flat-roofed blocks of varying height – the tallest sections rise to twelve storeys – are interconnected by enclosed bridges at the third, fifth and seventh floors. All stairwells, offices and corridors have natural light thanks to a total of 170,000 square metres (17 ha) of glazing. The ensemble suffered heavy damage during the war, but the reinforced-concrete structure survived intact, and renovations – the area was declared a UNESCO World Heritage Site in 2002 – are currently under way. A small museum tells the story of the Gosprom's construction and the urban planners' vision for the New Kharkov. If the director happens to be there when you visit, you may even be invited to use the still-functioning original lift and touch the historic brass handles and heavy window frames. You can imagine how traffic coursed through the 'canyons' between the streets towards the square. A little further down, another set of high-rises was rebuilt after the war in altered form, their massive earth-coloured volumes a bow to the Stalinist-empire style. So was the elongated structure of the Hotel International, now Hotel Kharkov, which garnered a gold medal at the 1937 Paris World's Fair; next door, the Stalinist-empire style is on full display in the headquarters of the project and construction organizations from the 1950s. The square's eastern end is marked by the monumental building of the oblast administration with its facade graced by fourteen Corinthian columns, which replaced a Constructivist masterpiece completed in 1932 and destroyed by the Germans. Photographs of that earlier building from the occupation period show hangings being carried out above its portal. Further south lies the rambling municipal park with the monument to Taras Shevchenko – the meeting spot of the Maidan supporters – and numerous pavilions and cafés. The unceasing brisk traffic of students and other pedestrians leaving and entering the University metro station beneath the square softens the impression of overwhelming monumentality. As the urban planning of the 1920s would have it, the area behind the Gosprom complex is taken up by an affluent residential neighbourhood built for the nomenklatura, grouped, in keeping with Stalinist social engineering, by professional categories – chemists, workers of the word, senior managers in the tobacco industry, and so on.

Travelling to Kharkov with Lev Kopelev

We know a great deal about the Kharkov of those years because, as the capital, it naturally attracted many members of the country's political, scientific and cultural elite. Exploring it, we encounter master builders such as the engineer Pavel Rottert, who would go on to direct the construction of the Moscow Metro, and the natural scientists who worked at the Ukrainian Institute of Physics and Technology under the direction of the prodigy and *enfant terrible* Lev Landau to build the world's first nuclear reactor. We meet the engineers of the Kharkov Tractor Plant, including Mikhail Koshkin, chief designer of the legendary T-34 tank (he lived on Krasin Street) and Aleksei Beketov, the *spiritus rector* of the Kharkov school of architecture, whose work still defines the look of entire streets. A memorial plaque on a villa on Pushkin Street is dedicated to the great Ukrainian film-maker Oleksandr Dovzhenko. Kharkov figures prominently in the memoirs of a descendant of the Bosses, a Baltic German family of industrialists. And, of particular interest to Germans: Lev Kopelev, the Russian Ukrainian Jewish writer, who was born in Kiev in 1912 and died in Germany in 1997, spent his formative teenage years in Kharkov. We can entrust ourselves to the recollections he published under the title *The Education of a True Believer*, use them as an itinerary, to gain access to Ukraine's first capital. 'Ukraine,' Kopelev writes in his memoirs, is the country of my childhood and youth. I spoke Ukrainian with my nanny Khima; she told folk tales, nursery rhymes. Sang. It was she and Mama who sang those songs that will always be inside me. The boys with whom I became friends, played and fought with in the villages where father worked spoke Ukrainian. And my father himself spoke Ukrainian with his friends and comrades – other agronomists. At school and in the university I studied the Ukrainian language and literature. I learned to love forever the mighty poetry of Shevchenko, the poetry and prose of Franko, Lesia Ukrainka, the books of Panas Kulish, Kotsiubynsky. And I felt at home in the more recent Ukrainian literature. Close to me and necessary for me were the wise and sad dramas of Mykola Kulish, the verses of Tychyna, Zerov, Rylsky, Sosiura, the poetic prose of Khvylovy, Yanovsky. Up to 1935 I never missed a new production of Les Kurbas in the Berezil Theatre, I took pleasure in every new film by Dovzhenko.

Being bilingual was, to him, a natural fact of life: 'Some of my students spoke in Ukrainian, others had come from Russia, but the majority made themselves understood in that mixture of Ukrainian and Russian heard in the outlying towns, which you could consider a dialect of one or the other language, whichever you wished.'

Kharkov was also where the young Petro Hryhorenko (in Russian, Pyotr Grigorenko), who would become a general of the Red Army and, in the 1960s, one of the Soviet Union's most prominent dissidents, began his career; he graduated from the city's Polytechnic Institute. The engineer Viktor Kravchenko, whose escape to the West triggered the 'Kravchenko affair' in France, a scandal that rocked the country's scene of intellectual members of the Communist Party and its sympathizers, has left us a detailed narrative of his life as a student in Kharkov, where he resided in the 'Gigant' student hall. Last but not least, the author of one of the earliest and most important eyewitness accounts of the Stalinist purges, published in 1951 under the title *The Accused*, the Austrian physicist Alexander Weissberg-Cybulski, a friend of Arthur Koestler's, had moved to Kharkov in 1931 to work at the world-famous Ukrainian Institute of Physics and Technology and got caught up in Stalin's dragnet. He was freed after Albert Einstein and Irène and Frédéric Joliot-Curie intervened with the dictator – only to be extradited to Nazi Germany in 1939 (he jumped off the train in Poland and joined the underground). Kharkov also left traces in the work of Vasily Grossman, whose novel *Everything Flows* (published in the Soviet Union in 1989) – about collectivization and the Holodomor – likely would not have been written had the author not lived in the city as a student. With so many prominent lives intersecting here, we realize Kharkov is not as distant from our own world as we may have thought at first. Their recollections guide us to 78 Chernyshevska Street, where Lev Kopelev and his family lived in apartment no. 3 after arriving from Kiev. A scholar rummaging through the university's archive recently came across the protocol from the hearings before his enrolment. We can accompany the young Kopelev to the Comintern locomotive factory, where he was in charge of the plant's internal newspaper and radio station; or to the opera, where the literary celebrities of his time, such as Mayakovsky, appeared on the stage; or to the Gosprom building, where he got to know virtually the entire leadership of the Ukrainian Communist Party in person when he interviewed them for his factory gazette. Kopelev met Mykola Skrypnyk, the head of the Ukrainian Communist Party during the 'Ukrainian Renaissance' of the 1920s, before he and his ilk were denounced as 'bourgeois nationalists' (in 1934 he put a bullet in his head). He was also introduced to Pavel Postyshev, who executed Stalin's policies in Ukraine only to fall victim to the purges himself in 1939. And Kopelev, who wrote his first poems in the Ukrainian language, met the major Ukrainian poets of the 1920s who were later killed during the Great Terror. His memories of Kharkov can teach us much about the difficulties of a multiple identity as well as its potential – Ukrainian, Russian, Jewish: not so unusual in a city that, though the majority of its population speaks Russian at home, crosses effortlessly between languages and cultures.

To the young Kopelev, the Kharkov of the 1920s and early 1930s was the door to another world and a new era. 'Kharkov is the capital. You can tell right away. There are so many people that there aren't enough sidewalks for them, they have to walk in the street. I've never seen so many automobiles before, both cars and trucks. In Kiev you see them come by one at a time, but here there are probably just as many as there are horses and buggies.' He sketches a topography still identifiable to the visitor today. 'In Kharkov they already have new houses. We ride by a big red building called "The Arcade" and a grey one – the editorial offices of the newspaper *Communist*. A statue of a worker with a hammer stands high up on the roof. An old fellow we meet tells us they have started building a real skyscraper.' Compared to Kharkov, Kiev now feels sluggish and backward. 'After Kharkov, the capital, after conversations with Mark about the prospects for the country and the world revolution, Kiev seemed a quiet backwater, and all the school and troop doings seemed petty, childish.' He starts learning Esperanto – then the idiom of universal human brotherhood – though under Stalin it will be condemned as the language of the foreign enemy and espionage. He is entranced by the flourishing polyglot literary life in clubs and associations called 'Youth', 'The Plough', 'New Generation' and 'Avant-Garde'. The city of the New Economic Policy – a tumultuous, if short-lived, renaissance of trade and capitalist entrepreneurialism – had comedy shows, cabarets, casinos named Chemin de Fer or Seventeen and Four, dandies wearing Chekhovian pince-nez, Henri-Quatre beards and velvet gaiters – characters from the world of yesterday. 'NEP – it was the private stores and shops stocked far more abundantly and decorated far more colourfully than the drab Central Workers Co-ops. Dolled-up men and women in restaurants with orchestras blaring through the night. Casinos with spinning roulette wheels and croupiers shouting: "The bets are down!" Brightly painted girls in short skirts slowly strolling the streets at night approaching single men, or laughing shrilly from the phaetons of their cabs.' The young Kopelev also observes one of the earliest show trials, against the 'Union for the Freedom of Ukraine', which was held at the opera house in 1930, and as a Trotsky sympathizer he spends ten days inside the Kholodnaya Gora prison, which figures in other memoirs as well.

The prison was a four-storey brick building. Inside, narrow iron galleries along the walls led to the cells; in the corners were platforms on which the guards stood. Steep iron stairs ran from storey to storey. Wire mesh nets hung between the levels. The glass roof above reminded one of the big department stores. The walls in the rectangular cells were painted green near the floor and white above, three cots to a cell. High above was a single window, but without blinds. Across, beyond the wall, we saw the wing housing the career criminals and heard them singing songs all day and sometimes even at night.

In the winter of 1929–30, Kopelev works at the Osnova rail depot near Kharkov, where one of his colleagues is a German communist emigrant from Berlin; they will meet again years later, when Willi Husemann, a precision mechanic by training, guards the entrance to the building of the Central Committee of the East German Socialist Unity Party.

Ukrainian Topographies of Violence

More than anything else, however, the early Soviet Kharkov remembered by contemporaries – Kopelev, Hryhorenko, Kravchenko and Weissberg-Cybulski – is a scene of monstrous violence: the trials against the 'bourgeois specialists' and 'parasites' that marked the end of the New Economic Policy; collectivization (some of our witnesses were involved in its forcible implementation in the countryside); the mass deaths of peasants during the Holodomor they observed with their own eyes; the increasingly blind fury of the witch hunt against 'Ukrainian nationalists'; and, finally, the Great Terror. With the right kind of information at your disposal, you can take a tour across Kharkov's topography of violence. All it takes is wide and careful reading, city maps, a taxi and plenty of time. A villa on Darwin Street that is now the House of Architects was the Cheka headquarters during the Civil War. The people's commissar Valery Mezhlauk, who was executed after a show trial in Moscow in 1937, resided on Olminsky Street. The palatial building with the ProCreditBank branch on the square where six streets meet was the centre of the secret police's operations. Number 6 Artyom Street was where Kopelev's cousin Mark lived before his arrest. The building on the corner of Chernyshevska and Radnarkomivska Streets now used by the Ukrainian Ministry of the Interior was the seat of the NKVD. Behind the construction site fence in the courtyard was the inner prison, whose inmates were killed before the Germans captured the city on 25 October 1941. A plaque on the facade recalls the fate of more than 3,000 Polish officers, Andrzej Wajda's father among them, who were taken to Kharkov in the spring of 1940, slaughtered and hastily buried in mass graves on the edge of town by Bilhorod Highway, a thoroughfare lined with boarding-houses, villas and comfortable hotels; a joint Ukrainian Polish memorial at the site notes their names, occupations and dates of birth and death. We know quite a bit about the prison in which the young Kopelev was held for a few days, where up to 12,000 detainees were jammed together at the time.

Weissberg-Cybulski shared a cell with hundreds of prisoners representing more than a dozen different nationalities – there were few Russians
or Ukrainians, but all the minorities living in Kharkov were represented:
Poles, Jews, Germans, Armenians, Georgians, Latvians, Lithuanians,
Finns, Assyrians, Chinese, Greeks, Turks, Macedonians, Bulgarians,
Koreans, Hungarians, Tatars, Bashkirs and Belorussians, and not one
of them knew the reason for his arrest. 'The Kholodnaya Gora prison
sat on the edge of town,' Weissberg-Cybulski writes in his memoirs.

> In the past, I had driven by it on my daily way to the laboratory
> station. At the time, you could espy half-naked prisoners cling-
> ing to the bars of their windows. They looked barely human,
> and I often shuddered to see them . . . The building dated back
> to tsarist times. At first the car transporting the prisoners was
> admitted through an iron gate. We stepped off and walked to
> a second wall, in which a small door opened as we arrived.
> The guard examined our papers and signalled us to go on.
> My escort walked me to unit no. 2, a four-storey building on
> a T-shaped plan. Lined up along the stem of the T were fifty
> solitary cells on four storeys. The crossbar consisted of twelve
> large group cells. I was assigned to a single cell, no. 37, I believe.
> Actually, it had been a single cell in the tsarist era. Now it slept
> three. The cell measured 4 by 2 metres. There were iron cots
> (two along one wall, one across the room) that could be folded
> up. At night, when they were folded down, there was a 30-cm
> clearance between them. I was alone in my cell.

In the evenings, girls and boys sat outside the neighbourhood's residential buildings; some played the harmonica or danced. 'From our cells
we could overhear their music.' You can see the massive whitewashed
building with its window blinds, which dates from the era of Catherine
the Great, from up close; it is still in use as a prison.

The most important lead, however, will take you out into the countryside, to the Ukrainian villages, the scene of collectivization, which
brought clashes resembling a civil war, the deportation of hundreds
of thousands of peasant families, and the death from starvation of
between 3.5 and 5 million people. Out where the road leading to the
Ukrainian Russian border, which is a mere 38 kilometres away, inter-
sects with the ring road, near the village of Ruska Lozova, a monument

to the victims sits on an artificial hill. It was installed after a years-long bitter controversy that divided the city into two camps: should the Holodomor be described as similar to the Holocaust, a genocide of the Ukrainian people deliberately engineered in Moscow, or as 'collateral damage' in the grand experiment of agricultural collectivization, which upended the lives of Russian farmers and Kazakh nomads as well? The subject was taboo for decades, but by now a wide range of sources have been published in critical editions and the scholarship is extensive. Looking back on the tragedy, Petro Hryhorenko remembered:

> I for my part was perfectly able to perceive what was going on. In the summer of 1930, the Party sent us Komsomol members at the Polytechnic Institute in Kharkov out into the country to 'help' with the harvest. And that short preparatory meeting before we would go out into the field should have told me everything I needed to know about the real menace to my people. I merely needed to listen to the brief Stanislav Kosior, the general secretary of the Ukrainian Party, gave us.

Hryhorenko spent time in the countryside on several occasions – his father was an agronomist – so he was aware of the developments there. He saw desolate villages in which not a soul lived anymore, railway stations black with half-naked people wandering about and utterly emaciated children besieging the wagons.

> The scene was the same at every station in Ukraine, and the throngs of the hungry grew larger the further south we came. After that trip I was no longer surprised by anything I now saw in Borisovka. The village streets lay deserted. The few people I encountered passed me without responding to my greeting – unheard-of in a Ukrainian village. My father was at home. He had difficulty standing up: due to malnourishment, he was showing the first symptoms of oedema – swelling of the body and limbs. There was absolutely nothing edible left in the house beyond a small pumpkin, and this was in the middle of December.

In *Muss Russland hungern?* (1935), a German observer, Ewald Ammende, summarized the reports of travellers returning from the famine area, which were long thought to be anti-Soviet propaganda: 'The streets of the former Ukrainian capital were strewn with the bodies of farmers who had died of starvation; they had arrived on earlier trains hoping to beg for something in the city but had been so frail that they had fallen over dead. In the industrial towns of the Donets Basin, too, the hungry farmers laid siege to the apartments of comparatively well-off technicians and engineers from morning to night.' A German economic specialist who managed to obtain permission to travel throughout the Soviet Union as late as 1933 offered this account:

> The train having pulled into the station, you step off and enter the hall. It is clean and there is no one to be seen except the railway officers and the GPU operatives. But when you go outside, the entire square in front of the station is covered with corpses. Terrifying skeletons lie in the dirt on the pavement. Some still stir, the others are motionless. When you step closer to the latter, you realize that they are already dead. All victims of hunger. They fled the hunger in the villages, but in the city they succumbed to it.

Another report notes:

> Corpses in the streets! That was beyond my ability to absorb. At first I wouldn't believe my eyes. Children pulled themselves together, gathering whatever strength they had left to scour the street for something edible. Yet they were so weak and exhausted that they fell down and remained where they lay. The poor children were the most powerful impression . . . In Kharkov I saw a boy who was nothing but skin and bones lying in the middle of the street. A second boy sat by a pile of garbage from which he pulled eggshells. Children trudged along the streets in hordes, looking for edible refuse, for leftover food or fruits. They perished along the way like wild animals . . . When the spectre of hunger hovered over the villages, the parents led their children out into the city, where they deserted them, hoping that someone there would take pity on the poor little ones.

Kopelev writes about his work in the village: 'Naturally, I berated all kulaks and their ilk, cursing them and threatening them with the contempt of the people, the hatred and the punishing sword of the proletariat, which would strike all those who, maliciously or out of sheer ignorance, hid crops.' He goes on to depict the situation in Kharkov:

> Friends who visited me as I lay ill – in 1933 – told me that the railway stations were crammed with farmers. Entire families with elderly parents and children were trying to get on trains, no matter the destination, to escape the hunger. Many crept around the streets and begged. At night, special cars collected the bodies at the stations, beneath bridges, in doorways and driveways. These trucks, covered with linen tarpaulins, drove around in the late hours of the night, when no one left their home. Other cars collected the homeless; the sick and utterly exhausted were taken to hospitals. The city's clinics were all filled to overflowing, as were the morgues. Children who had lost their parents were taken to orphanages. Adults who had some strength left were simply transported out of the city and left to their fate.

Driving through depopulated villages, he observes:

> Skinny nags drag two sledges along the street. Three men plod along beside them. They have wrapped coarse cloths or women's headscarves over their fur caps in the manner of bashlyks. Belts made out of twisted rags hold their dirty brownish caftans tightly closed. The men, their legs thickly wrapped in bags, slowly put one foot before the other. One sledge is loaded with two longish bast sacks covered with bast mats and sackcloth. The other is empty. When a house's windows are smashed or boarded up, they pass without stopping. Other houses have undamaged windows, but the doors are open, swaying in the wind. No one lives here anymore.

The great writer Vasily Grossman, who studied chemistry in Kharkov between 1932 and 1934, drew on similar experiences for his novel *Everything Flows*.

The city's territory is marked by violence; every one of the mass graves – now often surrounded by disused cemeteries, parks or industrial compounds – stands for an epoch in the history of calamitous experience. Even the monument to the 'liquidators' who received lethal doses of radiation in Chernobyl and the conspicuously desecrated grave of members of the post-1945 Ukrainian Insurgent Army in a municipal park – the area, formerly a Jewish cemetery, was converted into the Komsomol Park and recently renamed Memorial Park – are links in this unending chain of violence.

The question of how the city should commemorate these dead is the central point of contention in the so-called 'remembrance war' that broke out during Perestroika and continues to be fought today. Which dead, which victims should be remembered? Which streets and squares should be 'purged' of their Soviet patron saints, and which names should be kept in place? Which public holidays from the Soviet era should be retained, and which new memorial days and public celebrations should the independent Ukraine introduce? As Tatiana Zhurzhenko has shown, the fight over names in the public space has been about more than unearthing historical facts that were kept secret for so long: both parties – primarily, the pro- and anti-Maidan activists – have implicitly sought to harness the past in their struggle to define the terms of the political debate and assert their influence.

The Germans in Kharkov

As though the Holodomor and the Great Terror had not been enough, within a few years Kharkov came under German occupation. The austere memorial to the city's defenders and the Red Army soldiers who died in battle, also on Bilhorod Highway, brought the Soviet War Memorial in Berlin's Treptower Park to my mind. The city was in German hands from 25 October 1941 until 23 August 1943. The topography of German-occupied Kharkov, too, is documented in considerable detail. The municipal museum has a German-made city map from 1942 – it is marked 'for official use only' – and pictures of Soviet citizens thrown from balconies or hanged in the entrances to banks and hotels, but also group shots of German infantrymen in front of the Gosprom complex and a 'Café München'. The Gestapo operated from a modern brick building at 100 Sumska Street, across the road from a noble family's home that now houses a 'wedding palace'.

The Germans lost no time: in November 1941, the city's remaining Jews were herded together in a ghetto on the grounds of the tractor plant and exposed to death from cold and hunger. In the *Black Book of Russian Jewry*, which Ilya Ehrenburg and Vasily Grossman compiled as the Red Army liberated Eastern Europe, Maria Sokol wrote: 'It is difficult to describe the scene: fifteen thousand people, maybe more, walking down Old Moscow Street towards the Tractor factory. Many were dragging various things along with them. Among them were the sick and even paralytics, who were carried in the arms of others. The road from Old Moscow Street to the Tractor factory was strewn with the bodies of children, the old, and the sick.' When they left the hell of the camp, it was for the Drobytsky Yar ravine, a few kilometres further out of town, now on the highway to Chuhuiv, where a monument and a memorial site inform the visitor about the murder of the city's Jewish citizens. A rust-brown menorah rises from a field of stones and red sand. The plaque reads *Hic locus ubi mortui docent vivos*. The landscape is peaceful. The wind sweeps over the meadows, the smell of blossoming locust trees hangs in the air, as everywhere in Ukraine in spring. The inscription on one of the steles marking the path to the site commemorates the more than 16,000 Jews of Kharkov who were killed by the Germans – 'old people, children, and women, because they were Jews'; the other reads 'We bow in memory of the victims of fascism.' The memorial proper, a tall arch all in white, bears the words 'Thou Shalt Not Kill' in several languages. The names of the victims are recorded in a crypt-like room underneath. To learn more about the life of Kharkov's Jewry before the war and extermination, visit the Holocaust Museum in the city centre, at 28 Petrovsky Street. Launched as a private initiative by Larisa Volovik in the early 1990s but now supported by the municipal authorities, the museum presents the interior of a Jewish home, pictures of victims as well as individuals who saved and aided Jews, anti-Semitic posters produced by the German occupiers and their Russian and Ukrainian collaborators, ordinances and salvaged relics such as spoons, buttons, shell casings, shoes, medicine vials and flacons. There is a spectator's ticket to the first war crimes trial held on 15–18 December 1943, four months after the city's liberation, at the opera house on Rymarska Street, now home to the Kharkov Philharmonic Society, and a copy of the trial protocol, 'Procès de Kharkov'. Newsreel footage shows the defendants and witnesses as well as the correspondents Ilya Ehrenburg, Konstantin Simonov and

Aleksei Tolstoy. The defendants – several Germans and the Russian Mikhail Bulanov, who had driven the gas van – were found guilty and hanged before the eyes of 40,000 citizens on Blagovishchensky Maidan in the city centre.

The 'Fifth Kharkov': The Sound of the New City

The Ukrainian sociologist and journalist Tatiana Zhurzhenko, building on the ideas of George Shevelov, a famous linguist and native son of the city who taught at Harvard and Columbia, has spoken of the 'fifth Kharkov'. The first Kharkov, in Shevelov's portrayal of the city's history, was the seventeenth- and eighteenth-century settlement of Cossacks; the second Kharkov, the nineteenth-century capital of a governorate of the Russian Empire; the third Kharkov, the city of Ukrainian modernism in the 1920s, which perished in Stalin's terror. The fourth Kharkov, to Shevelov's mind, was the city reborn after the German occupation and the ravages of war, a city that had no recollection of its brief golden age. Has the time come for the 'fifth Kharkov', for a return into the circle of great European cities? Zhurzhenko lays out Kharkov's situation today: located near the border to Russia, it has become a city on the edge, a frontier town. The frontline is a mere 40 kilometres away. Before the war, people drove half an hour to visit relatives on the other side; the people of Belgorod used to come in the evenings to see a movie. That is all in the past. The buses that connect Kharkov to Moscow are often held up for two or three hours at the border. Passengers shuttling between Belgorod and Kharkov have to disembark – bus service terminates at the border – and cross the no-man's-land on foot. In the spring of 2015 both sides started digging trenches and building guard posts. Driving down into the city on the highway coming from the north, you are welcomed by a demonstrative forest of blue-and-yellow flags that signals to visitors from Russia: this is Kharkiv, a Ukrainian city, even though it is just a hop and a skip beyond your border. The simmering war interferes with the rhythm of life in the city: more than 130,000 refugees and displaced persons are registered in the city, and estimates of unregistered newcomers are much higher. The railway station with the monumental dome above the central hall, which used to be black with people, lies deserted now that no trains take Muscovites to Crimea and other southern destinations. The waiting room with its enormous fresco from the 1950s showing Kharkov as a city of skyscrapers has been converted into a help centre for new arrivals from the occupied areas around Lugansk and Donetsk. The refugees, who often carry nothing more than their documents and a few prized possessions, receive vital information, medical and psychological attention, and addresses for an initial place to stay. One representative each from the labour office, the Ministry of Temporarily Occupied Territories and Internally Displaced Persons, and the volunteer organization are seated at tables on which brochures are laid out, and the centre has access to databases designed to help refugees make the first steps in their new home town – most of them will not be able to return to the occupied territories. The city's hospitals absorb the wounded; the helicopters coming straight from the front-lines can be heard flying across the city. Walking through the neighbourhoods, you repeatedly see groups of people clustering outside public offices who hope to complete the bureaucratic procedures nec-essary for their integration into a new environment. Most of the work, usually invisible to the eyes of visiting foreigners, is apparently done by volunteers. Life in the city feels bafflingly normal in some ways, but the war is everywhere: in the newspapers and television newscasts, in the advertisements and appeals for donations, in the collection box on the counter at the hotel reception giving guests an opportunity to make a contribution to support those affected by the turmoil. Kharkov takes care of the fighters as well as it can, living in tense expectation that new developments might rapidly create challenges which would throw even stronger cities off balance.

Europeans and Americans have been able to travel freely to Ukraine for several years; they do not even need a visa. Nothing stops them from exploring this great and, in many ways, strange country, yet few have availed themselves of the new freedom. Everything is convenient, there is no bureaucratic red tape, and affordable and friendly accom-modations are easily found anywhere. Younger visitors can take the buses operated by Eurolines, which take them to Ukraine's remotest corners. A country awaits discovery that is unlike anything most Europeans have seen, with a history, that can be hard to grasp even for experts, that needs to be told afresh. Ukraine is a Europe in miniature, boasting extraordinary linguistic and cultural diversity and beautiful cities and landscapes. Outside Ukraine, however, there is a tendency to discuss such cultural wealth as the source of an alleged risk of dis-integration rather than an asset. Ukrainians, the young generation in particular, have criss-crossed Europe looking for work or education, and so getting around on English or German is easy enough. There is something for everyone: cities and towns are eager to strike up partnerships with their peers in the West – Kharkov is already twinned with Bologna, Cincinnati, Nuremberg and Rishon LeZion, among others – and the tourism and agriculture sectors need investors, who have good reason to distrust the talk of a 'failing state' and study the economic potential for themselves. Architecture aficionados who have seen it all – from New York's Rockefeller Center to Zaha Hadid's National Museum of the Arts of the XXI Century in Rome – but always lacked the time or energy to tour the monuments of Red modernism should finally come to see the Gosprom complex. Technical relief agencies and other humanitarian organizations will find an infinite supply of worthwhile missions in a country that has had to deal with Russian 'aid convoys'. A city like Kharkov is the right place for young adults who are tired of the Berlin club scene and want to do something different with their lives for a change. At its well over a dozen universities and other institutions of higher education, they will meet people of their own age with whom they share at least one language and who know something about the gravity of the situation the rest of Europe has been slow to catch on to. Ryanair and EasyJet might render a historic service to the continent and expand its horizon by adding Kharkov and cities like it to their list of destinations at long last. To get yourself in a Kharkov kind of mood, read Serhii Zhadan's novel *Voroshilovgrad* (unfortunately, his *Anarchy in the UKR* still awaits translation into English). His writing vibrates with the sound of the new Kharkov, a city that knows only too well what is at stake, aware that everything might be lost from one moment to the next.

(2014)

EIGHT

DNEPROPETROVSK:
ROCKET CITY ON THE DNIEPER
AND CITY OF POTEMKIN

To the traveller arriving from Central Europe, Dnepropetrovsk – in Ukrainian, Dnipropetrovsk – initially feels vaguely American. The impression is prompted first and foremost by the gleaming office towers, bank buildings and housing blocks projecting above the city's downtown. The skyline looms over the mile-wide river: 'Manhattan on the Dnieper'. Judging by the glazed facades and the style of the architecture, these high-rises were all built in the past twenty years. They seem unconnected to the urban fabric around them, almost demonstratively so, as though to signal: we have no business with the city of the past, we wish to leave the Soviet Dnepropetrovsk behind, we mean to transcend it. They are symbols of the energy with which the city has launched itself into a new era; the traditional name has widely been supplanted by 'Dniprocity' or, even shorter, 'Dnipro', the version used by the locals, who are forever pressed for time. Dnepropetrovsk, that was the Soviet Union's metallurgy and mechanical engineering hub, a city closed to foreigners for decades due to the concentration of missile manufacturing and arms industries. Dnipro is high-tech, finance and banks; the city has emerged as Ukraine's financial centre.

City Maps for Tourists and Terrorists

But it is the summer of 2014, and the country is at war, although the visitor might not notice at first. The Donbass Express with its blue-and-yellow carriages, which reached Donetsk in less than two hours in peacetime, no longer travels on schedule and sometimes is cancelled altogether. At the international airport, flights for Sharm el-Sheikh and Abu Dhabi still take off, but entire squadrons of helicopters sit on the apron, having just come back from deployments or being readied for the next engagement. Separatists in the area around Lugansk recently shot down a Ukrainian aeroplane carrying elite troops stationed in Dnepropetrovsk. Traffic is congested on the city's thoroughfares; crowds have descended on European Square and the adjoining new shopping arcade, and joggers are out and about in the spacious parks, of which the city boasts several. Dnepropetrovsk is doing business as usual. But then the visitor is struck by the fact that it has attired itself in yellow and blue. The colours are flown everywhere, in endless variations. And the steady stream of news reports about new incidents speaks to a level of alertness, a tension barely held in check: something is going on that might bring the city's life to a sudden halt and disrupt the precarious calm. 'Dnepropetrovsk is not Donetsk,' Hennadii Korban, the deputy governor of Dnepropetrovsk Oblast, will say in an interview in October 2014. The city is prepared to fend off attacks and attempts at subversion. Thousands of soldiers and reservists equipped and paid by the municipal authorities and private individuals are ready and vigilant. A personal observation during my visit in the spring of 2014 teaches me that the apprehensions that prompted these preparations are far from unwarranted. I entered a basement bookstore on Lenin Street to stock up on city maps and plans. The saleswoman was bewildered by my request: that same day alone, several other patrons had asked for maps of Dnepropetrovsk – the more exact the better; plane-table sheets and ordnance maps would be best. What was happening? She had formed a theory: tourists need maps to orient themselves in the urban space, to navigate its historical strata and find objects of interest. But there was another class of outsiders who likewise needed maps, and exact maps, to guide them through unfamiliar terrain, as they identified strategically important points, urban infrastructures, places of symbolic significance or perhaps even the home addresses of prominent residents. There has been ample evidence of such terrorist rather than touristic interest in Dnepropetrovsk's topography: the storming of the oblast administration building by anti-Maidan protesters in February; the raising of Russian flags on public buildings; attempts to intimidate and terrorize Maidan activists. Yet the city refuses to let itself be thrown off balance: thanks to the initiative taken by its leading oligarch, Ihor Kolomoisky, now the governor of Dnepropetrovsk Oblast, it has emerged as the centre of Ukrainian self-defence.

Ekaterinoslav: 'Petersburg of the South', 'Athens of the North'

Dnepropetrovsk is only one of many names the city has borne in its not very long history. The first settlement on the Dnieper, just upriver from an extended stretch of rapids, was a fortress of the Zaporozhian Cossacks built in 1635 that was known as Kodak. After Catherine the Great disbanded the Cossack Hetmanate in 1775, Novomoskovsk was founded on the left bank of the Dnieper in 1776 to signal the commencement of the Russian colonization programme; a monastery with a historically important wooden church can still be seen today. The modern city's real founding date is 1783, when Ekaterinoslav – the name means 'Glory of Catherine' – was established where the centre of Dnepropetrovsk now stands. Travelling to the 'New Russia', the empress herself had passed through the area where her protégé Prince Potemkin then laid out the street grid and started construction for the city. For a brief interval, it was called Novorossiysk: that was during the reign of Catherine's son Paul I, who hated his mother. Its emergence as a major administrative and industrial centre in the last third of the nineteenth century coincided with the rise of the revolutionary movement. The city wanted to shake off the association with the empress, and another attempt was initiated in 1917, when, for a short period, it adopted the moniker Sicheslav in honour of the Cossack tradition. A fully official and more lasting rechristening came in 1926, when, in consultation with Moscow, the city named itself after a prominent son, the professional revolutionary Grigory Petrovsky, a Party stalwart throughout his long life – he was unwavering in his loyalty even during the collectivization campaign and Stalin's terror and was buried near the Kremlin wall in 1958. The largest metallurgical facility, formerly known as the Bryansk Plant, also took his name. His monument stands on the square in front of the station. Whether the city will continue to bear his name, a symbol of Soviet Ukraine and the Stalin era, remains to be seen. Of late the controversy has flared up again.

When the first stone was laid in Catherine II's presence on 9 May 1787, it was far from obvious that the new city would prosper. She had arrived from Kiev with a flotilla of eighty ships carrying a crew of 3,000 and hundreds of musicians, singers and actors to inaugurate nothing less than the centre of the 'New Russia', a 'Petersburg of the South' or 'Athens of the North', the cornerstone of her 'Greek project' to defeat the Ottoman Empire. Prince Potemkin was to realize

Catherine's vision of the transformation of the Pontic steppe's 'Wild Field' into a 'garden full of flowers'. The 'Potemkin village' that later became a proverbial figure for the manufacture of illusions not backed up by any real accomplishments was merely an instance of a practice that, though expensive, was widespread in absolutist Europe: an elaborate mock-up of the city to be built in the future. And there can be no doubt: Potemkin's project – from his own palace to the city's chessboard street grid and the uniform eaves heights – did not remain a vision on paper or a set of facades, it became reality. The foundation stone for Transfiguration Cathedral was laid at the highest point of a hill overlooking the river where it sharply bends towards the south. The original plans called for a church larger than St Peter's in Rome; the building as it stands, designed by Andreyan Zakharov, the eminent architect best known for the Admiralty in St Petersburg, and initially intended as a temporary solution, was converted into a museum of atheism in the Soviet era. Descending from Cathedral Square towards the Dnieper, the visitor reaches the Taras Shevchenko Park of Culture and Recreation (formerly the Park of Communist Youth) and the old governor's palace Potemkin had built for himself in 1790. After the revolution, it was used first as a convalescent home and later as a cultural centre for students at Dnepropetrovsk State University. The elongated Neoclassical edifice, which suffered heavy damage in the war, has a fine view of Monastyrsky Island (called Island of Youth under communism), the site of a monastery that existed centuries before the city's foundation, today a park with beaches to which thousands flock in the summer. The Dnieper, which was impassable for ships on this stretch until the rapids were flooded after construction of the DneproGES dam in 1932, is now as wide as an estuary, with the city sprawled out on both banks – on summer nights, a visitor walking on the promenades might almost think himself on a Mediterranean shore.

To those who attended the ceremony in 1787, the Habsburg emperor Joseph II among them, much about it may well have felt like a 'Potemkin village', and for a long time it did not seem that Ekaterinoslav – made capital of a governorate in 1803 – would ever amount to much. But then the discovery of coal in the nearby Donets Basin and sizable iron-ore deposits in Krivoi Rog made the city the 'Russian Empire's boomtown', as Rainer Lindner put it. Besides the Dnieper – river navigation was by far the most important form of transportation well into the nineteenth century, and 1,400 ships touched at Ekaterinoslav every year – the city was soon also connected to the ever denser network of railways, the most prominent projects being the Catherine Railway and the bridge across the river, which was opened to traffic with great pomp in 1884. The city's industrialization gathered speed in the 1860s. The first metallurgical plant, the Bryansk Joint Stock Company's Alexander Factory, now known as the Petrovsky Metallurgical Plant, was taken into operation on 10 May 1887; with up to 30,000 workers, it would be the city's largest employer for decades. In the autumn of 1889 Chaudoir, a French Belgian conglomerate, opened a pipe mill, soon followed by the Gantke Plant (named after Karl Liebknecht after the revolution), Chaudoir-B (later Comintern) and the railway repair workshop (later the Kirov Plant). The Belgian company Esau & Co. started manufacturing agricultural equipment in 1895 (the factory later became the Voroshilov Harvester-Thresher Plant). Ekaterinoslav was a major destination for foreign investment in Russia, and at one point international corporations controlled 90 per cent of the metallurgical industry and 63 per cent of the coal output. One culmination of this development – what was envisioned as a 'Petersburg of the South' now more closely resembled a Manchester of the Russian Empire – was the South Russian Regional Agricultural, Industrial and Manufacturing Exhibition in 1910. A few years later, the evacuation of manufacturing facilities from the empire's western provinces in the early months of the First World War further added to Ekaterinoslav's industrial base. Eighty per cent of the labour migrants who swelled the city's population

The Dnipro bridge, 18 March 1884.

came from rural Russia; many of the tradesmen, small merchants and professionals among the newcomers were Jews who had left the Pale of Settlement. Fast-paced industrial development, the original accumulation of capital, and the mass immigration of peasants went hand in hand with the astonishingly swift formation of an urban society. The best place to study its history is the central avenue laid out in the eighteenth century by urban planners in St Petersburg: for 12 kilometres (7.5 miles), from Cathedral Square to the railway station, the 100-metre- (330-ft-) wide thoroughfare originally called Ekaterininsky Prospect – it still bears the name it was given by the Soviets, Prospect Karla Marksa (between 1941 and 1943 the German occupiers called it Breite Straße) – is a panorama of the ravages and corrosions of the twentieth century.

A Timeline in Stone

The no. 1 tramway line connects the two ends of downtown Dnepropetrovsk: Cathedral and Station Squares. The trip from one to the other makes for a vivid experience of the city's defining features: set on three hills, it has strikingly steep streets. The elevations command views of the surrounding vast urban landscape, which stretches out over 24 kilometres (15 miles) north to south and 40 kilometres (25 miles) west to east. The avenue's 12 kilometres (7.5 miles) are Dnepropetrovsk's median axis, as envisioned by Catherine's master builders. After the name change in 1926, a general plan for the growing city's development drawn up in 1933 proposed shifting the centre as well. The new city would have embraced the river that its two halves straddled as its true axis. The result might have been a revival of the idea of a 'Petersburg of the South': the Dnieper, like the Neva, as a central artery coursing through the urban space. The planners of the 1930s imagined imposing structures, including a Red Army tower block. The idea of moving the city's life closer to the wide river continues to circulate in the urban planning debate. As it is, the kilometres-long broad promenade with walkways, piers and a fine view of the Dnieper is among Europe's most beautiful riversides, despite the concrete colossus of the Hotel Parus. Construction work on the building, set on a salient jutting out into the river and shaped to recall a sail, began in the 1980s but was never completed, presumably because the structure is unsuitable for any use by today's standards. At night, the empty shell is illuminated in blue and yellow, the Ukrainian national colours, while an enormous moon rises above the far bank – a closer look reveals it to be an artist's installation on the grounds of a factory owned by the oligarch and art collector Victor Pinchuk.

The Dnieper never became the city's central axis – that was and still is the role of Ekaterininsky Prospect alias Prospect Karla Marksa. A trip in Dnepropetrovsk, whether by foot, by car or by public transit, almost invariably leads to the avenue that resembles a long park, with paths, flowerbeds and a market where artists sell their pictures. The no. 1 tram not only traverses the city, but travels through the centuries. The thoroughfare was the focus or anchor of every significant development in the city's history; every major event took place on it or in its vicinity. Each successive generation contributed to the ensemble, and each generation broke a piece out of this urban space or lost a part of it. Some events, some losses are remembered, but a veil of silence is cast over many more, all traces of them effaced. And this paradigmatic urban scene has remained the prime stage for today's protagonists. In the spring of 2014 brutal clashes between Maidan supporters and their adversaries broke out on the almost intimidatingly vast squares in front of the oblast administration and city hall. The pedestal that supported a statue of Lenin now stands empty, fenced in by hoarding covered with a picture of a girl in Ukrainian national attire. An artist's installation on the same square in the shape of an oversized mousetrap is presumably meant to exhort the citizenry to be wary of Pied Pipers and demagogues.

For a succinct introduction to Dnepropetrovsk's history, the visitor might go to the Historical Museum, which grew out of the collection of Alexander Pol (1832–1890), the pioneering mining and railway construction entrepreneur. Known as the 'Columbus of New Russia', he was one of the most important industrialists of the nineteenth century. From his death until well after the revolution, the growing collection was overseen by Dmytro Yavornytsky, a distinguished scholar who embodied the distinctive qualities of urbane society, its conviviality, its active involvement in civic and learned societies, its philanthropic initiatives and municipal self-government. At the time of my visit, the museum is preparing an exhibition on 'The Great War and the Governorate Capital Ekaterinoslav'. The section dedicated to collectivization is surprisingly small. On view are photographs of farmsteads being searched and grain seizures as well as transcripts of trials against individuals accused of cannibalism. A farm tractor manufactured in

1931, the black paint contrasting with the bright-red wheel rims, stands at the centre of the room, almost like a work of art. The eyewitness testimony of one Viktor Kravchenko, a student and Komsomol activist who was sent into the village of Petrovo, paints a vivid picture of the war waged on the peasantry in the countryside: 'The most horrifying sight were the little children, their skeletal limbs sticking out from their bloated bodies. Starvation had erased any trace of youth in their faces and left them grotesquely disfigured. Only their eyes were still those of children. Scattered everywhere lay the prone bodies of men and women, their faces and bellies turgid, their eyes utterly devoid of expression.' The horrors of the famine of 1932–3 were plain to see in the city as well:

> Despite the rigorous police measures designed to prevent the victims from fleeing their homes, Dnepropetrovsk was overrun by starving peasants. Many of them, apathetic and too frail even to beg, had collapsed around the railway stations. Their children were skeletons with distended bellies. It used to be that friends and relatives in the countryside mailed food parcels into the city. Now it was the countryside that was hungry. But our own rations were so small and the supply situation was so uncertain that few dared to give away what they had.

Another room in the municipal museum is devoted to the architect Alexander Krasnoselsky, whose work more than anyone else's defines the look of modern Dnepropetrovsk. On display are a bourgeois interior, diary entries from travels to Western Europe, sheet music and instruments, pictures from a 'world of yesterday'. Krasnoselsky designed the Univermag department store on Prospect Karla Marksa (1936–8).

Near the upper end of the avenue lies the city's wealthiest residential neighbourhood. Interspersed among the pre-revolutionary villas that line its streets – they were later taken over by the nomenklatura: Leonid Brezhnev, for example, lived at 11 Voroshilov Street – are several educational institutions established in the decades after 1890, such as the National Mining University. Enlarged in the period of Soviet industrialization, they usually occupy monumental buildings in the Neoclassical style of the time.

Photographs of old Ekaterinoslav show a multi-ethnic city. The names on shop signs and the wares in window displays bear witness to its Jewish, Russian, Ukrainian, Black Sea German and expatriate communities; the sizable presence of Belgian and French companies in particular is noteworthy. A ruse of history has allowed the tsarist eagle to survive on the meticulously restored facade of the National Bank of Ukraine building on the corner of Prospect Karla Marksa and Lenin Street. The names of the hotels on both sides of the avenue are a mix of international classics – Astoria, Bristol, Europa, the Grand – and Soviet-era standbys: Spartak, October, and so on.

The avenue is also where locals go for diversion and amusement, hence the cafés and numerous cinemas, including the Coliseum, later renamed October. Some buildings bear memorial plaques; one informs the passerby that the Ukrainian anarchist leader Nestor Makhno lodged at the Hotel Astoria in 1919. The Grand Hotel on the corner of Prospect Karla Marksa and Pervozvanivska is readily recognizable despite the damages it sustained in the Second World War: a Ukrainian version of Art Nouveau, distinctive enough and yet not altogether too different in its formal idiom from buildings the visitor has perhaps seen in Munich or Graz. The English Club became a rallying point for the revolutionaries and, much later, the local branch of the Volunteer Society for Cooperation with the Army, Aviation and Navy (DOSAAF). 'Power in Ekaterinoslav', Viktor Kravchenko remembered,

> changed hands between parties every month and occasionally several times within a single week. We gave up on trying to ascertain who was in control at a given moment – the Reds, the Whites, the Greens, Petliura's men, the troops of Hetman Skoropadsky, Batko Makhno or Grigoryev. For a few months, we lived under German occupation, then the Germans disappeared and the surges of the warring armies, most dressed in rags and showing little regard for their own or anyone else's lives, rolled over the emaciated body of our city.

The streets were strewn with corpses; soldiers sat down beside them to wolf down their rations. 'Almost every day brought horrible pogroms in the Jewish quarter, assaults by the brigands on banks, and train robberies. Each new government denounced the one before it as bandits and would soon be reviled as bandits in turn. For a week, or perhaps longer, everyone got worked up over Makhno's anarchist regime that had entrenched itself in Ekaterinoslav, then the Reds returned to power, and it was as though Makhno had never been seen.'

A plaque on the facade of the central post office, another edifice from the 1910s, lists some of the prominent protagonists of civil-war Dnepropetrovsk who used its services: the above-mentioned professional revolutionary Petrovsky; the writer Aleksei Tolstoy, who then still sided with the Whites and collected material for his novel of exile *The Road to Calvary*; but also the anarchist leader Makhno, Stalin's comrade Kliment Voroshilov and the commander of the legendary First Cavalry Army, Semyon Budyonny. The post office as a scene of history: it was here that the counter-revolutionaries fought their last battle against the Bolsheviks on 29 December 1917; but it was also here that, in 1918 and again in 1941–3, the German occupiers sorted the field post bound for the Reich.

Prospect Karla Marksa ends in a large square in front of the central station, where the no. 1 tramway loops around to head back into the city. The square is busy even at night, and the front of the building, which reprises the proportions of the original structure from 1894 – it was destroyed by the Germans – is illuminated. Another tram that departs in the opposite direction transports the visitor into the world of metallurgy and chemistry. Behind the railway yard lie the sprawling industrial installations that made Ekaterinoslav and then Dnepropetrovsk a centre of iron and steel production. For kilometre after kilometre the tram rumbles past rusty and soot-black factory halls. Fresh green is bursting from cracks everywhere, as though nature had begun to reclaim these forges of Vulcan. Even farther out, the city unravels into residential neighbourhoods that are no longer urban and not quite yet villages.

All in all, a trip down Ekaterininsky Prospect / Prospect Karla Marksa is a journey along a timeline in stone. One detail can be spotted within the tramway cars themselves: they were obviously decommissioned in Germany and sold off to Ukraine, and the original signs instructing passengers to press a button to let the conductor know they wish to alight at the next stop are still in place. The facades outside the windows likewise bear the imprint of the various periods. We dart past late eighteenth-century Neoclassical buildings from which the spirit of the Enlightenment speaks, past the products of a boom-era eclecticism that knew not what to do with its wealth. We are delighted to encounter surviving specimens of Art Nouveau, a style that was regarded with contempt in the Soviet Union, and stunned by the massive solidity of the edifices a city exhausted by war managed to raise in the years of reconstruction after 1945 – German prisoners of war toiled on some of the construction sites. The most recent additions to this pair of 12-kilometre-long sceneries are the brainchildren of postmodernist architects; few of them are as understated and well-crafted as the replica of London's Big Ben on a business and entertainment centre.

Jewish Ekaterinoslav

For a fuller picture, the visitor must get off the tram and stroll down the side streets branching off the major thoroughfares to explore the neighbourhoods. He may find himself drawn to the Menorah Centre, perhaps the most imposing high-rise complex in downtown Dnipro. Designed by Alexander Sorin, the ensemble of seven towers of varying height – the tallest is twenty storeys high – has some of the monumentality and austerity of a temple. It is located on Sholem Aleichem Street in what used to be Ekaterinoslav's Jewish neighbourhood in the city's central district, right across the street from the former Dormition Cathedral, which was dismantled in the 1930s and converted into a hospital (the church has not yet been rebuilt). According to the management, the Menorah Centre is the largest Jewish community centre in the world, with shops, hotels, conference halls, cafés and a museum detailing the history of Jews in Ukraine, and it is surely one major reason why Dnepropetrovsk has a reputation for being 'Ukraine's Jewish city', as the *Kyiv Post* put it. Integrated into the complex is the old Golden Rose Synagogue, one of over thirty synagogues and prayer houses that existed in the city before the revolution. Entering the centre, this visitor was baffled by the bustle and occasionally taken aback by the sumptuous interiors and precious materials. The Jewish Memory and Holocaust in Ukraine Museum closes a glaring gap in the exhibition in the municipal historical museum. In the late Russian Empire, around one-third of Ekaterinoslav's population was Jewish; the city had a strong Jewish labour movement and successful Jewish entrepreneurs. But it was also the scene of pogroms in 1883 and again in 1906. Prominent figures in Jewish history associated with Ekaterinoslav include Rabbi Menachem Mendel Schneerson, who grew up here and died as a highly revered tzadik in New York; Shmaryahu Levin, who studied at Berlin's Friedrich Wilhelm University before serving as the city's crown rabbi and later was a member of the first Russian duma; and Ber Borochov, a leader of the Labour Zionist movement.

The Menorah Centre's volume and shape add a distinctive accent to the Dnipro city skyline, especially at night, when spotlights illuminate the complex. It might almost be a memento: behold, this is the city that, after all the horrors of German occupation, is once again home to a Jewish community of 50,000, the country's second largest after Kiev. If the visitor takes the no. 1 tramway to the final stop and then walks a little farther, past the new building of Oles Honchar University, before turning right into a copse, he encounters a modest monument, a small concrete obelisk bearing the inscription 'To the Peaceful Citizens and Victims of Fascism. October 1941'. A second monument was erected in the old Jewish cemetery. Outside the city, by the country road that runs past the wooden church of Novomoskovsk, a commemorative stone was set in 2014 to mark the place where 4,000 Jews from Dnepropetrovsk were murdered.

The last days of Jewish Dnepropetrovsk are recorded in witness statements Ilya Ehrenburg and Vasily Grossman compiled after liberation. One of them, the testimony of a Mr and Mrs Indikt, leads us to an object so inconspicuous amid the posters advertising Givenchy and Hugo Boss that even an attentive passerby is likely to overlook it: mounted well above eye level on Alexander Krasnoselsky's Univermag department store, the most prominent building from the 1930s, a plaque notes that it was here that the city's Jews began their final trek towards the ravine in the old botanical garden, today's Gagarin Park. The Germans had entered Dnepropetrovsk on 24 August 1941. Many Jews, unaware of what was in store for them, had remained in their homes; many believed the lie that they would merely be 'resettled'. On 13 October, 11,000 Jews, obeying the public notice issued by the German city commandant, reported to the Univermag, whence they were marched through the city, down Karl Marx Avenue, Karl Liebknecht Street and Zaporozhye Highway. The killing operation, under the commando of the ss general Friedrich Jeckeln, who had also organized massacres in Kamianets-Podilsky, Kiev, Riga and elsewhere, lasted for two days. Of the 30,000 Jews who had lived in the city in 1941, no more than 702 were alive by February 1942. One of the few who escaped in the nick of time was Ilya Kabakov, now a world-renowned artist, who was evacuated to Samarkand in Central Asia.

Dnepropetrovsk under German Occupation

A history museum and diorama devoted to the war era, with a focus on the Battle of the Dnieper, opened its doors in 1975. The concrete edifice, a little out of the way and largely deserted, is surrounded by specimens of famous tank types from the Great Patriotic War. Children now clamber about on them. The display in room seven of the municipal museum, which is dedicated to the period of German occupation, includes uniforms, revolvers, letters and photographs of Prospect Karla Marksa and the ruins of buildings familiar to everyone in the city, such as the railway station, the bread factory and the mining college. A fire had gutted the 'Bavarian House'. On a map of Berlin, someone has marked the route into the 'Lair of the Beast': the Reichstag. The overcoats worn by Marshals Konev and Malinovsky are kept in a glass case like relics. Also on view is the parade uniform of Vladimir Sudets, later marshal of the aviation, and the mount of a Katyusha rocket launcher, a formidable piece of weapons technology.

The most comprehensive guide to the topography of German-occupied Dnepropetrovsk is the work of the urban historian Mikhail Shatrov, whose history of the city, written in the waning years of the Soviet Union, can be found at the book bazaar outside the theatre. As usual, the conquerors' first order was to remake the city's toponymy: Prospect Karla Marksa, for example, became Breite Straße. Then they commandeered the best hotels, such as the Astoria. Hitherto unseen cars cruised the city's streets: Platt, the chief of the local Sicherheitsdienst division, and the city commandant Major von Heldelmann travelled in black Opel limousines. The gallows for public hangings of hostages and partisans went up on Breite Straße. The Comintern cinema was now the Kino Viktoria, later the Thalia, and 'for Aryans only'; the Red Front became the Atrium, and the former Gorky, now Deutsche Lichtspiele, screened films starring Leni Riefenstahl, Marika Rökk and Harry Piel. The Chauffeurs' Club was converted into an officers' mess, while the Museum of the Revolution on the corner of Kharkovskaya Street and Karl Marx Avenue became an enlisted men's club. Franz Semerau cut hair at 32 Breite Straße; Hugo Garpoletto & Co. opened a branch store at 56 Breite Straße; Klapproth und Gross from Königsberg set up shop as well. The Petrovsky Plant was absorbed by the Hermann-Göring-Werke. Notifications and advertisements in German were everywhere – at the post office, outside movie theatres and in the shop windows.

Churches which the Soviet authorities had closed reopened. A Ukrainian theatre was established at the Railway Workers' Club. Ethnic Germans were requested to register at 30 Poltavskaya. Newspapers in Russian and Ukrainian were produced by emigrants who had returned from Berlin under the supervision of a Mr Teichmüller. The Gestapo operated from the two-storey building at 3 Lenin Street, right next to the theatre. Another site indelibly marked by the German presence is the playground of the school no. 9 on Mostova Street, where a mass grave from the occupation period containing five hundred bodies was discovered during construction work in the 1960s.

By the time the Germans were forced to abandon Dnepropetrovsk on 25 October 1943, thousands of flats and factory buildings had been destroyed; fires had ravaged the city, whose population had shrunk from over half a million in 1939 to fewer than 200,000 people. Thousands of prisoners of war and 75,000 citizens had been deported to the Reich for forced labour. In a true miracle, much of the industrial capacity that had been evacuated to the Ural Mountains was reinstalled and taken back into operation by early 1945.

Closed City: Golden Age / Stagnation

The three decades between 1959 and 1987, when Dnepropetrovsk was officially a 'closed city', were arguably its golden age. As early as the late 1940s, an automotive plant had been established on the grounds of a former aeroplane factory; a secret installation code-named 'Plant 586' and the 'Southern Design Bureau' later opened nearby. The complex grew into what remains the city's largest industrial operation: Yuzhmash, a leader in Soviet missile and aerospace design and construction. Much of the technology that made the Soviet Union a superpower and at times gave it an edge over its rival was developed at Yuzhmash.

In an open-air museum in the city centre that was inaugurated in 2013, the svelte white bodies of Cyclon-3, 8K11 and 8K99 rockets stand lined up like arrows pointing skyward. Cutting-edge technology went hand in hand with secrecy. Specialists from Moscow and Leningrad moved to the city, drawn by privileges, perks and bonuses. Yet although the city was closed, it was not out of this world: Beatlemania swept its youth clubs as elsewhere in the Union, rock concerts were held at Yuzhmash's own culture palace, there were Hare Krishnas and Christian celebrations; the Komsomol raised a generation of young people who yearned to break free of the oppressive conformism of the late Soviet Union. In that sense, communist Dnepropetrovsk, as the historian Sergei Zhuk, a native son of the city, has shown, exemplified both rapid progress and stagnation, rocket city and rock 'n' roll.

Rocket city was also the birthplace of the 'Dnepropetrovsk clan', an unusually influential cadre factory. One of its alumni, Leonid Brezhnev, rose to the apex of the Soviet hierarchy; Leonid Kuchma, Yuzhmash's general director, went on to become president after Ukrainian independence. Prime Minister Yulia Tymoshenko laid the foundations for her commercial career with a music and video rental business. The billionaires Hennadii Boholiubov and Viktor Pinchuk graduated from the Academy of Civil Engineering and Architecture and the Metallurgical Institute, respectively; the latter school also produced Ihor Kolomoisky, one of the country's wealthiest men, an active member of the Jewish community and governor of Dnepropetrovsk Oblast in difficult times.

To the visitor today, the enormous factory halls and large administrative buildings from the 1970s stand as evidence that the 'closed city' was much more than merely a large Soviet provincial town. Critical masses formed here that patiently awaited the moment when they would be set free or unleashed, when the time for action would come. In the newly independent Ukraine, Dnepropetrovsk, like other cities across the former Soviet empire, needed to reinvent itself. The rise of Ekaterinoslav was the work of enterprising individuals such as Alexander Pol. Today's Dniprocity has no shortage of entrepreneurs in his mould.

(2014)

NINE

DONETSK:
TWENTIETH-CENTURY URBICIDES

EVEN AFTER the occupation of the oblast administrative building in downtown Donetsk on 6 April 2014, it was far from obvious that it would come to this: that the thriving capital of the Donbass would within a year's time become a ghost town – indeed, a dying city. One observer who saw clearly what was happening was a blogger who, a few weeks after the violent storming of the building by pro-Russian separatists, wrote a 'letter to everyone who doesn't live in Donetsk':

> Dear reader, you can't imagine how eerie and horrifying it is to watch as a city dies. Donetsk will never again be the city I remember; you'll never again see the city that was. To all appearances, it is still a lively city now that spring has arrived – with verdant green and children playing in the streets, with open grocery stores, blossoming flowers, and wide streets. Outside the window I can hear the ball hitting the tennis court. Donetsk has the look of a person who has taken a lethal hit but doesn't know yet that he will soon be dead. The city is almost as it was. Almost – because the cancerous growths are already there to see: checkpoints, concrete barriers with sandbags, masked armed men, and machine guns. On the weekends, there are almost no cars in the streets, and the silence is shocking and depressing. The city is dying. Not a single shop is open after ten in the evening, no pharmacy, there's no one in the street, and the only cars are taxis. All coffee shops, all public facilities are closed. I once accompanied a friend home after ten, a distance of not even half a mile, but we took our passports, and we both had a queasy feeling

because of the curfew. You have to be a fatalist or drunk to do what I did and walk through town – and I live in the centre – carrying a guitar in its case . . . I'm scared and frightened in my own city . . . No one believes that the people who live here are needed by anybody. We've been cast off, and Donetsk has become a cage, a prison, from which one can still escape if one abandons everything – apartment, property, work, hopes and plans for the future – so as to survive, which is the most important thing. Everyone understands that this will go on for a long time. That things will get very, very bad. That many will die. Just as the city will die.

When I returned from a trip to Donetsk around Easter 2014, I did not want to believe that the small gang that had stormed and occupied the administrative building at the end of Shevchenko Boulevard would succeed in taking control of the city. What I saw gave the lie to the reports in the Russian media about the chaos in the Donbass: the city was running normally – trains were on time, and traffic on Artyom Street, its main thoroughfare, named after a local-born Bolshevik who was killed in the civil war, was congested (the majority of the cars were foreign-made). There was no sign of war or civil war, let alone a 'genocide' of the Russian-speaking population in a city where Russian was in any case the dominant language. Yet even the images that played on foreign television stations failed to capture what I saw with my own eyes: the steady rhythm of business as usual, the tranquil, even relaxed atmosphere of a city going about its daily routines, unfazed by the posse of oddballs who had taken the oblast building. Couples in elegant attire sauntered along Pushkin Boulevard with its fountains and flowerbeds; mothers took their children for a stroll beneath the illuminated advertisements for Italian restaurants and international brands from Apple and Gucci to Siemens. *Adventurers* had just opened in cinemas; the opera presented *Aida* and a new production of the *Flying Dutchman*. The bookshop looking out on the square where the city's fate would be decided showcased interesting new publications, including a compilation of documents from the local archive detailing the terror of the Stalin years; the bookseller suggested that I order online and promised timely delivery to Berlin. In short, the city I saw was a place where children did their homework, teenagers went to sports practice and students were flirting with the idea of doing a

Donetsk Regional Administration.

semester abroad in Poland, while others were already making plans for the summer holidays.

After the turmoil of the past several months, after the Euromaidan Revolution in Kiev and the lightning-speed annexation of Crimea, all was not well in Donetsk, where the ousted president Yanukovych and his Party of Regions had their main base of support. Rallies had been held for and against Maidan; the altercations in Donetsk had claimed the first life, the student and Svoboda activist Dmytro Cherniavsky. But there was something of a theatre troupe about the people who had congregated around the Lenin monument, put up their tent and then stormed the building; without a mass movement, an entire city rallying behind them, the incident was no more than a paltry imitation of Maidan. Slogans like 'Europe get out!' and 'Immediate withdrawal of the u.s. security mercenaries!' were emblazoned on tyre barricades by the main entrance. Everyone wore masks. They let some people pass and turned others back as they pleased. No one worked anymore in the huge twelve-storey complex; the administration with its computers had moved into various hotels. Icons and flags of the 'Donetsk People's Republic' hung on the facade. Elderly women and retirees demonstratively guarded a first aid tent, although far and wide there was no one who might charge the 'fort'. The tattooed men who passed through the entrance wore improvised camouflage uniforms and headbands and carried truncheons or, in some cases, whips with metal studs of the sort a concentration camp guard in a film might wield. There were no speeches, only songs from a tape booming across the square that relied heavily on rhyming 'Donbass' with 'working class'. The pedestrian zone, the art museum, the oblast library, the best bookshop in town and several institutes of the university were all nearby. How could a gang of nutcases possibly discompose and upset a major city! A few more days and the occupation would be over, soon to be forgotten as an inconsequential episode! The unvarying and interwoven routines at the heart of urban life, the force of habit that keeps a community going, would soon enough swallow up the incident and expel the hooligans. That was the impression I got in the cities of eastern Ukraine after the occupation of Crimea.

Still, it should have been clear then that the seizure of a central building in Donetsk – and similar incidents around the same time in Kharkov, Lugansk and Mariupol – were not spontaneous and coincidental but coordinated elements of a targeted action: the *coup de main* in Crimea was to be followed by the no less rapid takeover of the territory of the self-proclaimed entity Novorossiya, or New Russia. Following the Crimean model, the rebels would then apply to Russia for military 'protection'. For an outsider, these machinations were difficult to see through at the time, but since then some of the protagonists have been quite voluble about their roles, offering detailed accounts that confirm the existence of the larger plan. None more so than Igor Strelkov AKA. Igor Girkin, who, after the coup in Crimea, engineered the seizure of Slavyansk – a well-chosen target: a comparatively small and easily captured town that is also a railway hub. His success triggered a wave of occupations that allowed him to gain control of numerous cities and towns in the Donbass: Artyomovsk, Enakievo, Konstantinovka, Krasnyi Liman, Gorlovka, Khartsyzsk, Makeevka and, most importantly, Donetsk and Lugansk. While normal life continued as before, a clique seized key points and established a kind of shadow regime. A city of well over a million people was hijacked and taken hostage. In those first days and weeks, none of that was foreseeable – or I certainly did not foresee it, but then the new government in Kiev, it seems, was just as in the dark. The train I took from Kharkov to Donetsk passed through Slavyansk and Kramatorsk on schedule; in both towns the platforms were neat and clean and crowded with commuters headed home. Girkin/Strelkov's men already controlled Slavyansk, but the passengers in the air-conditioned open-plan carriage took out their laptops to watch American blockbusters or work. When I got to Donetsk, the cabbie – 'because of the unrest' – took a slightly different route to the hotel I had booked online and – 'because of the unrest' – demanded a slightly higher fare.

Kidnapping: The City as Hostage, Death of the City

Efforts to quash the terrorist occupations of public institutions in Donetsk and Lugansk came to nought, for a variety of reasons – perhaps the new government in Kiev, unsure of its powers and responsibilities, failed to seize the right moment for a resolute intervention and underestimated the extent to which these actions corroded the state's monopoly on the use of force; perhaps local police refused orders or shrank from confronting the ruthless terrorists; perhaps there really was no viable military option in the face of demonstrative readiness to use violence. Be that as it may, it appears that the kidnappers reached a sort of point of no return beyond which de-escalation was no longer possible. The ineluctable dynamic of the evolving crisis pointed towards ever greater radicalism: from symbolic to actual seizure, from the conquest of selected points to entire areas, from control over the public sphere to the suppression by force of any opposition, from the flouting and flagrant violation of all rules of engagement to the establishment of a despotic regime under which looting, rape, torture, even executions became common practice.

It is hardly the first time Europe has witnessed the death of cities and urbicide, but we still find it difficult to give a comprehensive account of the phenomenon. The long list of examples includes cities that were razed to the ground, incinerated, burnt to ashes and dust: Stalingrad, Warsaw and several German towns hit hardest by Allied bombardment. Others survived as empty shells, their walls and facades undamaged, even as their human substance was destroyed – by deportations into camps or gas chambers or, in some instances, by a complete exchange of their populations, as in Vilnius, Lviv, Łódź and Wrocław. After the cataclysm, these cities still stood, but in a sense they had ceased to be. The example nearest to us, both in time and in space, is presumably Sarajevo, where a community with a centuries-old tradition of multi-ethnic coexistence was destroyed before our very eyes. Most recently, one of the very oldest cities built by human civilization has fallen victim to urbicide: Aleppo.

Those who find themselves in the eye of the storm confront more urgent challenges than how to properly describe the processes that claim their lives. The sketches we do have show that each city perishes – or perhaps survives – in its own distinctive way. Blockaded Leningrad slowly starved to death, as remembered by Daniil Granin, Ales Adamovich and Lidiya Ginzburg. Miron Białoszewski's Warsaw, by contrast, was turned into a ghetto and then systematically torched. Ursula von Kardorff's diaries give us a sense of life in Berlin during the bombing raids; Hans von Lehndorff's of the last days of the 'Fortress Königsberg'; Herman Kruk's writings, of the horrors of occupied Vilnius.

To fully understand what is happening to the people of Donetsk, we must listen to their voices. They know better than anyone else about the sapping of their vital energies, about their precarious mental balance and the sources of their perseverance. They see the villainy and hubristic confidence of their masters from up close, and they know that the time will come when everything that is now covered up will come to light. The menace to their lives has sharpened their senses, and so they register the smallest details of a reality that outsiders cannot begin to imagine. Theirs is the duty to record everything and bear witness. Some blogs from the city already read like the self-scrutiny and self-analysis of a patient undergoing open-heart surgery.

Despite the density of the information that constantly bears down on us, we who watch from afar struggle to keep up to date on the evolving situation. Ever since my return from the Donbass, stacks of maps of widely different scales have sat on my desk – national and regional maps, city plans with street indexes and directories of local institutions. Taking a pen to them, one can enter everything: the detonated bridge, the shelled neighbourhood, the damaged electrical substation or railway station, the impact crater of the stray missile, the factory set ablaze in the crossfire. More technologically adept observers can do the same more quickly and conveniently – and perhaps also with greater precision – using Google Maps and Google Earth, tools that allow them to keep track of developing events, to render the situation on the ground in real time in a multifaceted representation that incorporates as many different perspectives as there are pairs of eyes, which is to say, a virtual infinity of vantage points. Photograph, map and annotation: the conjunction of these three media forms a constantly changing panorama illustrating the transmutation of a city into a battlefield. Modern mapping technology is an enormously powerful instrument, especially when it is used to integrate the abundant information that circulates in social networks. A striking example was the reconstruction of the itinerary of a Russian Buk transporter erector launcher from its base near Kursk into separatist territory, where it fired the missile that downed the Malaysia Airlines plane. This analysis was pieced together not by a nation's professional intelligence service, but by the professionals of the independent British investigative network Bellingcat.

The transformation of a city into a landscape of war takes place on all levels and affects all senses. People learn to pay attention to sounds and recognize the type of projectile and direction from which it was launched; the boom of the detonation tells them how far they are from the point of impact. Adults have become inured to the wailing of the alarm sirens that once startled them, and children can no longer sleep without the now-familiar acoustic background of battle noise. Even civilian ears can distinguish ordinary lorries from military convoys. Urbanites who had rarely descended into the basements of their prefabricated housing blocks have turned their compartments into shelters that increasingly look like homes: the regression from flat-dwellers to cave-dwellers is a characteristic phenomenon in civilized cities under assault from modern warfare. Windows are boarded up with plywood; adhesive tape protects against splintering when explosions shatter glass panes. Communication networks become vital, and mobile phones serve as basic relays for early warnings and all-clear signals – as long as people manage to recharge them despite the frequent power outages. A city that was perfectly safe disintegrates into corridors where residents believe it is safe to go and areas they dare not enter. At times they can venture out to take the dog for a walk, while at other times they must not set foot out of doors. Familiar streets have become hazardous, and people chart alternative routes to avoid encountering the loathsome and erratic strangers who have taken over their city. Those who live by themselves are especially at risk when leaving the house is dangerous: they cannot get needed medications, and hundreds have died of hunger or cold in the winter. In peacetime, the question of what would happen if power were cut, the taps ran dry or the sewer system failed never crosses anyone's mind, but when a shell hits the substation or a water main, people are abruptly thrown back into an era without lifts or running water. The most basic chores become intractable challenges, and urbanites find themselves living in a kind of new Stone Age. A single targeted – or stray – grenade can turn a bus stop or other place where people gather into a blood-soaked crater. Buses and tramways are still running, and they, too, are sometimes hit, the explosion perhaps recorded by a surveillance camera. Fires are no longer put out because the fire brigade cannot be alerted quickly enough or a power outage has disabled the pumps and so there is no water. Firemen work to exhaustion trying to contain the blazes and repair infrastructure, but they are hopelessly outmatched. In the summer, fields in the Donbass burned after shelling. Those who do not have compelling reasons to go out stay at home. Residents withdraw from their cities' public spaces and barricade themselves in their apartments as the streets and squares are increasingly the domain of military personnel. The Russian these men speak often sounds different from the local dialect, and they travel in cars with registration numbers from Vologda or Saratov, Russia – if they even have plates; the traffic laws do not apply to them. Young men avoid the streets because they might be pulled from their cars and forcibly recruited 'to defend the People's Republic'. Drivers who had never used the automatic door locks now hope they will offer a measure of protection against kidnappers. Along the arterial roads, the auto repair shops and car dealerships representing all the major international brands and the full palette of vehicle types have adapted to the needs of the uninvited visitors in camouflage wear, who also seize vehicles at will for their own use or to resell or smuggle them across the nearby border, as though in a revival of the Bolshevist rallying cries about 'expropriating the expropriators' and 'stealing what was stolen from you'. This practice of arbitrary usurpation is especially widespread in housing: thousands of residents have left town, some for good, others temporarily, hoping to hunker down with relatives in the unoccupied parts of Ukraine, across the border in Russia or in a hostel down on the Black Sea 'until this blows over'. Strangers move into vacant apartments and hotels are converted into cantonments for roaming mercenaries and their girlfriends. Apartments are looted, as are supermarkets and car dealerships. Where money was power, the Kalashnikov rules. The pre-revolutionary idea of 'black repartition' is back in vogue: anyone can take whatever he wants, provided he can muster the necessary brute force. The places where the city used to get together sit empty. Cafés – some of them have been damaged in the fighting – close early or are shuttered altogether. Church congregations adapt to the curfew and no longer hold services. Cinemas change their screening times because the streets are too unsafe in the evening. Residents have nowhere to retreat to, not even temporarily. A shell explodes in the gravel pit where the kids play; another has struck the reservoir, and now thousands of dead fish float on the surface. At some point the cash dispensers are no longer in service, then the pension payments stop, and the barter economy returns to the city centre.

The hostage-taker has the upper hand in this struggle; at least for a while he dictates how the victims of his extortion respond to the dilemma in which they are caught. The Ukrainian volunteer corps and army did mount an 'anti-terror campaign', but they have no viable strategy to counter the terror of the insurrectionists. Firing across large distances with imprecise artillery is hardly going to quash the separatists' urban warfare – on the contrary, it only fans the hatred of those who are held responsible for the whole disaster: the government in Kiev and its defenders. Entrenching oneself in a city, retooling its factories as repair workshops for tanks and other military equipment, setting up howitzers and grenade launchers in the middle of residential areas and using the inhabitants of entire housing complexes as human shields: in the Donbass, tactics we had long seen in other parts of the world have made inroads into Europe. Weaponry and equipment from the occupied arsenals of the Ukrainian Army, followed by daily shipments of brand-new matériel supplied across the Russian border, have transformed a civilian world into a military camp. Khaki is the dominant colour in the otherwise deserted streets, with personnel easily outnumbering normal pedestrians. Camouflage has replaced the outfits people used to go to work in. Thousands of apartments have been damaged, many are no longer habitable, and thousands upon thousands of people have been wounded. What was a city is turning into a training ground for military logistics, for the construction of defence works and the repurposing of schools and hospitals as sickbays.

It is easy to determine the points an assailant seeking to set a city, a region, on fire must home in on. Travelling in the Donbass, the visitor realizes that the landscape outside the train's windows is a steppe – especially in the spring, when the locust trees are in bloom, their pollen covering the industrial installations like a white veil – but also, and more importantly, that it is a human-made landscape of iron and steel. It is a stunning scenery, comparable only to other industrial landscapes around the world, from the Kuzbass to Pittsburgh, with kilometre upon kilometre of factory halls, with railways converging in vast junctions, with railway and road bridges stacked atop each other, with canals and pipelines. Yet this Cyclopean landscape is as vulnerable as it is awe-inspiring, and the course of the war in the Donbass can be neatly mapped onto the struggle to control or destroy the strategic objects, the nodes and edges of this network. Demolishing the right railway tracks at a single blow cripples large parts of the Donbass organism. Blowing up bridges severs vital connections. Capturing important road and railway junction towns such as Ilovaisk and Debaltsevo is a sure way to dominance in the terrain, mooting any agreements detailed by cartographers in Geneva and Minsk. When Donetsk Central Station was hit, a mass panic ensued, since many thousands had depended on it as the gateway that would allow them to escape from the besieged and shelled city. The longer the battle for the airport lasted, the more it became fraught with symbolic import – whoever would prevail here would win the larger war – but it was also fought over an object of real practical significance, whose destruction would render the city inaccessible, would cut it off from the rest of the world and plunge it back into a provinciality from which it had only just emerged. And, most importantly, once the collieries and large industrial installations would be hit or shut down, the 'heart of the Donbass' would stop beating, with all the industries that once gave work to city and region. Many coal pits have been flooded because blackouts shut down the pumps, and taking them back into operation will be cumbersome. Powerhouses and substations have sustained damage, while some large production plants have so far remained unscathed, by sheer luck or, as in the case of the properties of Rinat Akhmetov and others, thanks to arrangements between the owners and the separatist leaders. The point in shelling the Donbass Arena, a glass palace that had alighted on an old brownfield like a spaceship and become the Donbass's internationally known landmark, was not just to strike at a sports facility, a stadium: mining and football are central to the region's identity and its people's sense of pride. The team itself is now in exile, holding its matches in Lviv in western Ukraine. But that is only the tip of the iceberg – beneath the surface, Donetsk's entire social fabric is undergoing radical and potentially irreversible alteration. The 'city of a million roses' into which the metropolis of the mining district had transformed itself since the 1960s is now a place where the khaki of uniforms is the dominant colour. Since the first death of a protester, fear has ruled the streets, and at times what resembles nothing so much as mob law – consider the case of Iryna Dovhan, an alleged traitor who was lashed to a lamppost as though to a pillory and berated, kicked and maltreated by passersby as others stood by and cheered them on; the captive Ukrainian soldiers who were paraded through the city centre and forced to pass through a 'corridor of shame' formed by an enraged throng; and the reports of torture in the separatists' prison cells.

Terror is effective. Those who can relocate do. Entire professions emigrate. There is no longer anything to do for lawyers, so they leave. Most of the university's staff – the separatists captured the directorate – have moved to Vinnytsia, where they try to keep classes and research projects going. The client base of the small and medium-sized businesses that sprang up in the post-Soviet years, especially in the IT sector, is shrinking now that the laws of economics are increasingly superseded by the terror-political imperatives of a command economy that is primarily about divvying up the spoils and redistribution. Major corporations have moved their staff to other cities. The malls that were built in recent years have fallen silent as demand has collapsed. Qualified personnel who see no future for themselves and their families in a city of warlords have decamped, as have the doctors and hospital workers. Construction work has dried up. The new townhouses sit empty, and if you want to – and are ruthless enough – you can occupy one. In September 2014, Alexander Polkvoi called Donetsk 'Ukraine's Detroit', a city from which those with money, the high-income households, had emigrated to other municipalities. 'To the extent that it was not tied to the place, business has left Donetsk. That has nothing to do with politics – business requires unambiguous and understandable rules of the game, a place where one can make plans for the future and have confidence in the present.' The wonderful Donbass Arena, he wrote, was no longer needed and sat there like a monument, a glass Pyramid of Cheops commemorating the city vibrant with energy that was, covered with graffiti, abandoned to dilapidation, falling dark 'like the buttons in the elevators of the towers'. The Russian journalist Yulia Latynina has proposed a different comparison, arguing that Donetsk is undergoing what she calls *palestinizatsiya*: the proposal to surround the Donbass with a border wall in order to stop the spread of violence and anomie reminds her of the strangulation of the Gaza Strip. Yet others have been put in mind of Somalia by the de-facto rulers' arbitrary and despotic decisions.

The self-proclaimed People's Republics of Donetsk and Lugansk clearly will not survive on their own; their authority was secured in the battles of Ilovaisk and Debaltsevo – which concluded in massacres of the defeated Ukrainian troops – with help from Russia in the form of special forces and weaponry. They were dependent from day one on the influx of people and matériel from Russia because the arsonists' hopes that the people of the Donbass would rise up foundered. None other than Igor Girkin/Strelkov, the Russian expert in igniting insurrection, once complained that the Donbass was incapable of mustering even 20,000 men; and the referendum itself was transparently a pure PR operation without any representative value. We have every reason to doubt that the two republics' leaderships could build their para-states without outside help, or that their so-called governments will ever be more than puppet regimes led by quislings.

The posse that has reported for duty under the banner of the People's Republics is as colourful and disparate as the self-designed uniforms. Much about it is reminiscent of the marauding lansquenets and irregular militias of the past. In a distant or not-so-distant future, these activists – their rhetoric, their life choices and their mentality – will find their biographers and analysts, and eventually they will meet their judges as well. Terms like 'lowlifes' or 'dregs of society' are manifestly inadequate to comprehend and explain them, although certain types are disproportionately represented among them: small-time criminals sprung from the prisons by the 'uprising', thugs, former bodyguards and martial-arts devotees, drug addicts – people who need no idea or ideology to be game for anything. More consequential is the involvement of battle-hardened veterans of the late Soviet and post-Soviet wars and civil wars in Afghanistan, Tajikistan and Chechnya, and deployments in Transnistria and Yugoslavia. They are professionals against whom the dutifully trained recruits and reservists of an army inexperienced in battle such as Ukraine's were initially no match. Going through the list of warlords, self-appointed governors, chiefs and commanders of the two People's Republics, one notices the large number of dubious-to-outright-pathological characters and hit men. Their tattoos are a record of the scenes where they gained their experience. There are many, too many, in the 'post-Soviet space', especially in Russia, who never found their way back into civilian life – and what was 'civilian life' in the chaos of the 1990s! Joining the fray in Crimea and the Donbass was, for them, an obvious choice: it was where they felt at home – war was the world they knew. Nor should we forget the idealists and romantics who agonized over when Russia would finally 'rise from her knees' and only waited for the opportunity to put in practice all the pent-up resentment stoked by books and pamphlets. This group includes history buffs (Girkin/Strelkov is one of them); those who sought their salvation in the Orthodox Church and in fealty to an Orthodox oligarch like Konstantin Malofeev (one example is Alexander Borodai, the Moscow-born 'prime minister' who helped prepare the coup in Crimea and eastern Ukraine); students who absorbed the teachings of the neo-Eurasianist guru Alexander Dugin and constructed a worldview out of radical right-wing and racist ideas years ago (like the neo-Nazi and 'people's governor' Pavel Gubarev). One striking detail is how often a career in advertising or public relations seems to have been a springboard into the separatists' upper echelons: all it took was a fast mouth and a knack for homing in on the already existing contradictions of a populace exploited and humiliated by oligarchs, on people's feeling that they were being defrauded of the fruits of their lifelong labour. An intuitive sense for these weak spots and a talent for demagogy were enough to catapult individuals no one had heard of until recently into the spotlight not just of the Donbass's but of the world's attention. Over the course of the past year we have had ample opportunity to get to know them: the 'people's mayor' Vyacheslav Ponomaryov, for example, who had OSCE representatives detained and led diplomats with international experience and journalists from around the world by the nose. Almost all of them had spent time abroad, in France or the United States, and their sartorial choices and rhetoric were clearly inspired by the style and design of postmodernism; others donned colourful exotic costumes for their turn in the limelight – there were Cossack atamans, commissars in leather coats, and aficionados of the blue-and-white sailor shirt that has been a symbol of Russian-Soviet masculinity ever since the revolution and Eisenstein's *Battleship Potemkin*. Throw in, for good measure, a detachment of Islamist fighters from Chechnya sent to the Donbass by Kadyrov.

Thanks to the revolution in the field of media technology, we know the faces and identities of these characters fairly well. They have long stopped feeling the need to hide behind masks and are self-confident enough to share their selfies with tanks and howitzers with the entire world. There are thrill-seekers among them who cannot think of anything better to do with their holidays than going to war: the Donbass as an adventure playground that beckons with rich booty and, more importantly, with the camaraderie and *esprit de corps* that have vanished from their ordinary lives at home. War, to them, is an extra-curricular activity, and jeans, fashionable sunglasses and Kalashnikovs are the gear that goes with it. And we have pictures of the poor devils who were sent off into the war without being told where they were going; some of them would return to their home towns, to Pskov or Vologda, in coffins, shipped back from a country in which, officials insisted, there was no war and no soldier was dying.

Yet the abundant pictures should not distract us from those who remain unseen, the true specialists, the analysts and high-tech warriors who cannot be bothered with Cossack sabres and other military theatrics. These are people who bring expertise in data analysis, interception, counterintelligence and the operation of complex weapon systems to the table and have access to the resources Moscow provides. They prepare the analyses based on which the master in Moscow maps out the next move.

All these various factions together do not have the wherewithal to manage a city of a million people or an entire industrial region, to keep things running, let alone to foster development. Their existence depends on arms shipments and aid convoys from outside, and on an influx of people who see opportunities for themselves in the crisis – it is not the first time the Donbass has experienced this kind of rule.

The End of the Donbass Museum

On the evening of Friday, 22 August 2014, the Donbass Regional Museum of Local History was hit by several shells and sustained heavy damage. The two sides, the separatists and the Ukrainian army, blamed each other. Photographs show a gash in the facade, shattered glass cases and ceilings that had caved in. Taxidermied animals including deer and a wild boar stood under the open sky; the mammoth was allegedly unharmed, as was the gallery devoted to the Donbass under German occupation and the Great Patriotic War. The director, Evgeny Denisenko, was aghast – one of Ukraine's most important local history museums, which had been established exactly ninety years earlier, in 1924, was forced to close until further notice. His staff started cleaning up and securing the exhibits without delay.

I had last seen the museum in April. It was an establishment of a peculiar kind that exists only within the boundaries of the former Soviet Union: a pedagogical institution that, in the absence of publications, was often also the only source of information on a town's history. Museums of its kind offered guided tours for groups, often from schools. Devoid of the technologically advanced multimedia and interactive mumbo-jumbo of their Western counterparts, they were also time capsules preserving the history of museum culture. The visitor was left to his own devices and free to take notes. Across the Union, these museums without exception proffered the same narrative of historical progress that was first framed in the nineteenth century. They imparted basic knowledge about the history of the Earth, the natural world, the plant and animal kingdoms, the various eras of the past and, most importantly, the achievements of socialism and the Soviet land, the culmination of all history. The major lacunae were easy to spot; crucial historical events were missing, and certain figures had apparently been declared non-persons. A similarly robust conception of museum work spoke from the presentation of the exhibits, a naturalism of physical presence that was bound to arouse suspicions in a visitor schooled in postmodernism, although now that the study of material culture has become fashionable its charm is evident. The museum in Donetsk had the flat-bottomed boat on which the Cossacks once raced down the Dnieper rapids, the blind singer's bandura, and the Thonet chair that was obligatory whenever Soviet exhibition-makers sought to illustrate a bourgeois interior. When the Soviet Union disintegrated, the narrative these museums presented also broke apart or at least became creaky, revealing gaps, throwing up questions that could not be asked before.

The Donetsk Regional Museum of Local History was an archetypical example of this characteristically Soviet institution, and its destruction came just as the changing political situation created an opportunity to reimagine it. And yet, all simplification notwithstanding, it presented the overwhelmingly rich and dramatic history of its city. Founded in 1869 by the Welsh industrialist and Bible-believing Christian John James Hughes (1815–1889), Donetsk was initially named after him and grew at breakneck pace: the population rose to 57,000 by 1917 and 300,000 on the eve of the Second World War. Yuzovka – the name was emblematic of a capitalist success story – became Stalino in 1924 and then, with de-Stalinization, in 1961 was given the name it bears today, after a tributary of the Don River.

In Donetsk, the galleries that are typically reserved for the natural world take on added meaning. Geological strata, the dynamic forces that forged the earth's crust, the whole below-ground universe: these are key to the natural resources that made the city and region a centre of heavy industry of vital importance first to the Russian Empire, then to the Soviet Union, and now to Ukraine; exceptionally rich deposits of anthracite coal, iron ores, graphite, dolomite, gypsum and kaolin have been identified in the Donbass. Rivers provide the water needed to process these riches and a cheap mode of transportation. The discovery of mineral resources beneath the steppes along the River Kalmius sparked a breathtaking economic development. The museum's diorama – another characteristic format of Soviet museum culture – illustrates how pits and ironworks were the beating hearts around which an extensive agglomeration of industrial villages sprang up and eventually grew into large cities: Enakievo, Makeevka, Alchevsk and others. The head frames above the shaft mines, which are now sunk to depths of up to 1,402 metres (4,600 ft), and the kilometres-long compound of the metallurgical plant are still the defining features of the Donetsk cityscape. The chessboard street grid laid out by English planners in the nineteenth century served as the point of departure when the city was redesigned in the 1930s. Scattered between these landmarks is everything that a city striking roots in the 'Wild Field' required: factory halls and, next to them, the director's villa; the fire tower and the hospital; the commercial college, the grand hotel, the bank; churches and houses of prayer for the various creeds the labour migrants brought with them to the nascent city: imperial subjects including Russians, Ukrainians, Jews, Armenians, Tatars and Greeks – and more than a few foreigners, primarily Englishmen, Scots, Belgians, Frenchmen and Germans. As the company nameplates, plaques on engines and desk utensils on display in the museum show, Yuzovka was a melting pot populated by 37 nationalities, a European city, a 'Machine in the Garden' (Leo Marx) of the Cossack lands. Besides the metal works of Hughes's New Russia Company Ltd, there were the companies of E. E. Olivier and Eduard Bosse, a Baltic German subject of the tsar from Estonia who had obtained his engineering degree in Zurich, as well as Belgian and French companies. When the Russian scholar Dmitri Mendeleev inspected the Donbass in 1888, he found a 'future America'. A bourgeois interior including a bureau and a harmonium complete with music by Johann Strauss (the instrument was damaged in the recent attack) as well as group pictures of the strength sports association give an impression of late imperial Yuzovka. Then the visitor moves on to war, revolution and civil war, represented by an armoured train named 'Karl Liebknecht and Rosa Luxemburg' from Starokramatorsk, brass-plated spiked helmets worn by the imperial German troops who occupied the city in 1918, photographs of the arrival of the social bandits led by the anarchist Nestor Makhno and of General Denikin's Whites marching in. Each successive ruling clique left its mark on Yuzovka, with looting, pogroms and executions of hostages. The 1920s, with their semi-free market and rapid reconstruction, are symbolized by a well-stocked village store and the insignia of modernity: an iron plough or the telephone on the desk of the Red director. After the revolution, Donetsk and the Donbass remained the great melting pot and forge of the Union. Among those who had moved here for work was a native of Kursk Governorate, Nikita Khrushchev; he laid the foundations for his meteoric rise as a rebellious worker in Bosse's factory and then as a young communist at the mining college. The museum has his rimless spectacles, a golden fountain pen and a melancholy portrait from his retirement years. Other characters of the Donbass myth, exemplified by the poster bearing the inscription 'The smoke from the factory chimneys is the breath of Soviet Russia', include the 'heroes of socialist labour' Aleksei Stakhanov and Nikita Izotov.

Although the period of industrialization is a subject treated with considerable pathos, the museum in Donetsk has room for the great

disasters of Soviet Ukraine as well: the campaign of forcible collectivization and the Holodomor, the famine of 1932–3 in which millions died;
the explanatory notes accompanying the exhibits even use the word
'genocide'. The room is designed almost like a memorial, with a display
including deportation orders, photographs of peasant families being
arrested and children scouring fields after the potato harvest, medical
certificates listing the symptoms of starvation, statistics tabulating the
numbers of victims. A separate section is devoted to the Great Terror
of 1937–8 in Ukraine, which, according to the information in the exhibition, claimed around 25,000 victims; on view are portraits of factory
directors, scholars and poets who were executed. The German assault
turned the city into a battlefield and the entire Donbass into scorched
earth. The visitor learns about the topography of German-occupied
Donetsk: the Gestapo operated from today's Donbass Palace, while the
city commandant officiated in what would later be the theatre café.
The display pinpoints the places where thousands of Soviet prisoners
of war starved to death and where the city's Jews were rounded up
and murdered. Toni Graschberger (from the Staatstheater in Munich)
directed a production of the Front-Oper company of Léo Delibes'
Coppélia and the *Faded Dream* after Pushkin at the Stadttheater Stalino,
now the Donetsk State Opera on Artyom Street. When it was all over,
German soldiers were interred in cemeteries on brownfields and columns of German war prisoners were marched past the ruins, later
joined by Transylvanian Saxons, ethnic Germans from Romania, who
were deported to the Donbass as forced labourers; Oskar Pastior and
Herta Müller have helped us grasp their suffering.

The most extensive and most lavish sections are devoted to the restoration of peace and reconstruction after 1945, with a particular focus
on the tenure of the mayor and Red manager Vladimir Degtyaryov,
a powerful and, it seems, widely popular provincial potentate who
led a building campaign – housing projects, supermarkets, stadiums,
schools and athletic facilities (he was an active footballer himself) – in
the 1960s and 1970s. Besides the city's 'famous sons' such as Nikita
Khrushchev, the composer Sergei Prokofiev (the airport destroyed in
the recent fighting is named after him) and the Russian Jewish writer
Vasily Grossman, who was born in Berdychiv and studied in Stalino,
it is athletes like the pole vaulter Sergei Bubka, several world-class
boxers and the football club Shakhtar that embody the city's self-image
and pride.

The long post-war era appears to have been the happiest time in Donetsk's and the Donbass's history. Regular flats and apartments were given priority over the bombastic palaces that had been built for the new labour aristocracy; consumer goods took precedence over the communism that was still in the Party's platform. The legacy of this period is impressive: schools, hospitals, blocks of flats, department stores, kindergartens and culture palaces, all embedded in parks along the Kalmius, which is dammed to form a lake in the city centre, and overshadowed by the cones of slag heaps, some of which are now overgrown with weeds. Although the city's existence has always been bound up with the coal pits and the huge metallurgical factory and other industries – some of which, like the toy factory, enjoy a legendary reputation – it is not a company town: it has its own centre, boulevards with representative buildings, most of them in the massive Neoclassical style of the 1930s and 1940s, and even a few structures that date from before the revolution, such as the old Hôtel Angleterre, one lyceum and the National Bank building. With its residential and office towers along a central axis, Donetsk reminded this visitor of Essen or Bochum – the latter is one of its twin cities, as is Magdeburg – and seeing it one might never know the tragedies it has lived through and survived. The boom during the empire's last decades ended in the crash of the revolution and civil war. The second wave of industrialization in the late 1920s and 1930s, marred by the Holodomor and the Great Terror, was brought to an abrupt end by the German occupation between 1941 and 1943, which destroyed in a historical blink of an eye what generations had toiled to build. In little more than two decades, the city died a twofold death. And statistical data are only the rawest and most abstract form that lets us begin to comprehend the catastrophe. Each date stands for a sudden end; each stands for a new beginning and, paradoxically, a peculiar continuity. The American historian Hiroaki Kuromiya studied the century-long history of the Donbass when the archives became accessible in the late 1980s; his analysis was published under the title *Freedom and Terror in the Donbass: A Ukrainian-Russian Borderland, 1870s–1990s*.

Yuzovka: Industrial Take-off and Downfall

The history of the Donbass as an industrial region begins with the discovery and exploitation of the coal and ore deposits in the mid-1800s.

Until then the area had been a 'Wild Field', a no-man's-land, settled late and gradually, a borderland between Poland–Lithuania and Muscovy in the north and the Ottoman Empire and its vassal the Crimean Khanate in the south, a transitional zone and territory of the Zaporozhian and Don Cossacks, finally integrated into the Russian Empire under Catherine II. Not unlike the American 'Wild West', the 'Wild Field' attracted all sorts of people who chafed under the conditions in the lands of the Polish crown, the tsar or the sultan: peasants who fled serfdom, Old Believers who sought to escape persecution by the Orthodox Church, criminals who hoped to avoid punishment, adventurers whom the pursuit of happiness brought to the vast undeveloped area, Jews terrorized by the pogroms in the cities and towns of the Pale of Settlement. The discovery of coal and ore deposits along the middle reaches of the Donets triggered not only an unparalleled industrial boom, but a no less staggering migration. By 1917 the 'Russian Empire's Ruhr' produced 87 per cent of the nation's total coal output, 70 per cent of the crude iron, 57 per cent of the steel, over 90 per cent of the coke, and over 60 per cent of the soda ash and mercury. The area's population soared: the 1897 census showed 700,000 people living in the Donbass; in 1920, despite the bloodletting of the war and civil war, that number had risen to over 2 million, and by 1959 there were no fewer than 7 million residents.

John Hughes received a commission from the Russian government to develop metal works in the region in 1869, established the New Russia Company for Pit Coal, Iron and Railway Manufacturing and, in 1871, smelted the first iron ore. His success in the new industry prompted others to get in on the action: landowners who became entrepreneurs, foreign corporations that wanted to be part of the enormous empire's incipient industrialization. The writer Konstantin Paustovsky, who spent time in Yuzovka, described the 'coal fever' that had seized the city. Twenty-six out of 36 joint stock companies operating in the Donbass were foreign, the majority of them French and Belgian. Many metallurgical operations in Makeevka, Konstantinovka and Enakievo that are still major brands today were originally founded by expatriate entrepreneurs. The giant Mariupol Metallurgical Combine started out as a Belgian-owned company named Russky Providans. Donetsk's Dongormash was originally the Bosse Plant; the French-owned Société minière et industrielle de Routchenko built a plant in what is now the city's Petrovsky District. Hughes had brought his own engineers, accountants and preachers from Britain, as well as football, which quickly caught on with the locals, and built the city's first European-style hotel. The Donbass of those decades, the historian Stanislav Kmet has observed, had more in common with Western Europe than with Poltava or Kharkov. And in fact the region had been 'European' even before Hughes arrived. The small town of Novgorodskoe, not far from Dzerzhinsk, was founded by German Mennonites settled here by Catherine II and originally known as New York. Today's Telmanovo, after Ernst Thälmann, was once the German community of Ostheim. Around 1800 there were 68 such German settlements.

The influx of capital raised the demand for manpower, and workers flocked to the Donbass from all over the Russian Empire. According to the 1897 census, of the population of the central Donbass, 52.4 per cent were Ukrainians, 28.7 per cent Russians, 6.4 per cent Greeks, 4.3 per cent Germans, 2.9 per cent Jews, 2.1 per cent Tatars, 0.8 per cent Belorussians and 0.4 per cent Poles. A 1917 statistic for Donetsk similarly paints the picture of a melting pot: there were 37 different nationalities among its 54,718 people, including 31,952 Russians, 9,934 Jews, 7,086 Ukrainians, 2,120 Poles, 1,465 Belorussians, 421 Armenians, 334 Tatars, 130 Kazakhs, 101 Englishmen, 96 Roma and seventy Germans. The Ukrainian poet Volodymyr Sosiura, a native of Debaltsevo, had Serbian, Hungarian, Jewish, French and Karachay ancestors. Khrushchev recalled dealing with Bulgarian farmers and German settlers.

General view of Yuzovka.

As in other industrial regions, workers' living and labour conditions during the first phase of industrialization were grim and defined by ruthless exploitation. Accidents in the pits were nothing unusual, and the managerial and working classes lived in different worlds. Payday regularly ended with excessive drinking, outbreaks of violence, brawls and organized fistfights between mineworkers grouped by ethnic backgrounds. Clashes with the Cossack militia were routine, as were flare-ups of the tensions between the different nationalities, especially between the Russians and Ukrainians flowing into the cities from the countryside and the Jews from the Pale of Settlement; the young Khrushchev witnessed one such bloody pogrom. A contemporary observer wrote about the misery wrought by backbreaking work, accidents, alcoholism, squalor and violence:

> Far and wide around the town of Yuzovka one feels the breath of Ekaterinoslav Governorate's mighty mining industry; one senses capitalism's thirst for raw power and sees quite clearly what it gives the masses and what it takes from them. Like symbols of the future struggle to which the meeting of capital and proletarian labour must eventually give rise everywhere, the sombre factory compounds with their heaven-assailing colossal smokestacks spewing columns of fire and clouds of smoke lie spread out at smaller or larger intervals throughout Yuzovka and around it, filling the air with incessant hissing and whooshing, shrieking and screeching.

The sense of shock this experience instilled was mixed with the fascination of modern industry, as Alexander Kuprin's story *Moloch* (1896) illustrates:

> Thousands of sounds merged into a long, galloping hubbub: the clear notes of stone-masons' chisels, the ringing blows of riveters pounding away at boiler rivets, the heavy crashing of steam hammers, the powerful hissing and whistling of steam pipes, and occasional muffled, earth-shaking explosions somewhere underground. It was an engrossing and awe-inspiring sight. Human labour was in full swing like a huge, complex and precise machine. Thousands of people – engineers, stone-masons, mechanics, carpenters, fitters, navvies, joiners,

blacksmiths – had come together from various corners of the earth, in order to give their strength and health, their wits and energy, in obedience to the iron law of the struggle for survival, for just one step forward in industrial progress.

The tensions between a young working class and a young capitalism repeatedly erupted in revolts, strikes and demonstrations. The patriotic and chauvinistic mobilization at the beginning of the First World War only briefly masked them. The collapse of the old order in 1917 then released forces that, although they devastated the 'Machine in the Steppe', ultimately drove the region's development forward. The years of revolution and civil war saw various masters come and go. The radicals, the Bolsheviks, won the majority of votes in Donetsk and Lugansk, but at first the Donbass was conquered by General Kaledin, whose White troops spread terror wherever they went. More generally, the area around the Don became a hub for counter-revolutionary forces of all stripes, from the Whites to the liberals; a short-lived Donets–Krivoi Rog Soviet Republic that opposed the Tsentralna Rada was ousted by German and Austrian occupying troops, who left in the autumn of 1918. Where the Reds brought nationalization and expropriation of the bourgeoisie and expelled managers and engineers, the Whites restored the old order, with strike bans and corporal punishments. Each shift in the balance of power was accompanied by looting, mass executions and horrendous atrocities as well as pogroms against the Jews, whom all sides identified as the enemy.

In the industrial cities of the Donbass, this turmoil led to a collapse of output. Not a single one of the 65 smelting furnaces that existed in 1913 was in operation by the time the civil war ended, and production had virtually come to a halt. Eighty per cent of the region's horses, which were indispensable for transportation, were dead, and the railways had been destroyed. Each changeover of power further decimated what had been the Donbass's society. The *burzhui* fled into White-held territory; many businessmen went into exile. Open season was declared on engineers and specialists. Communications networks, the telegraph system and the connections to the centre broke down, and the region was left to fend for itself. Urbanites hoping to survive moved out into the countryside and stole the harvest from the peasantry. The adversaries in the civil war and the German occupiers also pioneered destructive and punitive tactics that would subsequently be employed again and again: mines were flooded; political enemies, dead or alive, were plunged down the shafts. What had coalesced into a city fell apart. As industrial labour dwindled, so did the class of industrial workers, as a Bolshevik correctly observed in 1919: 'The economic centre of the Soviet Republic has been turned into a cemetery on which the Donbass's miners and metalworkers lie.' Everything had to be rebuilt from scratch.

Stalino: Symphony of the Donbass and Great Terror

After a brief delay, the city in 1924 officially renounced the name of its founder John Hughes, the 'British capitalist', and adopted a new one, in premature or prescient obeisance: Stalino. Following a strikingly quick recovery in the years of the NEP, Stalin would be the rising star guiding its further development. What played out after 1929, in the impetuous early years of the planned economy, was effectively a refounding or remake of the city. As everywhere, new street names were the first portent of profound changes that ultimately amounted to the construction of a community from the ground up. Despite the damages wrought by the Second World War, the structures the general plan for Stalino envisioned are still landmarks in its urban fabric: the Ordzhonikidze girls' lyceum (1937), the Hotel Donbass (1938), the restaurant Moskva (1938), the Komsomolets cinema (1937), the First Pioneers' and Students' Palace (1932), the National Bank building, schools and culture palaces. Many of them are arrayed along Artyom Street. In 1939 a local newspaper proudly reported: 'Little remains of the old Yuzovka. In the years of Stalin's five-year plans, a new socialist city has been created. Where lowly huts oppressed by destitution stood, where land lay waste, hundreds of multi-storey blocks of flats as well as social and cultural facilities have been built; blooming parks, gardens, and green spaces extend between them.' What had been a 'colony of foreign capital' was now the 'pride of the Soviet land' and 'all-Soviet boiler house', and the mineworker had become an indispensable cinematic and cultural-political icon. The Donbass was the cradle of the heroic figures of an entire era, perhaps even of a distinctive civilization: the civilization of the Soviet world. Dziga Vertov came to shoot for his documentary film *Enthusiasm: Symphony of the Donbass* (1930). The New Man was born and forged – the backward peasant transformed into the progressive proletarian or engineer – in the Donbass. It was in the Donbass that Aleksei Stakhanov – who was a native of a village in the area and worked in a mine in Donetsk for some time – and Nikita Izotov set their best-worker world records. The area provided the settings for feature films about the rough but warm-hearted proletarian milieu – see, for example, *Miners of the Don* (1951) – with whose characters more than a generation of Soviet citizens would identify. The young Petro Hryhorenko, who would rise to the rank of general and later become a prominent dissident, gave a description of the new city's layout that is still by and large correct:

Donetsk today is a modern large city. In the 1920s it was an agglomeration of workers' settlements around the giant ironworks at the centre. The divisions of the plant were scattered across the entire huge natural basin, with the workers' neighbourhoods on higher ground along the periphery. The only arguably old part of town was the quarter that lay north of the mill. It was transected by sixteen 'lines' (streets) that began at the plant and ran south to north. The heart of the city was a large square – around 800 or 1,000 feet wide and an entire 'line' lengthwise. Standing at its centre, the mill in one's back, one looked at the first and second 'lines', which circumscribed the area of storehouses and granaries, of market halls and the hay market at the centre. The remaining edges of the square were taken up by the workingmen's school (the former lyceum), the mining college (formerly a commercial school), and other official buildings.

He also had a keen eye for the city's social mixture and internal barriers:

The social differentiation among the workers in Stalino was indeed incredibly rigid and reflected in the geographical structure of its neighbourhoods. Maslovka, south of the mill, was the centre of the working-class suburbs. Its streets formed parallel belts around the plant compound and were lined by company-owned red-brick houses where one or two families lived, all foremen and especially skilled technicians. The upscale neighbourhood, with the engineers' single-family homes and the former plant director's villa – in my days, it was where the workingmen's association held its meetings

– adjoined Maslovka to the east. In the centre of Maslovka, right by the mill, rose a sprawling building: lecture hall, stage, foyer, assembly room all in one, known as the 'auditorium'. West of Maslovka and still south of the ironworks compound was Larinka. Although there were no industrial installations here, the land was plant property, and the plots were exclusively reserved for qualified members of the staff. Further west was Aleksandrovka, also with company-owned plots, on which the permanent staff of unqualified workers lived, unskilled labourers, heavers, etc. Yet another neighbourhood, called 'Smolyanin Hill', lay south of Maslovka, with company-owned houses accommodating the families of four white-collar or medium-qualification blue-collar workers each. Finally, a few detached homes – again, owned by the company, of course – between Maslovka and Smolyanin Hill were reserved for especially important and hard-to-find specialists. As regards the plebes, the lumpenproletariat, casual labourers without regular incomes or in the bottom wage groups, they dwelled in what can only be called rabbit hutches, which the owners let to them at usurious rates. Or they built 'wild' settlements on the outskirts. The residents of all these neighbourhoods had raised moral barriers between each other that were more rigid than any social barriers that had existed in the old Russia. For example, on no account must a girl from Maslovka marry a young man from Aleksandrovka; even a greeting or a handshake were regarded as improper, as I experienced at first hand.

The new society that formed in the Donbass, the 'all-Soviet boiler house', bore all the hallmarks of a precipitate, frenzied and violent industrialization that went hand in hand with the destruction of the traditional world of the Ukrainian and Russian village. As is well known, the forced collectivization of agriculture culminated in the great famine of the Holodomor. Although industrial workers were privileged in the distribution of foodstuffs, the city was connected to the countryside by a thousand threads, and so urbanites were aware of what was going on out there: of the deportations, the mass deaths, the NKVD operations that resembled a civil war. The Union's industries needed manpower, and so the peasants' basis of existence was destroyed. Millions of them streamed to the cities. Stalino was among the destinations of this rural exodus, and its population multiplied within a decade. By 1939 the city had almost half a million inhabitants. Forced mass migration and chaotic industrialization turned the forge of the New Man into a pressure tank that might blow up at any moment. The Donbass offered hundreds of thousands an escape from the village and plunged hundreds of thousands more into the abyss first of the Holodomor, then of the Great Terror. Amid so much adversity, violence, dashed hopes, people clung to the utopia of an earthly paradise and brooded on vengeance. The 'Wild Field' became a haven for those whose lives were in danger or who faced persecution, those driven by ambition or hatred, those who had suffered and hoped to settle old scores. Every hand was needed, and so it was a place where one might disappear: the farmer who absconded because he was slated for deportation, the former White army soldier or member of a revolutionary party who needed to erase his past, the cleric or member of one of the ethnic minorities – the Polish, the Germans, the Greeks – who woke up one morning to find that the secret police targeted his people as 'agents' or 'spies'; engineers and managers who served as scapegoats for industrial accidents and when production fell short of the plan were charged as 'parasites' and 'saboteurs'. The Great Terror swept over the Donbass with murderous force, and none other than Khrushchev, who had laid the foundations for his career at the technical college in Yuzovka, offered a justification of lethal concision in 1938 (he was just 44 years old!): 'The Donbass exerts a powerful attraction on enemies and agents of whatever stripe – Trotskyites, rightists, spies. They all engage in activities hostile to Soviet power. We must be more vigilant and get rid of all traitors . . . Kulaks flock to the Donbass because it is easier to hide here. The kulak wears the miner's shirt and the worker sees that they toil together for three years and thinks that they are of the same kind. But that means nothing.'

The final tally of the Great Terror in the Donbass – the dark flipside of the 'Symphony of the Donbass' – is monstrous. The numbers that are given for 1937–8 vary. Hiroaki Kuromiya has calculated that 50,000 death sentences were issued in the 'bacchanalia of terror'; the Donbass, with 16.5 per cent of Ukraine's total population, accounted for one-third of all executions in the republic. Tanja Penter has counted 37,146 individuals arrested by the NKVD and 9,729 death sentences but believes the actual totals may be higher. The Ukrainian historian V. Nikolsky has written that 20,000 people were killed in Donetsk Oblast alone. The death toll was especially high among the class of younger people who had rapidly risen through the ranks in the 1930s: engineers, technicians and Red managers. Several sites of repression and the NKVD's mass crimes were identified in the Perestroika period of the 1980s, including today's Prokofiev Conservatory at 44 Artyom Street, then the NKVD's headquarters, and a mass grave in Ruchenkovo that is now marked by a memorial.

Ground Zero: The Germans in Donetsk

The Wehrmacht conquered Stalino on 20 October 1941; the city was liberated on 8 September 1943. Two years of occupation reduced the population to a third of the pre-war number: of the 462,395 people who had lived in Donetsk in 1939, 148,507 were still there by 1943. Around 65,000 were able to escape or evacuated in time, but the great majority had to weather the occupation's regime. The widespread hope that the situation might improve with the Germans in power proved to be a fatal illusion. The Donbass was key to Nazi Germany's plans of colonial exploitation and geopolitical reorganization, which called for the elimination of large parts of the population. Even residents who were willing to work with the Germans quickly realized that the kolkhozes would not be disbanded, the ban on small businesses would not be lifted, and the terror would not end. All that the Germans – who, it should be noted, had received large amounts of primary commodities from the Donbass after the Nazi–Soviet Pact of 1939 – cared for was to restart the local industry to serve their purposes of resource extraction and arms production. To this end, the coal pits were reorganized under the roof of the Berg- und Hüttenwerksgesellschaft Ost (BHO), mining specialists from the Ruhr were deployed to the Donbass and a campaign of unbridled terror began. In a historical study of the Donbass, Tanja Penter has analysed this world of hunger, reprisals, forced labour and mass murder, showing that the area was ground zero for German policies in Eastern Europe. The retreating Red Army had left scorched earth, damaging shaft mines, hauling engines, boiler houses and workshops to render them unusable. Under the pretence of searches, the Germans – military personnel as well as civilian employees of the occupation regime – plundered what was left. The first transport of workers into the Reich departed in January 1942; all in all, more than 335,000 people were deported from the Donbass for forced labour, 252,239 from Stalino Oblast and 83,757 from Voroshilovgrad (now Lugansk) Oblast.

In Stalino Oblast alone, 150,000 Soviet prisoners of war died. From the first day, the Donbass's Jews and 'gypsies' were targets of a systematic campaign of extermination. A ghetto briefly existed in Stalino's Belyi Karer neighbourhood. The Jews of Stalino, Mariupol, Voroshilovgrad and Kramatorsk who had not managed to escape were murdered; around 16,000 in Stalino, between 8,000 and 9,000 in Mariupol. Official investigations have tallied mass graves containing over 323,000 bodies in Stalino Oblast; 174,000 of the dead were civilians, 149,000 captured Red Army soldiers. Many of the prisoners of war who survived the German terror regime found themselves branded as 'traitors to the motherland' upon their return and disappeared into Stalin's camps. One of the largest mass graves was located in shaft 4–4bis in Kalinovka; others were identified in the Stalino prisoner-of-war camp on the grounds of the Lenin Club, which was destroyed in the war and not rebuilt until 1965. Kalinovka was also where those who had died of suffocation in the gas vans were taken. A witness later testified to these and other mass killings: 'Several vans arrived every day. The vans backed up to the shaft. Then the people had to undress, keeping on only their underwear or sometimes not even that. One by one the SD men took them to the pithead building, where they killed them. The bodies were thrown into the shaft.'

Like the scenes of Stalinist terror, the sites associated with the Germans (and their allies: the Italians had their 'Italian Casino' where the central market hall stands today) in Donetsk are still there if the visitor knows where to look: the Hotel Donbass was the head office of the Gestapo; the Hôtel Grande-Bretagne was a brothel 'in excellent German order' (admission: 3 marks); there was a 'labour bureau' and the city administration led by a mayor named A. A. Eichmann. In 1946–7 Stalino's municipal theatre and opera house hosted the trials against German war criminals and their collaborators. 'The hall is full to bursting. Workers, kolkhozniki, educated citizens and housewives have come. But they are not mere spectators . . . Not one who is here has not suffered from the defendants' crimes in one manner or another . . . Present, too, though invisible, are those who can no longer testify to the atrocities committed by Hitler's men because they were shot in the anti-tank trench outside Mariupol, flung into the shaft of the Kalinovka mine, or tortured to death in the prisoner-of-war camp in Novoekonomicheskoe.'

In the ten years beginning in 1943, over 320,000 private citizens in the Soviet Union were charged with collaboration, 93,590 of them in Ukraine; hundreds of thousands of Red Army soldiers and forced

German infantrymen fighting in a village near Donetsk, 1943. Here they have
blown up the basement of a house to 'burn out' Russian soldiers.

labourers released from German captivity were sent off into Stalin's
camps. In Stalino alone, 2,569 people were convicted of espionage for
the Germans, treason and collaboration. The Soviet narrative after the
war was for the most part structured by a simple antithesis: collaborators on one side, partisans on the other (Alexander Fadeev's novel *The
Young Guard*, in which their exploits take on mythical proportions, is
set in the Donbass city of Krasnodon). What this rigid formula fails to
acknowledge is the actual conduct of the majority of the population,
people who neither joined the resistance nor sided with the enemy but
simply tried to survive day after day in the occupied cities – a painful
problem for all of Europe, not just for Ukrainians and Russians.

The devastations, loss of human lives and chaos wrought by the
Second World War left the Donbass a radically different place. Matters
were made worse by a famine in 1946–7 that killed a million people.
The fruits of the Herculean development efforts of the pre-war decades
lay in ruins; society had to start again from square one. A country
that had emerged from the 1930s bereft of its best people, a nation of
terrorized and traumatized citizens, had been shattered by the war; not
a stone had been left standing. Virtually every horror imaginable had
been visited upon the Soviet citizenry: targeted starvation and extermination, mass deportations and mass migrations, slave labour in its

German and Soviet versions, mass terror and genocide. As some fled the Donbass, others sought refuge in it. The continuity of generations was broken because the war had devoured entire age cohorts; it would take decades for the country to return to a balanced gender ratio. A society that had been unstable and in flux as it was, whose structures and identities had been liquidated, was, after the destructions and upheavals of war, embroiled in flagrant disintegration – and was saved only by the unifying bond of a patriotism born from the battle for survival. Yet the yearned-for end of the war turned out to be no more than the transition to a new, the Cold War.

Escape routes and the routes of the deportations intersected in this ground zero of the post-war Soviet Union. Conscripted labourers had arrived from the western lands that Stalin had occupied in 1939 – Galicia, northern Bukovina and Bessarabia. The Germans had in turn deported hundreds of thousands of forced labourers. The front-line had passed over the city, and each side had identified its chosen victims in advance. Each side had had its enemies and its collaborators, and some had played both parts. The Donbass had become an underground that defied control, a haven for all those who had made it out alive: Red partisans and members of the nationalist Ukrainian Insurgent Army, deserters, deported peasants who had returned, Jews who had survived but were no longer welcome at home and were chased away yet again, uprooted individuals of all nationalities – a veritable society of 'displaced persons'. Donetsk had been a laboratory for German planners who saw the opportunity to put their dreams of a new Europe into practice: experts in transportation who laid out arterial roads to Stalino and Krivoi Rog and oil pipelines further out, to Maikop and Baku, mining specialists and specialists – more than a few of them with advanced degrees – in 'Eastern population policy', which is to say, genocide. Millions of German soldiers of all branches had come to know the areas where today's battles are being waged. Every place now mentioned in the nightly news about the fighting in eastern Ukraine already figured in the reports of that other war's progress and announcements of victory on German newsreels. And still the Germans, who are so proud of having 'come to terms with their past', block out the fact that what is colloquially known as the *Russlandfeldzug*, the Russian campaign, was also a campaign against Ukraine. The Donbass was among its battlefields.

Donetsk: Reconstruction and the Return of War

Stalino has been Donetsk since 1961, and the place where a statue of the dictator once stood is now taken up by a monument to the city's founder, John Hughes (his ruined residence is marked on Google Maps, but I was unable to find it in the actual city). The area was resettled, its infrastructure repaired with astonishing celerity, but it was also

Artyom Street, Voroshilovsky District, Donetsk.

the scene of repeated protests and skirmishes between the authorities and a working class that, conscious of its strength, no longer put up with every new humiliation. It is perhaps no wonder that the Donbass became the cradle of a new labour movement: its workers were sick of being the transmission belt on the wheels of the state, the union bureaucracy and the factory directors. By the late 1970s, miners such as Vladimir Klebanov and Aleksei Nikitin, inspired by the experiences in Poland, harnessed spontaneous resistance in the pits to push for the establishment of independent unions. Unlike in Poland, however, the gulf between the rebellious workers and the intelligentsia in the capital proved unbridgeable; even Andrei Sakharov dismissed Klebanov's initiative because it allegedly focused solely on 'material issues' such as wages, housing and consumer goods. The nascent Ukrainian national movement Rukh likewise did not take a particular interest in the workers in the Donbass. Still, the strikes that broke out in 1989 and quickly spread were among the developments that precipitated or at least expedited the end of the Soviet Union. The Donbass also produced prominent dissidents and representatives of the civil rights movement such as Viacheslav Chornovil and the poet Vasyl Stus. The high turnout for the referendum on Ukrainian independence and the large majorities that supported it – 84 per cent voted in favour in Donetsk, 83.9 per cent in Lugansk – reflected the hope that an independent Ukraine would swiftly resolve all the problems that had plagued the Donbass's population for years. Disappointment set in soon enough; the communists regained much of their erstwhile influence and, postponing overdue structural reforms, banked on forcing the new government in Kiev to keep the subsidies coming indefinitely. The Party of Regions and the oligarchs who had risen to power in the chaos of the transition were adept at mobilizing the myth of the mineworker and securing government grants, but they had no interest in modernizing the Donbass, which would inevitably have entailed shutting down unprofitable factories and pits. Instead they eviscerated the remains of the socialist economy, stashed their wealth away, mostly in (Western) foreign countries, and used the miners to exert pressure on 'Kiev' to accede to their demands. 'Kiev', for its part, was long content to look down on the Donbass as a backwater, a reservation inhabited by people who were stuck in the Soviet mentality. Both sides miscalculated, with disastrous consequences. The gamble with the Donbass's concerns and anxieties that had long allowed the Party of Regions and Yanukovych to exploit the region slipped – or rather, was wrested – from their hands. Others have taken the reins and, amid chants of 'For Novorossiya!', turned the Donbass into a stomping ground for failed existences and imperialist adventurers who care nothing for the region's future and a testing area for Russian military experts trying out new forms of warfare. The history of the German Freikorps of the interwar years teaches us that the centre of power cannot forever remain unaffected by this kind of exportation of violence. It is only a matter of time until the crisis escalates. The damage and the loss of lives will be horrendous – in the Donbass, but not only in the Donbass.

(2015)

TEN

CZERNOWITZ:
CITY UPON A HILL

THAT REAL PLACES are eclipsed by their literary prominence, their significance as metaphors, would appear to be a price that cultures focused on words and texts must pay. Still, it is always a loss of concreteness, a curtailing of the registers of perception, that not even the most dedicated exercise in exegesis can make up for. The case of Czernowitz, however, was compounded by something else: the city that, thanks to its association with Paul Celan and Rose Ausländer, will forever be inscribed on the map of world literature had really vanished, first into the Nazis' mass graves and gas chambers, then into Stalin's empire. Once the Iron Curtain went down over Central Europe, it was virtually inaccessible. So my rediscovery of Czernowitz/Chernovtsy/Cernăuți/Chernivtsi in the 1980s virtually necessitated a description of the borders that I had to cross or overcome as I sought to locate not just the literary but the real topos. That is why the account of my journey that follows is also a story of decelerated time, practices of border-crossing, and the overwhelming encounter with an urban fabric that had endured all stages of Sovietization and provincialization and yet had borne up. Many of the changes that were in the air even then arrived soon enough, and to transformative effect: the borders cutting it off from Romania and all of southeastern Europe are open; Chernivtsi emerged as a central hub in the network of small traders and bazaars; the literary world started coming, and the writers and artists who arrived for the annual Meridian Czernowitz literature festival discovered that poems have places where they were written and that interpretations can only benefit from the reader's familiarity with these places as he pores over the texts. A tourist equipped with a Soviet-era city map would lose his way in today's Chernivtsi. Lenin

Street no longer exists; all it takes to rename a street is a decree. Taking possession of the city's rich and complex cultural heritage, preserving and nurturing the culture of Czernowitz as part of Ukrainian culture: that is a far greater challenge.

(2015)

✛

CZERNOWITZ IS REAL and not merely a topos of the literary world. It is a modern-day city, and not even a small and insignificant one, with a population of around 260,000. Czernowitz leads a literary existence, as it were, in books about the life and work of Paul Celan, the poet, who was born and raised here; it figures in the poems of Rose Ausländer, and students of Georg Büchner's writings know that the novelist and scholar who produced the first complete edition, Karl Emil Franzos, grew up here. That Czernowitz lives on in pictures and illustrated books, usually produced by the organizations of the Bukovina Germans, who are fond of apostrophizing it as a 'German city'. But Czernowitz is real, not just a memory, a backdrop, an archetypal example of what has been lost. It is a place one can travel to.

The trip is not an easy one. The difficulties begin with the question of how to get there. On the railway map in Baedeker's guide to Austria–Hungary from before the First World War, Czernowitz is sure of its place in the world; though located on the eastern edge of the Habsburg Empire, it is fully integrated in the network of lines that, in the Austrian and Czech lands, is so tightly knit that it becomes difficult to tell the various connections apart, while the Galician crown land and the plains of Hungary still leave much room for development. Back then, Czernowitz was a well-known destination, reached from Kraków via Lemberg. It was also an interchange station for travellers coming from Lemberg and bound for Odessa or making the long trip from Bucharest to Warsaw. Today, by contrast, the would-be visitor has trouble chasing down a map that gives him so much as a sense of the city's location. Chernovtsy is where contemporary maps end, making it impossible to envision how it is, or was, connected to the rest of the world.

Chernovtsy, which was Austrian once upon a time, is far away from today's shrunken Austria, on the far side of several borders. A Romanian map – and between the wars, the city was Romanian – ends at the border from which it is just over 32 kilometres (20 miles) to the former Cernăuţi. On a map of the Soviet Union, or even of the Ukrainian Soviet Republic, it is a tiny border town, barely visible amid the tangled web of larger cities and more important connections. Chernovtsy is a city marginalized, almost excluded, by cartography. To get a feeling for where it is situated, one must purchase a map of Central Europe that, though it may be imprecise in many respects, gets this one crucial fact right. One must disregard the new borders, must set the perspectives of the new capitals aside, to ascertain its place – and I am not referring to the intersection of the 26th degree of east longitude and the 48th parallel.

Modern-day travel agents, even ones that specialize in destinations off the beaten track, are utterly out of their depth when asked to help prepare a trip to Czernowitz, now officially known as Chernovtsy. I am advised to take a train from Berlin to Brest and continue southward, even though – in this respect at least, the network map in the old Baedeker is still correct – there is a railway line from Berlin via Kraków, Lvov and Chernovtsy to Bucharest. Hotel reservations must be confirmed by Intourist headquarters in Moscow, almost a thousand kilometres from Chernovtsy. The travel agent cannot issue a through ticket because the leg to Kraków is operated by the Polish State Railways; the Soviet Railways takes over at the Polish–Soviet border. Yet what happens when the Soviet train to Lvov and Chernovtsy is fully booked, which it is apt to be, but I cannot linger because I have only a transit visa for Poland? This sort of voyage is in many ways incalculable from the outset, a gradual approach from city to city. I work my way forward. Looking at the map, I am acutely aware of how small and intricately nested Europe is, even if the intervals stretch out indefinitely and time slows to a crawl. I must readjust my internal clock or I will lose my nerve.

And so it is good that the trip begins in East Berlin, at the Lichtenberg station. The queues before the desks at the Friedrichstraße border checkpoint, where the natives of West Berlin are sundered from those of East Berlin and the citizens of West Germany from those of other nations, move so slowly that, even though I have left home early enough, I worry that I will miss my train, which departs within sight of my city and yet from a different country. It is good that I have to pass through the checkpoint at Friedrichstraße because it delivers with a punch the experience that will repeat itself again and again over the next several days: people laden with suitcases advancing centimetre by centimetre, the official glancing into the passport and the list of wanted persons, the ponderous business of stamp and ink pad, the imposingly momentous scrutinizing of dates and foreign currencies, the tenseness that builds up inside me as time is painfully dilated. Border-crossing and transit as Procrustean procedures that forcibly accustom me to foreign rhythms of time.

Variations on this game will play out over the next few days: the crowds of passengers will be of different compositions – Polish parents and children with backpacks on the train from Berlin to Kraków; Soviet tourists who have crammed their compartments with television sets and jeans from Poland's black markets on the leg from Kraków to Lvov. When the train will leave Chernovtsy for Bucharest, almost all passengers will be Soviet Jews; some will be headed towards the airport, where they will board an El Al aeroplane, and some will never return. The play of expressions on the officials' faces, too, will vary: distrust will remain the keynote, but each border policeman will add a touch of national flair. The Polish will make sure the Russians understand that they cannot keep shopping until nothing is left in Poland without paying outrageous customs duties, a cruel game they like to play with harmless day-trippers; at the Soviet–Romanian border, the Soviet guards will let it be known that the car full of emigrants is no longer even a nuisance because it has been coming through late in the evening for some time now; their Romanian colleagues will be eager to offer advantageous exchange rates for hard currencies and friendlier to foreigners than to their countrymen.

The journey from Berlin to Czernowitz: that is a night spent on an overheated train via Wrocław to Kraków, a trip through the dark, the compartments crowded with young people and workers, as though the whole country were working the night shift, the platforms cold and empty in the neon light that is too dim to illuminate the wide arches of Wrocław Central Station. It is a night on an iron nerve cord singing with the incessant motion of endless freight trains from the Upper Silesian Industrial Region around Katowice towards the coast, now passing by in slow motion so that I can read the inscriptions on the cars, now rushing past, their compression waves bursting in upon the compartment and jolting the dozing passengers awake.

Kraków in passing: the fog rising from the Vistula on this late autumn day is so thick that it obscures the steeples of the churches and towers of the Wawel even when the visitor stands at their feet – the skyscrapers of the Middle Ages. The air is heavy with the smoke and scent of the dead leaves that city workers have raked up in the parks encircling the old town and set on fire.

Lovely Lvov, that city of broad streets and handsome buildings, is feverish with people; one might think that a million live here. Burning leaves, again, before the pompous facades of the Hotel George and the old Diet of Galicia and Lodomeria. The autumn foliage in the municipal park is thinning.

And then another night on the train – almost twelve hours for a distance the Austro-Hungarian Empire's engines covered in five and a quarter. The steady rattling of a slow-moving train might be lulling, but this one is too slow for comfort and makes frequent stops; the stations blinking into the rainy autumn morning's light are no longer the Habsburg ochre but a luminous red and white. Still, we have not fallen out of time: the train's intercom, which is set to an unbearably high volume, broadcasts the news – this or that functionary in Kazakhstan has been deposed, another has stepped down 'for reasons of age', a new production is about to premiere at the Mayakovsky Theatre in Moscow. The youngsters in the neighbouring cabin are in a rebellious spirit and scold the conductor, who is everywhere but where she is supposed to be: serving the passengers. In my own compartment, a robust blonde is putting her husband, who has downed a whole bottle of vodka, to bed, consoling him that their day of shopping in Lvov was a success. They offer me one of the ten bottles of beer they bought. When I show them photographs of Czernowitz's city hall and the old Jewish temple, they ooh and aah – no wonder, for as I will learn later, there are no pictures, no old postcards to be had anywhere in Chernovtsy, not even of what were once the most representative buildings in the city. I am coming to a place that has no picture of itself.

Colonial Town

It is more easily said than done: forming a picture of a city that spoke and still speaks many languages. But why not start with what is plain to the eye? Chernovtsy is a svelte city, that is something I notice on my very first taxi ride from the station to the hotel, which, contrary to my expectations, is not in the centre but far out in a new neighbourhood. The complex has only just been finished, with everything one could wish for – bars, restaurants, a sauna, a retail shop for travellers who can pay in hard currencies – and at fifteen storeys it is so tall that at night it almost touches the moon. One is relieved that the planners who put it here and the Hungarians who built it stayed away from the city proper.

Pulling out of the square outside the station, which has the look of an ocean steamer that has cast anchor by the tracks that converge here, white, grandiose, with a mighty dome, the taxi driver steps on the accelerator as the street ascends steeply towards the centre and the old town square before levelling off when we head out into the suburbs. Chernovtsy sits on an elevation, a narrow ridge, and this situation above the valley of the River Pruth lends it an air of lightness and elegance: rather than thronged and densely built up like so many medieval towns hemmed in by hills, it is airy, spacious and spread out like a carpet. Only around Tsentralnaya Square do the buildings rise to three or five storeys, and there Chernovtsy is a city of the nineteenth and early twentieth centuries through and through, every square metre put to some use, the facades vying for the passerby's attention.

To go downtown in Chernovtsy is to go uphill. Then again, that hill itself is merely a foothill of the nearby Carpathian Mountains, and one can see the nearest higher hills and ridges from various vantage points in the city. The landscape lives in Rose Ausländer's poetry:

> Green mother
> Bukovina
> Butterflies in the hair
>
> Drink
> Says the sun
> Red milk of melons
> White milk of maize
> I turned it sweet
>
> Violet pinecones
> Air wings, birds and leaves
>
> Back of the Carpathians
> Fatherly
> Invites you
> To carry you

Four tongues
Four-tongued songs

People
Who understand one another

The city is quickly traversed, even on foot, and the visitor soon realizes that its *leggerezza* is not just due to its situation on a hilltop. It is in large part a result of planning, the spaciousness of the colonial town whose architects took the long view and were sure to lay out squares and parks. This is not a city that outgrew the narrow lanes and cramped houses of an overcrowded medieval town. Czernowitz was born the moment it became the Austrian monarchy's easternmost outpost. Tsentralnaya Square, formerly known as Ringplatz, is the signature feature of any urban structure on the Habsburg continent – it is where all ventures begin and all roads converge. Mehlplatz or Flour Square, Getreideplatz or Corn Square, Holzplatz or Wood Square; old names that point to the trades that catered to the growing city; Sturmplatz signals that Czernowitz was not least importantly also a garrison town. These squares have been renamed several times since and are no longer quite so accurately rectangular, but they continue to define the urban relief. What followed was merely a process of compaction; buildings were enlarged until the gaps were closed, the city attained a new solidity. Yet all of that happened within less than a century. The city we see today was complete by 1930. The Czernowitz that was the legacy of the Habsburg monarchy consists of the characteristic structures of a colonial town in the empire's eastern reaches: city hall, central post office, university, stock exchange, customhouse, police and prison, the revenue authority, barracks, hospitals, lyceums and the Chamber of Commerce and Industry. And then there were the buildings of a city that had come into its own, that was no longer just an administrative seat but a flourishing cultural and economic centre: middle-class homes, tenements, villas, department stores, hotels, restaurants, newspaper publishers' offices and schools. Most saliently, Czernowitz was a city of many creeds and nations: see the enormous residence of the Bukovinian and Dalmatian Metropolitans, the minster said to have been inspired by St Isaac's Cathedral in St Petersburg, the Russian Orthodox, Greek Catholic, Armenian and Protestant churches, the Polish monastery, the splendid Israelite temple and the old synagogue.

Czernowitz postcard of the Chamber of Commerce and Industry, Chernivtsi, 1910.

The city is not overly large and lies before the visitor like an open book, perhaps especially in the spring and autumn. Even in the densely built-up old town, the facades are aglow with the red leaves of the grapevines that grow everywhere. Chernovtsy is translucent like the autumnal parks. It has enough room for spacious single-storey homes surrounded by gardens – meadows, really – with apple trees. It has room for large courtyards the visitor glimpses as he walks along the streets. Open to the sun, with loggias and verandas on all sides, lushly overgrown with grapevines, they momentarily transport him to more southerly climes. Only the most luxurious amenities, it seems, persuaded the people of Czernowitz to forsake life in the garden for the newly built apartment houses. A community of detached-home dwellers must have had more than its share of individualists. To grow up here was to be an urbanite and yet know the nightingale's song. Rose Ausländer allows us to hear the rushing of the cold river coming down from the Carpathians:

> The pebbles chirred in the Pruth
> Carved fleeting patterns into
> Our soles
>
> Narcissuses we lay in the water's blank surface
> Held ourselves in our arms

At night covered by the wind
Bed teeming with fish
A goldfish the moon

Whisper of sidelocks
The rabbi in caftan and shtreimel
Surrounded by bliss-eyed Chassidim

Birds – we know not
Their names their cry
Beckons and startles
Our plumage too is complete
We follow you
Synagogues pitching and tossing
Across fields of maize

Little Austria

The town on the hill above the Pruth is the capital of Bukovina, which, like the German 'Buchenland', means 'land of beeches'. What I know about the city and region I learned from my Intourist guide, from books published by former Bukovina Germans in West Germany, from a history of the Jews of Bukovina that came out in Tel Aviv, and from the almost indecipherable secret language of its poets. That is hardly all there is to know – I would have to read Romanian and Ukrainian and perhaps even Armenian to round out the picture.

Czernowitz is first mentioned in a document in 1408, but its history goes further back. Scythians and Dacians, Huns and Hungarians, wild Pecheneg and Cuman tribesmen on horseback traversed the hill country between the Pruth and Siret rivers. The town's name indicates that it was a Slavic settlement before it became a provincial capital in the Habsburg Empire. Several trade routes converged at the ford across the Pruth, connecting Constantinople to Nuremberg and the towns of Transylvania to Kraków and the Baltic Sea. Part of the Principality of Moldavia for several centuries and briefly Polish, the area was the scene of frequent skirmishes between Turks and Poles, and King Charles XII of Sweden stopped here in 1709 after his defeat at the hands of Peter the Great in the Battle of Poltava. So the town had a history before the Austrians arrived – a Slavic, Moldavian, Turkish,

Polish and, with the immigration of Jewish refugees from Western Europe, Jewish history. Still, the city that greets the visitor today came into being on 31 August 1774, the day the Austrian general Gabriel Baron of Splény marched in; Karl Freiherr von Enzenberg was the first head of the newly established military district. A *Kreis* within the Kingdom of Galicia and Lodomeria from 1786 and a separate crown land from 1849, Bukovina was part of the Habsburg Empire from 1775 until 1918, when it was annexed by Romania, whose troops moved into the northern part in November of that year. After a Soviet ultimatum in June 1940, the Red Army occupied northern Bukovina and Bessarabia. Only a year later, in June 1941, Romania retook Cernăuţi with help from German command units: the war against the Soviet Union had begun.

On 29 March 1944 – the war had turned against the Germans – Soviet troops returned, and Chernovtsy became the capital of Chernovtsy Oblast, a division of the Ukrainian Soviet Socialist Republic, while southern Bukovina remained Romanian. The boundary runs 32 kilometres (20 miles) south of the city, and residents who want to visit the former centres of Chassidism on the other side must obtain the usual special permits for border zones. These dry dates and facts begin to suggest what the city has been through, especially in the twentieth century.

Czernowitz's rise as a capital with its own character began with the establishment of the Austrian administration. Around 1800 the town had no more than 6,000 residents – 'Germans, Moldavians, Jews, Armenians, Ruthenians'. That number grew to 47,000 by 1900 and 120,000 by 1930. The city's population consisted entirely of large minorities, a fact that was crucial to its development. The 1930 census lists around 45,000 Jews, 30,000 Romanians, 14,000 Ruthenians, 12,000 Poles and 18,000 Germans, most of whom lived in Rosch (Rosha), a suburb predominantly inhabited by Swabians that still felt like a village unto itself; there were also several dozen smaller nationalities who had found a home in the area: Armenians, Georgians, Roma, Hutsuls, Turks and Hungarians.

The city today is still ethnically mixed, the wordsmiths organized in the local writers' guild still haggle in four languages, the television station broadcasts in Ukrainian, Moldovan and Russian, and it is not difficult to meet locals who speak Romanian or German. Still, as the Intourist guide declares, Chernovtsy is now a Ukrainian city: Ukrainians make up almost 70 per cent of its population, which has grown to 260,000 residents; Moldovans account for 9 per cent, Romanians for 10 per cent and the Jewish community numbers around 10,000.

Compared to the uniform cities of post-war Europe, that may seem like a colourful mélange, but those who knew Czernowitz – a miniature replica of the multi-ethnic empire, a 'Little Austria' – would presumably not recognize today's Chernovtsy. It has become hard to believe that, as long as an ageing monarch in the distant and yet accessible capital watched over his subjects in the crown land, all its ethnic and religious groups got along.

> Back of the Carpathians
> Fatherly
> Invites you
> To carry you
>
> Four tongues
> Four-tongued songs
>
> People
> Who understand one another

Yet how can we, for whom no road leads back to the world before the rupture, imagine this place?

> Where
> In the time without Austria does my word grow
> Into the roots
> It is of the land of beeches
> I think
> Uprooted word
> Birds lost to the wind

That is how Rose Ausländer put it. It takes a bit of knowledge and historical imagination to envision, behind the facades, which are as handsome as they were, the differentiations of an intricately structured and diversely organized multicultural urban community. Yet the imagination finds purchase in documents: narratives, autobiographies, the protocols of the city's past life. Take, for instance, the university, which now occupies the residence of the metropolitans: a splendid ensemble with a beautiful park over which the scent of cypress trees wafts, built between 1864 and 1875 to the designs of the architect Josef Hlávka from Prague, with concessions to the stylistic vernacular of Greek Orthodoxy, with elements from Byzantium and Moorish Spain, with magnificent staircases and endless hallways, with unfired bricks and glazed roof tiles, with a church containing a gold-gleaming iconostasis.

Yet the residence, a reconstruction of the original that went up in flames when the Germans and Romanians retreated, did not become home to the university until after the war; the church is now a lecture and concert hall. The Alma Mater Francisco-Josephina Cernautiensis used to reside in more modest Neoclassical buildings along Universitätsstrasse, needing no outward splendour: it had an objective, and it accomplished that objective. Several generations of students benefited from the improbable peaceful coexistence of the many cultures that intersected here. Europe's easternmost German university was inaugurated on the occasion of the centennial of Bukovina's union with Austria on 4 October 1875. It initially had three faculties: Greek Orthodox theology, jurisprudence and philosophy. The first rector, Dr Tomaszczuk, already saw the need to defend the new institution against association with the widely maligned notion of Austria's 'cultural mission'. Classes and exams were held in German, at the theological faculty also in Romanian, Ukrainian and Church Slavonic. Some of the professors were native Bukovinians, while others came from Vienna, Graz, Heidelberg, Paris, Lvov, Riga and Sibiu. Of the 44 men who were elected to the rector's office between 1875 and 1919, there were 22 Germans, eleven Romanians, nine Jews and two Ukrainians. Instruction in German was more than an instrument of Germanization. Czernowitz attracted students from Galicia, Romania, Poland, Serbia, Hungary, Croatia, the Banat, Dalmatia, Bosnia, Bulgaria and Greece, as well as Germans and Austrians in considerable numbers. Of the students enrolled at the university in the last year of peace before the First World War, 458 said German was their native language; 310 had grown up speaking Romanian, 303 Ukrainian, 86 Polish and 41, another language. Yet 431 of those 458 German speakers, and two-thirds of all students, were Jewish. Hence the diversity of their associations and clubs; hence the multilingualism of the treasury of songs they performed at their *commercia*. The German fraternities were called Austria, Alemannia and Gothia; the Jewish ones, Hasmonea, Zephira and Hebronia; the

Romanians had their Junimea; the Ukrainians, their Soyuz, Zaporizhia and Mazepa.

Similarly, the city's athletic fields saw contests between clubs called Jahn and Makkabi, Polonia and Dovbush. Its squares and public spaces – especially the municipal garden with the casino and the markets – mirrored its social and cultural composition. Ice cream and matzos, pretzels and sunflower seeds were sold from stalls. Swabian peasant women from Rosch, Hutsuls from the mountains, Jewish pedlars encountered each other on the markets, set apart by their attire and their language. There were several 'national houses', including the German house, in the characteristic style of the turn of the century, a Romantic half-timbered multi-storey structure with large rooms, and, not far away, the Ukrainian community centre and the Polish house. Today, the German house is a children's movie theatre, and only a silver-coated stag's head with enormous antlers and the screening room's beer-hall architecture remain as evidence of its erstwhile function. The Ukrainian house, too, has been converted into a cinema. The house of Jewish culture on Theatre Square – the sprawling ostentatious neo-Baroque facade, painted blue and white, bears the year 1908 – is now used by the light industry workers' culture club. Two vertices have been clipped from the Stars of David in the banisters; disco parties and Mister and Miss Chernovtsy contests advertised on posters throughout the city are held in the mirrored hall on the ground floor, and at night, before the building closes, teenagers on souped-up motorcycles race past each other at breakneck speed as though in a medieval tournament, the deafening noise alarming the spectators leaving the nearby theatre. There was a time when Dr Repta, the metropolitan, arranged for safe storage of the Torah scrolls as the Russian army was closing in on the city in the First World War; when the German house's management offered its lecture hall because the Jewish house's was too small for the crowds who had come to hear Theodor Herzl speak. Allow me to quote at length from the memoirs of a native of Czernowitz who escaped to Tel Aviv. He remembered the area around the old Fountain Square, where the upper and lower towns abutted:

> The common people called the place where all the streets inhabited by Jews intersected the 'Ham'. It was a world unto itself. Already in the early morning hours it bustled with life. Men hurried to the prayer houses or to their businesses. Housewives did their shopping. There was Juda Feuer's shop, where all sorts

of necessities could be found. Across the street, Ruthenian farmers from surrounding villages who had come to town to find casual work crowded in front of a tavern where a Jew sold spirits. There were many arguments among them, some of which led to fistfights. A city policeman was constantly posted there. He never smiled because he was conscious of the dignity of his position. On Sundays, he wore his parade uniform and a rooster feather fluttered on his black hat. Unimpressed by his authority, the young people from the surrounding streets made fun of him, called him mocking names, and outran him when he tried to chase them down. The policemen, mostly of Ruthenian nationality, knew only a smattering of German: '*Abu gengen Sie, abu stehen Sie zur Seite*', one would hear them say.

The wholesale bakery belonging to Mordechai Weissmann's heirs was nearby. In the basements of the one-storey houses, women sold bread, pretzels, other baked goods and sweets to passersby and noisy children in whose outstretched little hands a red copper coin lent the necessary emphasis to their desire. On the eastern side of the square, a small alleyway led to the Jewish hospital and later to the home for the elderly. Shops of all sorts lined Springbrunnengasse. Several sold used clothing. Nearby, sharp aromas escaped from the butcher shops and fish stores. The transactions and bargaining took place with much loud conversation. The noise lasted until late into the evening. On the street that led past Altmarkt Square stood the tables for dressed poultry. Salesladies sold their wares on the small slope that later became Theodor Herzl Square. Eggs, vegetables and chickens were supplied by peasant women from the countryside whose white kerchiefs made them visible from a distance and the 'Swabians' from the suburb of Rosch, where their ancestors had settled since the reign of Emperor Joseph II. Craftsmen of all sorts had set up their businesses in the surrounding houses. There was also no lack of inns, taverns and canteens in which the regulars were offered fish prepared in the traditional manner in addition to a good drink.

The upper town with its stores, shopping streets, restaurants and parks was where the pleasanter sides of life were set – or so it seemed in retrospect:

One who thinks back with longing on his vanished youth cannot forget the small pleasures the city offered. One memory picture crowds out the other and all bring back magically happy experiences. Unforgettable are the Sunday strolls along the eastern edge of Ringplatz, known as 'Pardini Heights', which was not actually an elevation and got its name from Heinrich Pardini's university bookstore (later Engel & Suchanka). There stood groups of young officers from the garrison in their resplendent parade uniforms; students from Franz-Josephs-Universität ambled by, their caps making for a colourful picture. Coquettish girls smiled and chattered, accepting the challenging and admiring looks of the men as if they were homage due to them, and appeared not to hear the remarks addressed to them. Every Wednesday afternoon, the band of the Imperial and Royal Infantry Regiment No. 41 'Archduke Eugen' under Kosteletzky's direction played not far from the Tomaszczuk monument and opposite the garden restaurant, the 'Kursalon', in the municipal park. The beautiful main promenade was filled with people from one end to the other and there was little chance of getting a seat on one of the garden benches. The city had other public gardens. On 'Göbelshöhe', the planted slope between Franzosgasse and Steiner's brewery, outdoor parties of all sorts with confetti battles were held every summer. Joy and merriment ruled here, and many a high school student overcame his shyness and threw the contents of a full confetti container over his admired beauty to be rewarded with a fleeting smile. Strollers in need of quiet sought out the shade beneath the trees on Habsburghöhe (previously Bischofsberg), located behind the archbishop's palace, whose winding paths offered sweeping views of the Pruth valley. The cool and aroma-filled air in this paradise of evergreens was beneficial and refreshing in the hot summer months. The centrally located Franz-Josephs-Park with the grand statue of Empress Elisabeth and the seat of the state government in the background resembled a four-cornered island of green between heavily travelled streets. Children ran and shouted without cares in Schillerpark, whose freshly planted grounds lay along the road sloping down to the suburb of Rosch.

On summer evenings around the turn of the century, families liked to visit Katz's Garten on Russische Gasse (later Friedmann's milk bar and vegetarian restaurant). Entertainment was provided by the lively musician Schlomele Hirsch and his brother Leib, who played at all the weddings. Other 'garden taverns' included an establishment on Siebenbürger Straße, where a piano store and Gruder's ice-skating rink later stood, and the 'Beer Palace' on Rottgasse – after the building, which didn't look much like a palace, was torn down, this, too, became a popular ice-skating rink. During the hot summer months, a Jewish theatre would perform at one of these venues. The plays, mostly satires on the life of small-town Jews, satisfied only rather modest expectations.

Czernowitz was manifestly a healthy community, despite the conflicts and tensions that arose whenever one of the minorities tried to lord it over the others. And there was one language, German, that everyone in the city understood, although that did not make it a German city. Where the ethnic Germans lived among themselves, in Rosch, they spoke the Swabian dialect. High German was the idiom of Jewish Czernowitz, and the Jewish community donated the funds for the Schiller monument installed outside the municipal theatre, later relegated by the Romanians to the German house's courtyard. German was not just the official language of the Austrian authorities, it was the medium of social advancement, of progress, of intercourse with the wider world. It seems almost inconceivable today that a city located hundreds of kilometres outside the German-speaking lands was home to publishing ventures putting out a rich assortment of German-language newspapers and magazines. Of course, there were Romanian, Ukrainian and Polish periodicals as well, but the newspapers of record were in German, published by Jewish proprietors and edited by Jewish deskmen. Who would have imagined that a city of Czernowitz's size had five German-language dailies, not counting the evening editions? And that the better coffee houses held subscriptions to over a hundred papers and magazines? It takes a society of individualists to create the demand for such a wide range of competing opinions; it takes vital relationships with the outside world for the local papers to shake off the must of provincialism; it takes people who need communication no less than food and water to sustain a public sphere that seems almost hypertrophic today. And papers like the *Bukowiner Rundschau*, the *Bukowiner Nachrichten*, the *Czernowitzer Tagblatt* and the *Czernowitzer Allgemeine Zeitung* were read not only in Czernowitz but in Vienna and Bucharest. That is the sort of setting in which a distinctive new idiom is born. As Rose Ausländer put it,

> The various linguistic influences of course rubbed off on Bukovinian German, sometimes to less than salutary effect. But they also enriched it with new words and turns of phrase, endowing it with a peculiar physiognomy, a colour all its own. Beneath the surface of the sayable, deep and widely ramified roots extended into the various intertwined cultures, supplying the phrasing, the feeling for the sounds and imagery of language with sap and vigour. More than one in three inhabitants was Jewish, and that gave the city its particular hue. Old Jewish folklore, Chassidic legends 'were in the air', one took them in with each breath. This baroque linguistic milieu, this mythical-mystical sphere begot German and Jewish poets and writers: Paul Celan, Alfred Margul-Sperber, Immanuel Weissglas, Rose Ausländer, Alfred Kittner, Georg Drozdowski, David Goldfeld, Alfred Gong, Moses Rosenkranz, Gregor von Rezzori, the eminent lyric poet Itzig Manger, and others.

In a place like Czernowitz, language as such, language before any of its particular uses, was more than merely a means of communication. Where a single language is predominant, the linguistic community is, to those who grow up in it, a self-evident fact of life. Not so here, where one's relationship with one's mother tongue was a conscious allegiance.

And the residents of a city that stood apart from its environs like an island, that cast messages in bottles adrift and hoped to receive messages in return, inevitably formed a particular relationship with their world, which was distant and yet, paradoxically, one in which distances mattered little. What was thought and written in Bucharest, Vienna and Berlin was to them the thinking and writing of their peers, their neighbours. On their hill above the Pruth, they tuned in – the reception was crystal-clear – to conversations that took place far away and yet felt more connatural to them than the chatter of the peasantry in the surrounding countryside. This aloofness of an insular urban culture was what made it so rich and the cradle of an entire pleiad of German poets.

Czernowitz was a city of ecstatics and devotees. They were dedicated, in Schopenhauer's words, 'to the interest of thinking, not the thinking of interest'. The Orthodox Jews were pious devotees, 'Chassidim', of one or another 'holy' rabbi. The practical concerns of life were irrelevant to them. Many had no vocation and were supported by their wives, who were proud to be married to a 'man of learning'; they spent their lives 'learning' from the 'holy books' and blissfully hearkened to the wise words of their rabbi. The assimilated Jews and the educated Germans, Ukrainians, Romanians were devotees as well: of philosophers, political thinkers, poets, artists, composers or mystics. Karl Kraus had a large congregation of admirers in Czernowitz; you would see them, the *Fackel* in hand, in the streets and parks, in the forests and along the banks of the Pruth . . . A large flock professed the 'doctrine' of the eminent Berlin philosopher Constantin Brunner, who is only now coming to the attention of larger audiences thanks to translations into English and French. Nowhere else, not even in his own Berlin, did Brunner have more loyal followers than in Czernowitz . . . There were Schopenhauerians, Nietzsche-worshippers, Spinozists, Kantians, Marxists, Freudians; they raved over Hölderlin, Rilke, Stefan George, Trakl, Else Lasker-Schüler, Thomas Mann, Hesse, Gottfried Benn, Bertolt Brecht. They devoured the classical and modern works of literature in foreign languages, especially of French, Russian, English and American literature. Every disciple was utterly persuaded of his master's mission. They revered selflessly and with fervent enthusiasm: a word that modern criticism rejects as 'pathos' or sentimentality. In this atmosphere, anyone interested in the life of the mind was positively 'compelled' to grapple with philosophical, political, literary or artistic problems or to undertake his own attempts in one of these fields. – A city, a world that is no longer.

Pincer Movement

A city's spirit may be preserved in poems, but its topography is recorded in maps. When someone h as designs on a city, he puts his cartographers to work. The aggressor has sharp eyes, perhaps sharper than anyone

else's. He determines his objectives, he draws circles around the strategic targets, he marks the lines along which he will advance, he decides
what to capture and what to annihilate. City maps drawn by aggressors
are precise, unclouded by sentiment. The Nazis had such maps, and
preparing to travel to Czernowitz from Berlin, you can obtain them at
the Berliner Staatsbibliothek: 'Map of Czernowitz. Supplement accompanying the military-geographical survey of European Russia, file F
II, Ukraine, with Moldavian Republic and Crimea, ixth edition, 1941.
Special edition! III.41. For official use only.' This map was based on one
issued by Leon König, a Jewish publisher in Czernowitz. Bringing it to
Chernovtsy, you know more than any Intourist guide, and more also
than some locals whose families did not move here until after the war. It
registers everything: from the railway stations to the radio transmission
tower and the airfield; from the civilian authorities and the courts to
the statistical offices and school inspectorate; from the headquarters
of the constabulary to the jail. The aggressor has information on the
religious communities and has circled the churches and synagogues. He
knows where the schools are, the hospitals, the hotels: the Palast, the
Zentral, the Schwarzer Adler, the Gottlieb, the Bristol and the Pension
City, a boarding house where he will billet his staff officers.

And so the tourist explores the city with the aggressor's map in
hand, conscious that there is a second map he should ideally have as
well: the one compiled by the Soviet authorities. The moment the
German assault commenced and they needed to evacuate the city,
they deported thousands of residents to Russia in a single night –
saving some from the deportations to the camps of Transnistria that
the Romanians would set up. In both maps, the city appears as a trap
from which there is no escape.

Both conquering sides had their sights trained on the Jewish population, only the phraseologies were different. The ss-Brigadeführer Otto
Ohlendorf's Einsatzgruppe D persecuted the Jews as Jews, whereas the
Soviets arrested them as bourgeois and – unbelievably – as potential
Nazi accomplices. Never has a human group been hunted and elim-
inated with more absurd rationales. As Jews they bore the brunt of
nationalist and racist violence; as their city's middle class they drew
the hatred of its aggrieved poor, the 'masses'. Between the two surges
of violence, the Czernowitz that had been perished.

The buildings have not disappeared: except for an empty lot by
Tsentralnaya Square, the hostilities do not seem to have caused major

structural damage. The Germans set the Israelite temple on fire, but it was too massive, and even attempts to blow it up after the war could not shatter the imposing structure's walls. So the prominently located building now houses the October cinema; the walls have been white-washed, the dome and battlements are gone, but the outlines of the arched windows are still there. It is in fact quite unsuitable as a movie hall, since the mighty pillars supporting the roof block the view of the screen from large parts of the prayer hall. But does any one of the people standing in the ticket room or entering the lobby know – does anyone care – that this was once one of the most magnificent temples in all of Eastern Europe?

> Even from outside, it was a powerful sight to behold. It had a monumental main entrance and two side entrances (for women). One came into a spacious vestibule in which there was a memorial tablet on the wall with the names of the one hundred benefactors, among which were the oldest and most respected families of the city. From the vestibule – which also held a votive tablet for Heinrich Wagner – three doors led into the main room, which was distinguished by rich paintings and stuccowork. Ample light fell in through the coloured windows in both sidewalls. There were seats for the men on both sides of the main aisle as well as along both sidewalls. The women sat on two upper levels. The floors as well as the seats were made of oak and richly carved. The walls were light blue with paintings by pre-eminent artists. The dome had a blue back-ground sprinkled with golden stars. The altar and the Torah ark were sights to behold. On both sides of the stairs leading up to the altar were raised platforms for the chief rabbi and the chief cantor. At the centre of the bimah was a lectern for the preacher. Above the ark, which was provided with a red velvet cover embroidered with gold, burnt a silver eternal lamp. The temple had a capacity of one thousand people.

A red neon sign advertising the cinema now glows on the massive building at night; one might think that it is on fire. Services are held in a single one of the 88 synagogues the city had before the war. Others – especially those along the former Synagogengasse, now Henri Barbusse Street – have been repurposed as storage spaces; the imposing

Orthodox synagogue is used as a workshop by Goskino. Only the Jewish hospital is still in operation.

The map also shows the lane formerly named Wassilkogasse, and with the assistance of a clerk at the state archive in the former Jesuit church, its current name is quickly identified. This one, the reddish-brown house no. 5 with the Art Nouveau eagle on the facade, must have been Paul Celan's childhood home. And there, behind the municipal park, along today's Frunze and Fedkovych Streets, is the genteel neighbourhood that was the Jewish bourgeoisie's stronghold, with villas, almost mansions, a sampling of all the various styles in vogue around the turn of the century. Easily recognizable across the street from the temple is the Morgenroit building, where the Bund and other labour organizations worked to improve the common people's lot with educational programmes, lectures and libraries. A few buildings' functions have not changed: the prison, for example, is still a prison, though it is now obscured by a tall poster wall bearing Lenin's likeness that takes up the entire edge of the adjoining square, and the old constabulary headquarters is used by the KGB.

Each street, each building, takes on a different aspect. The Schwarzer Adler, now the Hotel Verkhovyna, had been commandeered by the Gestapo. The lift is currently out of service, as the porter kindly informs me. It is the one that appears in the diary of Dr Nathan Getzler, who lived in Montreal after the war:

> Wednesday, 9 July 1941. Neighbours who come into our hide-out report that 150 Jews were taken by the German Gestapo through the city to the target range and shot there. Among them was the chief rabbi, Dr Abraham Mark. Dr Mark along with the chief cantor Gurman, Jakob Galperin, Frühling, Josef Reininger and others had earlier been locked in the lift shaft of the Hotel 'Zum Schwarzen Adler'. The lift ran up and down and every time threatened to crush those imprisoned in the shaft. After these unfortunate people were tormented in this way for several days, they joined the group of those doomed to die and were taken to the Pruth near Bila and shot.

The staff of the Romanian Siguranţa and the German Gestapo comb Czernowitz's newspapers for the names of suspects. Fresh graves are dug in the Jewish cemetery. Hospitals are evacuated; the wretches living in the mental hospital are chased out into the street. Ukrainian and Romanian boys, cockades in their buttonholes, lead the patrols into the homes of Jews. The mob loots the abandoned apartments and stores. Romanian officers pad their salaries by selling passes, capitalizing on residents' mortal fear. When the deportations to the Transnistrian camps begin, the number of suicides reported day after day rises to around ten. A ghetto is established – there had never been a closed ghetto in Moldavia or Bukovina – and when its residents are led to the station, peasants are ready with their carts to earn a fare. An especially harrowing scene plays out on the corner of Dreifaltigkeitsgasse and Albertinengasse. The last members of the Boyan dynasty of rabbis leave their home to die in their finest clothes, their heads held high, the Torah scrolls in their hands. The spectators, Jews and Christians, watch in awe.

Tens of thousands died during the forced marches from Bukovina into the camps, in the quarries, labouring on road and railway construction sites. Very few found ways to stay in Czernowitz itself – either because they demonstrated that they were indispensable to keeping the city running or because the Romanian officials needed money. Rose Ausländer writes about this time:

> Linens of ice on Transnistria's fields
> Where the white reaper
> Reaped men
> No space no breeze
> Breathed
> No fire
> Warmed the corpses
> In the snowfield the corn slept
> Time slept
> On temples
>
> The heavenly balance's pointer
> A flashing icicle
> In 30 degrees Celsius below zero

No more than 6,000 of Czernowitz's 45,000 Jews survived. Time was frozen in those years:

Ice as far as the soul could reach

Daggers hung
From the roofs
The city was made of
Frozen glass
People hauled
Bags full of snow
To make frosty pyres

Once a song fell
From golden flakes
Onto the snowfield:
'Do you know the land
Where the lemons bloom?'
A land where lemons bloom?
Where blooms that land?
The snowmen
Did not know

The ice grew rampant
And sank
White roots
Into the marrow of our years

In less than three years, Czernowitz became a different city, although the streets and facades, the squares and houses were still the same. History falls apart: a time before, a time after.

We do not recognize us
Too wide between us
The Years
Fire
Burnt a hole
Into time

The stars
Too far between us

The fixed star
Knows only
Itself

'Before the Abyss of the Sky'

One wishes one could travel back in time to Czernowitz before the twentieth century's global wars, could get in contact with a community whose buildings, after all, still stand. But that would be no more than a conceit, an imaginary foothold where none exists: 'Fire / Burnt a hole / Into time'. That is why any search for traces of its history has an aspect of tourism, even if the visitor does not see himself as a tourist. There is no foothold, no vantage point from which what has happened could be made to make sense. Chernovtsy – and its fate was not singular; so many cities and towns of Central Europe suffered similar shocks – is a place where historical reasoning balks at historic madness. Hence the sense of resignation that colours the visitor's gaze upon the still-beautiful city, the aloofness with which he registers what was and notes the contemporary life that inhabits the extant structures. The houses along Tsentralnaya Square are beautiful – the savings bank building, for example, with the majolica frieze on the facade, designed by Hubert Gessner, an architect from Vienna, in 1920, signals the cosmopolitan spirit that left its imprint on cities across the monarchy. It now houses the local Party organization. The insurance buildings, the hotels, the stores on Tsentralnaya Square and the former Herrengasse speak to the energy and gumption that built this city, the entrepreneurial daring and unwavering will to succeed that animated its citizens. Each facade bears the features of the man who built it. The people who lived here cared for their property: they made sure that the brass mouldings and the glass display cases were polished to a shine, that the entrance radiated dignity and the interior breathed comfort. Nowadays such houses are mere branch establishments that might identically stand elsewhere.

People, things and homes were kernels of difference. To give just one example, there were ropemakers, carpenters, coopers, furriers, watchmakers, butchers, shoemakers, plumbers, bakers, barbers, coppersmiths, locksmiths, tinkers, glaziers, tailors, braziers, gold- and silversmiths, quilters, paperhangers, sign painters, stove setters, lorimers, cartwrights, blacksmiths, chimney sweeps, knackers, bricklayers, shochets, chazzans, solicitors and newspapermen. The street names reflected this immense diversity. Coming to Chernovtsy today, you know in advance that, like every city in the Soviet Union, it will have a statue of Lenin and a Kalinin Park, although nothing connects these namesakes to the city. The facades are individualistic, even excessively so – but the life in front of and behind them is the same as everywhere else: the peculiar slow-motion bustle characteristic of places where scarcity reigns; the resigned sluggishness that sets in when there is nothing to be discovered, only the same that exists everywhere else, the same canned fish, the same plastic bathtubs, the same books that are also sold in Kiev and Murmansk.

Such uniformity is conspicuous, almost painfully so, in a city that even today bears the imprint of individuation and difference. The shop windows and entrances are still embellished by the arabesques of advertising and brisk business, but there is nothing left to advertise or do business with. Splinters of what once made the region unique have survived in the cityscape: Roma in their colourful attire – here as elsewhere, the angels of nonconformity – can be seen on the avenues that were fashionable strolling promenades; Hutsuls are in town from the mountains, wearing what they have always worn, and not as folkloristic costumes, above their Soviet-made rubber boots. The markets, too, are such vestiges of the past. In the shadow of the old Hotel Bristol, now a student dormitory, between the low-slung Philharmonic Hall and mountains of cantaloupes piled up on the sidewalk, women sell live chickens, their feet tied together. Not a single book about Czernowitz is to be had in all of Chernovtsy, except for a guide to the local museum by the Ukrainian author Olha Kobylianska, who, a real Czernowitzer, also wrote in German and Polish, and a book in Ukrainian about the municipal theatre by Fellner & Helmer architects, Vienna. It is unlikely that the tourism organizations are trying to hide the easternmost capital of the Habsburg monarchy. Much more probably, the matter is far simpler: Chernovtsy, to them, is no more than a small provincial town in Ukraine, behind the times, in the middle of nowhere, a place where the newspapers from Moscow arrive in small batches and with considerable delay. They dream not of the Habsburg-era city but of a flat in the housing block on the edge of town. The new Intourist Hotel – to them it is the epitome of progress.

Residual or pseudo-forms of the typical business of a border town can be encountered in the vicinity of the hotel, where the Americans whose parents were born here and the German family who drove all the way from Moers to see the city of their ancestors have taken lodgings: Polish day-trippers who make no secret of what they are up to – they are hawking Western products; Romanian day-trippers stocking up on groceries; East German tourists who see I know not what in Czernowitz. The place feels more international than other cities of its size in the Ukrainian provinces. And where else would you find an old American-made Plymouth, now available for rent as a wedding car? Tens of thousands have emigrated over the past four decades – to Israel, to the United States, to West Berlin – and the winds that carried them off to faraway lands have not abated. The foreigners visiting the old homeland are easy to spot, at the Jewish cemetery, for example.

The surge that levelled everything struck not only the Jewish Czernowitz, whose synagogues were repurposed as workshops and storehouses. It struck the Armenian church, which has been converted into an organ concert hall. It seems the authorities insisted on turning the Sacred Heart of Jesus church in the centre into a museum of Bukovinian folklore and the Greek Orthodox one into a chess club. Nowhere else in the world are there as many secular facilities – cinemas, chess clubs, bathhouses and museums – that boast centuries-old frescoes and mosaics. The citizenry has no doubt gained the use of many a serviceable and beautiful building; but those buildings have been despoiled of their spirit. What was it that drove this great levelling? No evil intention, no dark machination, not even strategic objectives of the godless or militant atheism: it was the powerful momentum of the promises of a modernity that brought central heating and private bathrooms with running hot water – and turned the world ugly and grey.

How awkward the efforts are to restore some of the city's former splendour and individuality. Every evening, the orange-red glare of an illumination fills Tsentralnaya Square, a poor substitute for the sea of lights of a Western metropolis. But that is mere embellishment, decoration slapped on facades that no longer glow from within. The few years of the Second World War were the culmination of the drama that cities like Czernowitz lived through, yet that drama goes further back and runs deeper. It begins with the first Great War, which breached the barriers that sheltered the tumultuous process in which an urban culture accumulated. Without them, nothing shielded the city's civilization against seizure and destruction by order of those above and by the demand of those below who wanted to live better at others' expense.

Far away from the centres of its world, resting on the strong back of the Carpathian Mountains, Czernowitz is defenceless and indefensible. There is no direction in which its people could flee. The undefended cities and towns of Central Europe are where we can begin to contemplate, in absolute hopelessness, what has become of Europe.

One should not wish to leave this beautiful city without mentioning that there are things that made the sojourn 'before the abyss of the sky' bearable. Lingering on Chernovtsy's Theatre Square, this visitor encountered neatly groomed elderly gentlemen who made conversation in excellent German. He learned from the custodian of the future folklore museum that the plans may yet be revised, that the church may be restored as a church after all. The employees of the Goskino workshop told him that they would probably move to different premises soon so the Orthodox synagogue could be turned into a museum of Jewish history. He saw a poster for a performance of *The Golem* by the Kiev Jewish Theatre. He met a writer, Josef Burg, who was scheduled to give a reading of his stories in Yiddish in Berlin, where his publisher was based.

So there are relations between Chernovtsy and East Berlin. And Burg, in conversation, hinted at literary contacts in Bucharest as well: the German-language journal *Neue Literatur*, formerly edited by the highly respected writer Alfred Margul-Sperber, who discovered Rose Ausländer and Paul Celan. In the only synagogue that is still in use – built in 1925, it was left untouched by the Nazis and the Garda de Fier – the visitor spoke to the head of the Jewish community, who had just returned from Brooklyn and showed him the tefillin he had bought there. And before his departure, he attended a commemoration – it was the anniversary of the October pogrom in 1941 – on the Jewish cemetery. The roof of the synagogue there had caved in, but it remained an imposing structure. The occasion was already a tradition; flowers were laid on the grave of the fabulist Eliezer Steinbarg and the graves of the men, women and children who had been shot to death. Most of the mourners were elderly, but there were a few young people among them as well, and they spoke of things they had almost stopped believing in.

(1988)

ELEVEN

LVIV:

CAPITAL OF PROVINCIAL EUROPE

'IT IS A HUGE presumption to try to describe cities,' Joseph Roth wrote about Lviv – then called Lwów and located in the southeast of inter-war Poland – in an essay for the *Frankfurter Zeitung* in 1924. 'Cities have many faces, many moods, a thousand directions, colourful des-tinations, dark secrets, joyful secrets. Cities hide a lot and reveal a lot, each one is a totality, each one a plurality, each one has more time than a reporter, a human being, a group or a nation. Cities outlive the peo-ples to which they owe their existence and the languages in which their builders communicated with each other.' The cautionary remark cer-tainly applies to the following portrait of Lviv, now western Ukraine's first city, that I penned in the mid-1980s. At the time, it was, broadly speaking, a major Soviet city called Lvov, a place at the end of the world, overshadowed by the Iron Curtain, in the dead angle, beyond our horizon. But even then subtle changes had begun. Slowly, imper-ceptibly, yet inexorably, a region resurfaced whose name had ceased to signify for a post-war world cleft into East and West: Central Europe. Lviv was one of the cities marked on the map of that imaginary and yet real Central Europe, which had overwintered the division of the continent and the world during the Cold War. Lviv was proof that the dichotomy was false, that a third term existed, was not just a conceit, a fanciful notion: here was an urban body, a text in which one could read the fates of Europe's provincial heart. The region had indeed been ground up between the frontlines of the European civil war; what it had been had perished, its face altered beyond recognition. An erstwhile capital found itself on the margin. My trip to Lviv, a quarter-century ago, was an exploratory journey. What I sought was not the sweet wine of nostalgia but traces of the past. It was a time when guidebooks did not exist and maps that accurately represented the city's physical reality were impossible to obtain. I had to rely on Habsburg-era Baedekers, the recollections of survivors, the proceedings of trials against war criminals and similar materials to help me decode its text.

In the late summer of 2015, Lviv, far from being a city in a 'failing state', is abuzz with energy and people. In the centre, the streets have been torn up; they are scheduled to be repaved in time for the municipal elections in October. The farmers' markets brim with all the vegetables and fruits that grow in the gardens of the Carpathian foothills and the Podolian-Volhynian plain. The city is in the middle of a tourism boom. Buses from Poland disgorge nostalgia tourists, the children and grandchildren of ethnic Poles who were forcibly resettled after 1944, but one also sees many cars with registration numbers from Warsaw or Wrocław – the Polish middle class is discovering a neighbouring country where the pleasures of life are comparatively affordable. Many other visitors hail from central and eastern Ukraine: Crimea, where millions had gone on holiday before the Russian annexation, is difficult to get to, the beaches near Odessa are overcrowded, Mariupol is too unsafe. And Lviv is the gateway to the Carpathian Mountains. In the West, too, interest in Ukraine as a tourist destination has picked up. The flight from Vienna takes no more than an hour, and now there is a direct flight from Munich as well. Having fallen off Europeans' radar decades ago because of the Cold War, Ukraine's westernmost and, with over 700,000 residents, seventh-most populous city is back. A first push towards modernization came with the European football championship in 2012. Lviv boasts an international airport, whose steel and glass construction was visibly inspired by the work of Norman Foster; numerous new hotels; and a mayor under whose leadership the city has become the centre of Ukraine's booming and internationally competitive IT scene. Not yet fifty years old, Andrii Sadovy is not just the mayor but also a founder and leading figure of Samopomich (Self-Reliance), a party that emerged from the Maidan revolution and finished third in the most recent elections for the Verkhovna Rada in Kiev. He has nothing to do with the nationalists and 'Banderites' that, according to an extraordinarily persistent stereotype, run rampant in western Ukraine. Nor is he an oligarch: he advocates civic involvement, local self-government and decentralization as well as the indivisibility of Ukraine. So if the country is 'on the brink of collapse', there is another Ukraine, one that has no place in that defeatist perception: a nation that stands firm, despite the Russian threat and lukewarm European support. Lviv was a vital source of the civic energy that propelled Ukraine's quest for national independence and fuelled the 'Revolution of Dignity' on Maidan. And now it is a safe haven for many who have fled the war in eastern Ukraine.

Now, as the days are getting shorter and the city looks back on the summer, it can feel like the whole world stopped by. First there were the fans of Shakhtar Donetsk – the club has camped out here since its home stadium, the Donbass Arena, was destroyed – and Rapid Wien who came in large numbers to support their teams in the UEFA Cup match: one would have had to be blind and deaf to confuse the Austrians for nostalgics lured by the myth of Habsburg glory. Then a meeting of German and Ukrainian writers under the apt title 'A Bridge of Paper' presented an opportunity to hear some of the country's most popular authors: Yurii Andrukhovych, whose essays put Galicia back on Europe's intellectual map; Andrei Kurkov, the best-known representative of Russian-language literature in Ukraine; and Serhiy Zhadan, who travelled from Kharkov to recite poems about the war. Later on, Yurko Prokhasko, that subtle interpreter of urban spaces, led the Germans who were visiting Lviv for the first time on a tour of what Roth, a native of nearby Brody, called the 'city of blurred boundaries'. There is so much going on in just a few days that I, for one, acutely wish I could be everywhere at once. The Center for Urban History of East Central Europe – an institution appropriately housed in one of the finest Art Nouveau buildings – hosts a symposium titled 'Days of Modernity' at which urban planners, architects and historians, including one panellist from Moscow, speak about the modernism of the interwar years and its fates. Not far away, at Ivan Franko National University, in the splendid building where the Galician parliament once convened, a three-day international conference on 'East European Cataclysms and the Making of Modern International Law' brings together speakers from Kharkov, Leipzig and Stanford to discuss eastern Central Europe, that 'land in between', as an exemplary scene and laboratory of the twentieth century's excesses of violence. It has been a hot summer, and the constant military threat has strained Lvivans' nerves, but any concern that this programme might exhaust the energies of the city's audiences is laid to rest by the weeklong LvivKlezFest featuring klezmer bands from Warsaw, Kraków, Bucharest and New York, which transforms the entire city – the parks, but also the empty plot where the

Golden Rose Synagogue once stood – into a dance and concert stage. From dusk until late in the evening, the Rynok, the market square at the heart of the old town, is thronged with people who want to hear klezmer in all its diversity – from Jewish tango from Buenos Aires to the Kraków variant and Russian American jazz. Decades after Jerzy Petersburski's legendary Polish jazz orchestra performed in Lviv and made Eastern European music history, a sound has come home.

People are out for a stroll on Freedom Avenue, a wide street lined by trees and benches with a monument to the national poet Taras Shevchenko at its centre. It was for summer evenings like tonight, when the squares of Central European cities exude a Mediterranean flair, that this urban space, formerly called Karl Ludwig Street, then Prospect Lenina, was created. Between the illuminated neo-Renaissance opera house at one end and the Mickiewicz monument and Hotel George at the other, the citizenry basks in the glow of the undamaged fin-de-siècle facades, rendered doubly alluring by the warm light of the street lamps, and samples the souvenir vendors, ice-cream stalls and magicians. Neatly dressed urbanites mingle with holidaymakers in shorts, excited children, young women in high heels and men in muscle shirts. The colours, the murmuring of the crowd beneath the night sky – the scene does not yet quite resemble that on Prague's Old Town Square, which is packed with tourists, or Barcelona's Las Ramblas, but a hint of that larger world is in the air. Yet despite the atmosphere of friendly ease, everyone has been following the news; everyone knows what is happening elsewhere in the country. The city celebrates, but it does not party. Its people do not harbour illusions and diligently read the pages upon pages of advice in the papers on how to save electricity and gas to make it through the coming winter. The war seems far away and is nonetheless present. Many give up the Donbass for lost, at least for the time being, and are convinced that Ukraine needs to focus entirely on domestic problems, on reforming and modernizing itself. Lviv has taken in refugees, primarily Tatars from Crimea. One sees little khaki in the street, but during an excursion to nearby Zhovkva, a town on an ideal Renaissance plan and later a royal residence – John III Sobieski, the victor of the 1683 Battle of Vienna, was raised here – that had one of Galicia's largest synagogues, I see a group of men in their early twenties through to mid-forties who are on furlough and preparing to return to the front. Donation drives to support the army are held on the squares, and passersby stop outside a gallery that shows photographs of soldiers killed in action. A group of mostly elderly women and men comes together on the central avenue to intone patriotic chants, indefatigably, their voices subsiding only to rise again. A little farther down, a Slovak bard who has crossed the nearby border expresses his solidarity with his Ukrainian neighbours in song. A volunteer has spread out colour-fully painted shell splinters from the combat zone on the pavement, promising to donate the proceeds to the army. Serhii Zhadan reads poems about the war at the theatre and then boards the night train to Poltava, where he is expected at a benefit concert.

At this moment of menace, the city's historic beauty seems to meld with the character of its people: the urban fabric as a bulwark of stabil-ity at a time of uncertainty and targeted destabilization. The citizenry draws fortitude from the ruins of the High Castle and the medieval old town's chessboard street grid; from the churches and monasteries that are still the defining verticals in the city's silhouette; from the Renaissance houses built by patrician families around the Rynok, an ensemble that has few rivals among Europe's squares. Lviv's more recent history, by contrast, remains contentious. The 1941 pogroms in Lviv between the departure of the retreating Soviet troops and the installa-tion of the German administration, during which almost 7,000 Jews were killed, is one of the most atrocious chapters in the history of the collaboration between Ukrainian nationalists and the German occupi-ers; it still takes courage for historians in Ukraine to address it frankly, whereas the proposals to rename streets in honour of Organization of Ukrainian Nationalists activists do not appear to have encountered much resistance. Sites of violence dot the cityscape, including the Janowska labour camp, through which an estimated 200,000 Jews passed to be worked to death, shot in mass executions on the scene, or deported to the Bełżec extermination camp; the Janowska cemetery; and several prisons such as the infamous Brygidky and the Prison at Łąckiego. Plaques on their facades now commemorate the victims, and the Łąckiego prison has been converted into a museum that walks the visitor through the complete sequence of murderous outrages. The Lviv-based journalist and translator Yurii Durkot has written down its history. Built as a prison by the Austrian authorities, it was taken over by the Second Polish Republic, which imprisoned more than a few Ukrainian patriots and underground fighters in its cells. After the invasion by the Red Army in September 1939, the Soviet secret service NKVD used it to detain 'anti-Soviet and bourgeois elements' – Poles,

Jews, Ukrainians – many of whom were later deported to the Gulag. When the Germans attacked on 22 June 1941, the NKVD, taken by surprise by the enemy's rapid advance, murdered the 1,600 inmates. The gruesome sight of the decomposing corpses then served an anti-Semitic mob as a pretext for 'vengeance against the Jewish Bolsheviks'. After the city's liberation in the fall of 1943, the NKVD once again commandeered the prison, now for its persecution of the anti-Soviet Ukrainian underground, which persisted until the mid-1950s. Independent Ukraine's secret service SBU used the complex for a while until it was closed in 1996. Much of it remains as it was; visitors can see cells, an interrogation room, latrines and an execution chamber. Photographs of the bodies found in June 1941 are on display as part of the memorial in the courtyard.

It has been infinitely difficult to address this twofold experience of totalitarian violence at the hands of the Nazis as well as Stalin's henchmen. Lvivans have struggled to articulate what happened, do justice to all victims, and not flinch from an avowal of their own complicity, as the controversies over the erection of monuments and the renaming of streets and squares illustrate. The most recent bone of contention was a monument to the Ukrainian Greek Catholic metropolitan archbishop Andrei Sheptytsky (1865–1944). The scion of a Polonized ancient Ukrainian aristocratic family, he was a patron of Ukrainian culture; some criticize him for his proximity to the nationalist movement, while others revere him as a 'Righteous among the Nations' because he spoke out courageously against persecution of the Jews and was actively involved in saving many of them. When Adorno wrote, in *Minima Moralia*, that 'wrong life cannot be lived rightly', he had a very different quandary in mind, but perhaps the dictum was never truer than for the metropolitan of Lviv and all those who, like him, were hopelessly caught up between the twentieth century's frontlines.

By the time this sequence of catastrophes had run its course, the urban core that had borne so many names in its history was a different city. Now, in the 25th year of Ukrainian independence, Lviv tries to build on the legacy of its erstwhile prosperity and cultural florescence. Exhibitions like the one on the 'Myth of Galicia' that was shown in Kraków and Vienna have put it back on the map. It recollects the great names that were erased from memory and banished from commemoration for so long: Stanisław Lem, who was born and raised here; the Polish poets Zbigniew Herbert and Adam Zagajewski; the essayist

Józef Wittlin, to whom we owe the finest book on Lemberg. Lviv was the birthplace of the eminent Marxist theorist Roman Rosdolsky and a prominent symbolic figure of international communism, Karl Radek, as well as the leading thinker of classical liberalism Ludwig von Mises. The memoirs of the Polish writer Aleksander Wat, who fled to Soviet-occupied Lviv after the German attack on Poland, contain a portrait of life in the city between 1939 and 1941 and an account of his deportation. The city also left traces in the work of the German poet Günter Eich, who was deployed here as a soldier.

Unlike the organizers of the 'Myth of Galicia' exhibition, today's Lvivans are too concerned with the present to be preoccupied with their city's glorious past. They have almost everything that is needed to 'rebrand' Lviv. The enterprising mayor is aware of the significance of its abundant architectonic heritage and beauty and is adept at, in contemporary parlance, 'selling' his city. But Lviv will not be saved by tourism alone. Nor does it have an industrial base in the traditional sense; it is a city of administration, services and scientific institutions. It is not far to Kraków, Budapest, Prague and Vienna. The city is bilingual – Russian and Ukrainian – and understands Polish as well. Few cities are as linguistically open to all sides. Many Lvivans have worked or studied in the West. Its intellectuals are at home in European discourses and speak with confidence about issues in historiography, the latest academic trends and paradigm shifts in scholarship. Lviv might prove that strong regional identities and diversity, far from weakening a country, are signs of its vitality. And it might show those Germans who obstinately associate its name with 'nationalism' and 'Bandera' that a very different history exists as well, although the recent rash of new monuments to Stepan Bandera in several cities – Lviv has built an especially monstrous one, across the street from St Elizabeth's Church – is unnecessarily provocative. Members of my own generation who have never thought outside the box of German Russian relations might come to the realization that it would be worth their while to go and see for themselves. Younger Westerners will get to know people their own age who are in some ways more mature than they, having taken part in a transformative upheaval and learned lessons that television and newspapers alone cannot impart. Staying at one of the many affordable hostels, they may find the amenities rather spartan – metal bunk beds, one shared fridge for everyone – but will be awed by the wood panelling, the carved banister rails and Art Nouveau glazing from 1900. They might chance upon Villa Julietka, a fairy-tale mansion the architects and entrepreneurs Alfred and Julian Zachariewicz built for themselves. The Western discovery of Ukraine would be sped up greatly if Lviv were easier to get to – if Ukraine finally abolished the monopoly held by Ukraine International Airlines (UIA), which is controlled by one of the country's oligarchs, and conclude open skies agreements. Budget airlines would bring Europe's youth to the city. These changes will not happen in time for the events around the theme of 'The Mission of Culture during Crises' scheduled for the first week of September or the annual international book fair a week later. But it is not too late to come and witness the resurgence of this European city.

(2015)

✠

When Lvov Was the Capital of Provincial Europe

LVOV LIES AT the end of the world. The traveller is exhausted by the time he makes it here, for his voyage has been long, and the border crossings were probably arduous and time-consuming. If he boarded in Vienna, Budapest or Prague, it has taken him a day; the trip from Berlin via Kraków or from Bucharest can last up to two days. (There is an overnight train from Moscow, however.) Lvov is the final destination for civil servants and military officers on official business; for many more, it is an extended stopover on a transit route or an interchange station on the way to rest and recreation in the Carpathian Mountains. Lvov sits at the intersection of lines connecting the metropolises, but the geographical facts that define it are the nearby borders. A journey to Lvov takes the visitor into the forgotten slow-beating heart of Europe.

The difficulties he encounters are hardly technical or organiza-tional. The question 'Where is Lvov?' is answered easily enough by maps and timetable books. Even clueless travel agents are quick to learn. What makes this journey difficult is that Lvov is a city that leads a double existence: one in our minds and one in reality. The traveller is bound for a region that is almost impossible to characterize – it is both the centre of Europe and utterly peripheral. It is a city that is thoroughly of today, but visitors from outside come almost exclusively for its magnificent past. Lvov is Lemberg. But one should add at once that that is an illusion. The traveller who boards a train to Lvov arrives in a major Soviet city and not in a Habsburg-era mirage. Lemberg is the preferred destination of imaginary excursions, but those who actually go find themselves squarely in the world of today. Tourists are curious to see whether some of the fin-de-siècle's lustre still plays on the stones of today's Lvov; they want to know what has remained of a city that got caught up between the frontlines of the European civil war. We can identify its location on a map of the continent, but we are much less certain of its place in contemporary Europe's mental topography: it must be somewhere in that grey zone between nostalgia and ignorance, between a history that is long gone and a present that has fallen out of historical time. The journey to Lvov is a journey to the pole of doubt: is Europe, at its very centre, still conceivable?

Metropolis in the Transition Zone

The traveller trusts his eyes. When his train loops in a large arc around the city, which lies at the bottom of a wide valley open towards the north and ringed round by green parks, he knows that, after hours spent traversing plains and hill country, he has reached a metropolis. The countryside was expansive and almost devoid of human settlements, or so it seemed as he looked out the window, and he is unprepared for such a dense agglomeration of dwellings. Lvov is like an assault, a compact silhouette of innumerable towers, domes, spires and large complexes. After so much empty space, a sudden lack of room; maximum density and compression. Disembarking and walking into the station hall, he has left the country and arrived in the city, another world. It is where incoming traffic from the outlying districts merges, and the crowds seem twice as large because almost everyone is carrying a backpack or bags. Lvov is the uncontested centre of the region. The station hall is as large and airy as a cathedral; the sun's rays fall upon the jostle and the stuccowork, which, like the broad cream-coloured facade, dates the building to the early years of the century. This was the gateway through which passengers from Vienna passed when they first set foot on Galician soil and through which so many others left for the New World; a structure designed to be capacious and comfortable, to accommodate the brisk processing of voyagers, a bastion against a world ruled by the slow pace of horse-drawn vehicles. And a pompous station hall can be a manifestation of political power no less than a government building. In Lvov, the main station – which, it should be noted, is only one of altogether five – is a marker of an epoch: the late Habsburg Empire.

Monuments to Habsburg's civilizing mission dot the city. Most of them are complexes that, by virtue of their sheer dimensions, shatter the intricate and delicate medieval Lvov of narrow alleys and slender gables. They are the work of Vienna and of the era over which Vienna presided. The great city on the Danube built a replica of itself, a little Vienna. Early in the century, most of the walls that surrounded the old Lvov were razed and the river was covered with a broad promenade, today's Lenin Avenue, which is actually a spacious elongated square – and still the city's centre, the place where its residents' paths cross. At its northern end stands an opera house that had few rivals even in Austria-Hungary, an empire that surely did not lack for gorgeous opera houses. Designed by Zygmunt Gorgolewski in the 1890s, it is a splendid structure blending many styles, a finely wrought sculpture of pilasters, balustrades, Corinthian columns, statues and garlands. In the evenings, when the radiant light from the foyer of the Ivan Franko Lvov State Academic Theatre of Opera and Ballet falls upon the square, Lvov is, for a brief moment, a place on the Opernring. Tonight's performance may be a production of *Spartacus*, but you can imagine that Enrico Caruso appeared on its stage. One of the square's long sides is occupied by no less pompous and imposing structures: the former police headquarters, revenue office and district court; one of these buildings houses the inevitable Lenin Museum. The other long side belongs to business, to commerce and banks, to cafés and hotels. The facades are a mix of Neoclassical, neo-Baroque and Art Deco. Lemberg was where the flows of money throughout Galicia converged, hence the stately offices of mortgage and savings banks; and the capital of an imperial province whose residents and businesses thought they could protect themselves against vaguely imagined future menaces by taking out insurance, hence the no less prominent establishments of the insurance companies. And since this square marks the centre of the city, it is also where the hotels are clustered. Their names were the same as everywhere – Hôtel de France, Hôtel de l'Europe – and are the same as everywhere in the Soviet Union; the George, for example, has become the Intourist. The allegory of the continents on its facade illustrates that Lemberg, like Fellner & Helmer architects, whose creations are scattered throughout Central Europe, had a clear and definite idea of its place in the world. Other windows looking out over the square are unmistakably those of cafés whose denizens liked to keep an eye on the life of the city unfolding on the other side of the large panes. These must have been the coffee

Model of the Lviv Opera House.

houses where patrons could choose from over a hundred newspapers. The stores that sell books from the socialist sister countries must have been the bookshops and antiquarian booksellers that made Lemberg a hub of the book trade and a destination for connoisseurs of the printed word.

To this day, the representative edifices from the Habsburg era are salient in Lvov's countenance: the massive post and telegraph office; the Galician Sejm vis-à-vis the slightly unkempt municipal park, where the visitor can still espy the outlines of the circular plaza on which the band struck up in the afternoons; the home for the invalid on the edge of town, which might be the exact double of a similar institution in Trieste; the polytechnic; the Ossolineum, whose libraries and archives were a Polish national cultural treasure; the hospitals, barracks and casinos. Lemberg is a city erected by an empire that, even in its waning years, mustered the energy to create an image of itself: large and handsome, even imposing, and not altogether devoid of the colonialist gesture of progressive paternalism.

Yet this Lemberg of train station, citadel, banks, hotels and insurance buildings would be nothing without the old Lvov, which was complete before the Habsburgs arrived. Here the spires rise up that are etched into the sky over the city. It is as though carved into stone, with hard contours and dense as a crystal. No broad avenue welcomes the visitor who ventures into the old town; no boulevard awaits would-be flâneurs or parading soldiers. The narrow lanes form a chessboard pattern, but an ever so slightly irregular one. The visitor must find his

Postcard of Lemberg railway station.

way, and it would be pointless to be on the lookout for sights, since the entire ensemble, the place, is the sight. The Habsburg Lemberg is ochre and yellow; the pre-Habsburg Lvov is black like the large blocks of hewn stone of which the Renaissance mansions and patrician houses are built, or dove grey like the cobblestone pavement, worn shiny by centuries of use. The visitor losing his way in Lvov's heart is on the right track: he is approaching the primal cell of all European cities. His perspective changes with every step. Now a tower, a portal, a fountain catches his eye; now he glimpses a courtyard, ascends a perron, or heads down into an arcade; now he strays into a perfectly straight street that turns out to be a dead end. He must turn corners and balance on the kerbstone, must swerve around a statue or duck his head as he enters a low-ceilinged passageway.

Strolling, he leaps from one century into another and back. On the old Lvov's market square the merchants' houses from the sixteenth century press in upon him; in the suburbs he spots architectural embellishments designed by the Vienna Secession. He can immerse himself in the Latin Cathedral, that relic of Gothic Lvov, a city prone to devastating fires, or ascend a grand Baroque flight of stairs to St George's Cathedral. He can descend towards the Armenian Cathedral, whose base now sits considerably below street level, and see the headstones on the Armenian cemetery, some of which date from the fourteenth century. Or he can walk across the old town towards the Bernardine monastery. His wanderings take him deep into the centuries. The spires and domes seem to intertwine and coalesce above his head. This is the adamantine nucleus of patrician Lvov, which had ways and the means to purchase its freedom when Tatars, Turks or Vlachs stood outside the gates. It is a setting that even a King Charles XII of Sweden and the Sobieskis respected as a pinnacle of urban civilization, a hard shell fashioned by the industry of dynasties of artisans and craftsmen whose products, such as their gold work, were coveted as far away as Nuremberg and Constantinople. And despite this extraordinary compactness, old Lvov exudes the nonchalance that is at home where no generation feels under pressure to outmatch the achievements of those that came before. Buildings were extended and remodelled without much ado; they grew, sprawled and attained a new form in the process. Take the chapels of the Campiani and Boim families or the Korniakt Tower; all three were attached to existing churches. Lvov brought in master builders from all over: Peter the Roman, Peter Barbon, Jan de Wit, Nicola Gonzaga, Peter Stecher; some names are unknown today. Polish, Italian and Ukrainian architects designed parts of one and the same building. The funds for these edifices came from many sources and all directions of the compass: from Polish kings and Ukrainian hetmans, from Moldavian hospodars and Armenian merchants, and from Jewish and German bourgeois families. Where everything is melded to everything to the point of virtual indistinction and subtle nuances are key to a city's charm, all attribution ceases. Lvov fuses the Byzantine cross-in-square church with Gothic architecture; Italian influence transforms the iconostas into a masterpiece of Ukrainian Baroque art. The city's allure derives from the many cultures and peoples that have inhabited it. A vacant spot amid its density signals that some enormity must have taken place. One such spot is the octagonal central island on Stary Rynok Square. Elderly people sit on park benches and feed pigeons. A second is behind the Arsenal, where the firewall of a neighbouring building shows traces of another structure that once abutted it. A third is the nondescript expanse now taken up by a local kolkhoz market. These are the brownfields of Jewish Lvov, the sites of two of its demolished synagogues, among them the Golden Rose Synagogue, built in the sixteenth century and ruined by the Germans in 1941, and one of its cemeteries. Only the blue-glazed domes of a Moorish-style building that now houses a hospital remind the visitor that Lvov was once home to one of Central Europe's great Jewish communities.

Where Many Worlds Intersect

'Has Europe ended here?' Joseph Roth asks in his Galician travelogues, which appeared in the *Frankfurter Zeitung* in 1924.

> No, it hasn't ended. The relationship between Europe and this country, though it has been exiled, as it were, is constant and lively. Browsing the bookstores, I saw the most recent literary releases from England and France. A wind of culture carries the seeds and deposits them in Poland's soil. The contact with France is the most vigorous. Sparks fly back and forth over Germany, which seems to occupy a dead zone. Galicia slumbers in seclusion, lost to the world, yet it is not isolated; it has been exiled but not cut off; it has more culture than its poor sanitation system might make you think; it is rich in disarray and even more in oddity.

Lvov sits on the routes from Constantinople to Nuremberg and from Bologna to Vilnius. When an enemy force closed in upon the city, the alarm call was heard throughout Europe. Lvov was Ukrainian, Hungarian, Moldavian, Polish, Austrian, Russian, German and Soviet. Each new power that regarded the city as its possession added something to it; some despoiled it of everything. Not all provinces are created equal. Galicia was a province of imbrications, and Lemberg was a city of 'blurred boundaries', to quote Joseph Roth. Lviv, Lvov, Lwów, Leopolis, Lamburg, Lemberg: the city was founded by King Danylo Romanovych of Halych-Volhynia and named in honour of his son Lev, who first fortified Castle Hill. The oldest document mentioning it dates from 1256. King Casimir the Great of Poland conquered it in 1340 and granted it Magdeburg rights in 1356. The city grew into an important trading hub on the Via Regia from Santiago de Compostela to Byzantium and Kiev; it fended off the Tatars and the Turks and became a refuge for the burghers and tradesmen of other towns overrun and pillaged by attackers. It remained Polish until the Partition of Poland in 1772, a long possession punctuated by forays of Hungarians, Transylvanians, Cossacks, Vlachs and Swedes. After Austria gained control of the area, the Habsburg Empire's governors of the Kingdom of Galicia and Lodomeria held office here until 1918. Under the Habsburg monarchy, the city sampled the full spectrum of

Central European architectonic models and styles, from the mansions of the Polish aristocracy to bank and insurance palaces, music pavilions in the municipal park, a grand railway station, the polytechnic institute and the Galician Sejm building. Growing to around 200,000 residents on the eve of the First World War, Lvov was multilingual, multi-confessional and multi-ethnic, a city that married Byzantine and Latin influences, where the opulent local Baroque borrowed from the architecture of Ukraine's wooden churches and Viennese Art Nouveau met early functionalism – a uniquely rich culture, and one rife with tensions that, under pressure from outside powers, would explode in the first half of the twentieth century. The Great War turned Galicia into a battlefield and Lvov into a staging ground.

By the turn of the century, the city counted around 160,000 inhabitants, half of them Polish, plus circa 40,000 Jews, 30,000 Ukrainians and 7,000 Germans, as well as numerous smaller ethnic groups: Greeks, Hungarians, Bulgarians, Romanians, Italians and, notably, Armenians – the Armenian community, the largest in the Slavic lands, goes back to the thirteenth century. Lemberg was religiously diverse; Catholics made up roughly half of the population, while most of the remaining Christians were members of the Greek Catholic Church, with 1 per cent Armenian Catholics. Three archbishops had their seats in the city, which spoke many languages, primarily Polish, but also Yiddish,

Photograph of a street in Lviv, *c.* 1915–20.

Ukrainian and German. Its culture was necessarily polyglot and cosmopolitan. The great Ukrainian writer Ivan Franko was no less at home in Polish and German. Such an environment prompts reflections on the nature of language and a careful and deliberate use of one's native tongue. Alexander Granach, a leading actor on the stages of the German-speaking world of his time, arrived in Berlin after a stint in Lemberg, and Martin Buber spent his formative years in the city of Jewish Enlightenment and Chassidism. Lemberg was important enough for Niccolò Paganini, Franz Liszt and Maurice Ravel to come and perform. The Polish Lwów was almost a sister city of Kraków. Karl Emil Franzos's acerbic sketches introduced readerships in Berlin and Vienna to the province of his youth. The fault lines of national and social conflicts intersected in Lvov; one of the most eloquent spokesmen of the working class, Karl Radek, a native of the city, was actively involved in the Polish, German, Lithuanian and Russian labour movements. Lvov was also the gateway through which hundreds of thousands departed Galicia – which, despite the discovery of oil, never became another Pennsylvania – for the New World. For many, its name stood for the Europe they were forced to leave in order to survive. Joseph Roth's writings revolve around Galicia and its capital, no doubt because he was born in nearby Brody, but more importantly because they epitomized his Central European universe. Elsewhere, nationalism was only just becoming modern, but here it was already a lethal danger. In Galicia and Lemberg, many understood that 'the world is surely not meant to consist of "nations" and of fatherlands, which would not have the right to sacrifice so much as a single human life even if all they sought was to preserve their cultural identities.' And long before the great cataclysm, the people of Galicia and Lemberg exemplified what Joseph Roth meant when he wrote: 'We are all scattered fragments because we have lost our homeland.'

Disintegration Sequence

The Thirty Years' War that begins in 1914 and ends in 1945 turns Galicia into a battlefield and empties Lvov of its people. The city is caught up in an ever-accelerating maelstrom of changing rulers and shifting frontlines. After the collapse of Austria-Hungary, Lvov is, for a few months, part of a West Ukrainian People's Republic. In the summer of 1919, it becomes Polish; it will be the seat of a Polish voivodeship until

R60135

Russian troops at the monument of Sobieski in Lviv, 1914.

September 1939. Three weeks after Germany attacks Poland, the Red Army marches into the city and establishes a Soviet administration in western Ukraine, and on 1 November 1939, the Soviet Union annexes the Polish territory east of the Curzon Line. The German assault on the Soviet Union begins on 22 June 1941, and a mere eight days later, Lvov is occupied by German troops. Lemberg is now the capital of a District of Galicia, part of the General Government. General Konev's armies recapture it on 27 July 1944.

The unique equilibrium that characterized the city's life for so long has buckled under the tensions of the interwar years, but now it collapses under overwhelming outside pressure. 'Blurred boundaries' harden into polarization; civic coexistence is detonated by policies of extermination. Two sides are locked in mortal combat, but no proverbial third party has reason to rejoice. The violence they unleash is strong enough to blow a city to pieces that had matured to crystalline hardness. The explosives lie prepared. At the height of the Great Depression, more than one in three residents are out of work and have no source of income. The gulf between rich and poor adds fuel to the claims of nationalists. The liberation of Lwów, reintegrated into the Polish Republic after over 150 years of foreign rule, brought a pogrom against the Jewish Lemberg. In 1936 shots are fired on protesting unemployed workers. The Ukrainians who assert their right to the city are as anti-Polish as the Polish are anti-Ukrainian. The festering anti-bourgeois resentment blends into anti-Semitism. It is perhaps not a coincidence that Lvov furnishes Roman Rosdolsky with the material for his studies on capitalism, nationalism and anti-Semitism. Yet the city's fate is ultimately decided not on the scene but far away – in Berlin and Moscow. Lvov is destined to be ground to dust between the frontlines.

Assigned to the Soviet sphere of influence by the Molotov–Ribbentrop Pact, Lvov is one of the first cities to fall to the Germans after the Soviet invasion. More than a few people in the city harbour the nationalist illusion that the week between the NKVD's departure and the ss's arrival is an auspicious moment for the establishment of an independent Ukraine. The city is packed with refugees from German-occupied Poland and full of people whom Hitler and Stalin alike regard as suspect and unreliable: at the moment of retreat as much as offence, they are the predestined victims of bloodbaths. On the one side, these victims are Poles and Ukrainians who have been arrested as 'nationalists' as well as Jews branded as 'bourgeois elements' and Hitler's potential 'fifth columnists'. On the other side, they are primarily Jews, now accused of being 'bolshevist agents'. The NKVD liquidates thousands at the last minute; over 7,000 Jews of Lemberg die in a pogrom staged by Ukrainian nationalists and ss. Over the next two years, the city's Jewish community, whose history reached back to the fourteenth century, and the Jews of Galicia's other cities and towns are almost entirely exterminated by German *Einsatzkommandos*, with support from Ukrainians who see the German invasion as an opportunity to shake off the yoke of Soviet rule – a vain hope, as Bandera's arrest and imprisonment in Sachsenhausen demonstrate. In August 1941 around 119,000 Jews register with the Lemberg *Judenrat*. A ghetto is set up in which they are penned up in the spring of 1942; they are conscripted for forced labour while the deportations to Treblinka, Sobibór, Bełżec and Auschwitz commence. The ghetto is 'cleared' in June 1943. The city's 'German element' has already vanished in the winter of 1939–40, when the Galician Germans were resettled in the Reich in accordance with the agreement between Ribbentrop and Molotov. The German Protestant church served as the registration and repatriation office for the 7,000 Germans who left Lemberg: the end of a chapter that began under Maria Theresia.

The Red Army's return brings another horrendous bloodletting. The great majority of the Polish population is expelled to the westward-shifted Poland. Tens of thousands suspected of nationalism, mainly

Poles and Ukrainians, are deported to camps in the Soviet Union. Skirmishes between Soviet security forces and the underground fighters of the Ukrainian National Army continue until the early 1950s. Strangers move into a city depopulated by war. Today's Lvov is almost entirely Ukrainian.

All this occurred in the space of a few years, in a historical blink of an eye. It rendered all guides to Lvov, all Baedekers moot. The visitor who consults them is lost. The only places where he may find the Lvov that succumbed, the city that had been something like the Piedmont of civilian Central Europe, are the cemeteries. The inscriptions in many languages speak to hopes for a life after death. We must glean the splintered city's scattered fragments. Stanisław Lem's autobiography is a source, as are the poems of Zbigniew Herbert. The memoirs of Lemberg's Germans, who were resettled and then displaced yet again, give us a sense of the scene at the club 'Frohsinn', the centre of their community's social life. Exhibits in the municipal museum help us understand the erasure of the German language: Reichsbahn staff badges and the identity cards of forced labourers held in the camp on Janowska Street. We must go back to Germany and confront those who participated in the massacres against the Jewish people and the Polish and Ukrainian intelligentsia. We must read the newspapers of the Ukrainian diaspora and interview survivors of the deportations to Auschwitz, provided that they are still able and willing to speak to us. Lvov is a city where the language that might make sense of it all gives way to stunned silence.

The Young Lvov

Today's Lvov is a city after the cataclysm. The life that fills its streets is the life of those who came after the war or grew up in the peace that has reigned since. The city is projected to grow to a million residents over the next ten years. It has large factories making buses and television sets, and a radio and television station; it has dozens of theatres, museums and institutes; it has festivals and daily papers. Its is the ordinary life of an ordinary major Soviet city, although the new neighbourhoods are virtually invisible from the old town. It is, in a sense, a double city, a city divided against itself. The old Lvov is there, it is in use, but it has not been taken possession of by genuine citizens. Looking at the houses, the visitor can tell that they belong to no one because they are owned by everyone; the bookstores are recognizably those of a country where the production of books is in the hands of the government; the mission of the museums is manifestly to educate, not to lay out the historic material for the visitor to examine. The churches are 'architectonic ensembles'. Despite the large windowpanes through which one can observe the bustle outside, the coffee shops do not invite the patron to linger; they are supply stations aiming for maximum throughput. In the department stores, the discrepancy between shoppers' desires and the sparse offerings is obvious. The language one hears in the streets is a standard language spoken by everyone. The street names are familiar from other Soviet cities: Lenin Avenue, Peace Street, Frunze Street. The way passersby are dressed and comport themselves no longer signals their social class or profession. Today's Lvov is much bigger than pre-war Lemberg, but the rest of Europe knows less about it. There are no beggars, yet the city as a whole is poorer than it was when a person of some means could hardly walk a short distance without being accosted. Lvov has many more schools and educational establishments than ever before, but the worldview that speaks from the curricula has grown narrower. No one goes hungry, but the diverse cuisines from which visitors chose in the past have been boiled down to one. The old town may be full of pedestrians hurrying from one place to another, yet it has the air of a city that has been shut down. Lvov, once a town of burghers, is a city without *citoyens*. Far from being a place where time has stood still, it is a city that was plunged headlong into a new age, a piece of the modern world flattened by the gales of modernization. The young Lvov of the new neighbourhoods, a city built from scratch, is respectful of the old Lvov, which grew over centuries, but the gulf between the eras to which they belong is unbridgeable.

But, one suspects, perhaps these observations are the misperceptions of a foreigner who has no part in the city's life? It is entirely possible, since something undreamt-of is happening: Lvov has begun to engage in a conversation about itself and its provincialization in the age of progress. The municipal museum exhibits photographs from turn-of-the-century Lvov showing shop signs and advertisements of Polish, Austrian or Jewish stores. It exhibits newspapers from before the war, in all the languages that were written and spoken here. Also on display is a plan of the city in Polish. When a street vendor sets up his stall outside the museum and offers an illustrated book on historic Lvov, the volume sells out within minutes. A typescript circulates at an assembly, a draft platform for the Ukrainian Democratic Front, inspired by the initiatives in the Baltic countries. People read it with great interest and pass it on. A few months ago, private citizens mounted Lvov's first-ever exhibition of 'Jewish art' and thousands came to see it. A society for Jewish culture has formed; members discuss organizing Hebrew and Yiddish classes and launching dance and theatrical ensembles – and erecting a monument to the victims of the Lemberg ghetto. The design has been finalized and a donations account has been publicized. It has been proposed that the one undamaged synagogue, currently in use as a gymnasium by the university's department of physical culture, be returned to the Jewish community. On the square where the Golden Rose stood, an architect leads teenage volunteers as they unearth the foundation walls. All these initiatives have the approval and support of the city administration. Public life has begun to return to the public squares – and Lvov has some of the finest in all of Europe – in the persons of youngsters called, for simplicity's sake, hippies and citizens concerned with the preservation of historic monuments. The municipal park in front of the former parliament and present-day university, now called Ivan Franko Park, is once again the preferred staging ground for demonstrations in which an increasingly engaged citizenry articulates its demands. Lvov is emerging from the shadow of the border. The Polish nationals who cross it, to visit family or tend to graves, but also for business, number in the thousands. The elemental struggle for the smallest advantage brings both sides together, though the mistrust remains mutual.

If Lvov learns to have a frank conversation about itself, it will also find a language for what has happened to it. It will perhaps recover the multiplicity of voices that is needed to narrate the fate of this – and not only this – Central European city, a history that turned gateways of transit into final destinations. This new Lvov would have the where-withal to sketch a vision of what it might yet become: something new, presumably, not just a bit of Habsburg on Soviet territory; a city that, as our century draws to a close, would mature beyond its *fin de siècle*.

Nearing the end of its long post-war period, Europe is finding its voice. This Europe needs cities that outgrow the shadows of the Iron Curtain and the desolation of the West-Eastern provinces on both sides. It needs new boundary cities, cities of 'blurred boundaries'.

(1988)

TWELVE

THE SHOCK:
THINKING THE WORST-CASE SCENARIO

SINCE EUROMAIDAN the developing situation has taken a sharp turn for the worse. Looking back, it is still unclear, even mysterious to me why my voice failed, why no words availed in the face of what was happening. I perhaps sensed that anything I might say would seem pale and stale in comparison to the dramatic images. The situation resembled that on the late evening of 9 November 1989, when we left our apartment on Köpenicker Strasse in Berlin's Kreuzberg district and saw with our own eyes by Oberbaumbrücke and then on Kurfürstendamm what we would have refused to believe if someone had told us the news: that the Wall had fallen and the city's division was over. There are moments in life, it appears, when we stop as though thunderstruck; exclamations – 'That's incredible!' 'That's insane!' – or else complete silence are the most natural reactions. Perhaps I was reluctant to comment publicly because I feared that the conflict that had erupted and remained unresolved would escalate and result in irreparable harm, that I might be drawn into the fray and contribute to a development for which I would subsequently be held – intellectually, morally – responsible. Perhaps I wanted to avoid prematurely taking sides in a struggle that was bound to fail and in which others put their necks on the line. Perhaps I distrusted myself – I had been wrong before and my fingers had been burned.

I think – and the farther the events in question recede into the past, the more convinced I am – that the primary cause of the peculiar paralysis that I noted in others and observed and studied in myself was a sense of impuissance: we witnessed a swift and accelerating succession of events an adequate instant response to which would have required the ability to anticipate them, to think them through in advance.

Such nimble historical imagination, however, is formed not by reading history but only in the open and unsheltered space of immediate experience, in direct confrontation with a sudden menace. We who grew up in post-war Central Europe's peace of deterrence had been spared such experiences. Violence, to most of us, was an abstraction that figured in the discourses addressing what people had gone through in the past, a concept we could not match to anything we had felt for ourselves. Our silence and paralysis were an avowal: that we had become thoroughly unacquainted with the violent reality of the world out there. We had had no reason to let it come anywhere near us except in mediated form, as television images. We had examined the horrors of the past in considerable detail and read the documents and eyewitness reports; what they described struck us as more than any human being could bear, but they were descriptions from a time that was past, that lay behind us. It did not leave us unmoved, but we were able to discuss it in the safety afforded by historical distance. What, then, should we call what was happening now? An invasion of reality? A precipitate fall from the heights of the knowledge of the past we had accumulated into the immediacy of a contemporary experience we could no longer evade? The events crashed in on the circumscribed and well-ordered precinct from which our lives and thoughts did not stray, in which everything had its name; its barriers suddenly proved permeable and started to disintegrate. The novelty of this reality could not but come as a shock. We were reeling, overcome by events, forced to discard all the ideas about the world we had chosen to believe. The world had been 'in turmoil' for some time, since the 'watershed moment' of 1989, and the 'new complexity' was no longer so new but in fact a standing expression. But offering 'notes on the intellectual situation of the time' is one thing; being shaken to one's core by the concussions and convulsions that echo but distantly in that 'intellectual situation' is another thing entirely. However much we would like to believe that we are still above it all, we have suddenly been plunged into the thick of things and must cope with reality.

How fortunate must those be whose cool is imperturbable even now amid shocks and abrupt changes! The present bursts in upon them and still they stay above the fray, deftly and elegantly surfing on the enormous waves in which others drown. They never lack for theoretical concepts under which to subsume the new reality; their faith in the mind's primacy unshaken, they are always already ahead of that reality. Events that overmaster or at least stun others are, to them, merely fresh examples, new instances that, though perhaps not part of the programme, are nonetheless not truly surprising. What lets them look the situation squarely in the eye is not sangfroid but a distinctive resistance to being surprised, even indifference to the genuinely novel – which, in their view, is never truly unprecedented anyway because it is always analogous to some earlier phenomenon; because a comparative perspective allows it to be understood, which is also to say, disciplined, defused, rendered harmless. They have concepts ready for everything, be it 'geopolitics' or 'Western values', the 'new authoritarianism', perhaps even 'the Russian soul' or '*realpolitik*'. These are magic keys that make neat sense of a world that is about to explode such conceptual frameworks. But what if we hold no magic key, what if we do not have faith in their explanatory power?

In my case, more was at stake than merely a possible revision of a 'conceptual model', an idea of Russia and Russian history. Such revisions, corrections and amplifications are customary and part of the academic routine. But what if I was affected and concerned by the events not just as a scholar, a historian, but as an observer and witness who had travelled the region for decades, who had known – or had thought he knew – it better than most? 'Politics', which had long ceased to interfere with my work, or so it had seemed, was back in the spotlight (which, needless to say, it had never really left) and challenged me, not just as a scholarly authority but as a contemporary and citizen; for it is the citizen that is called upon in such situations to take a stand. The events themselves necessarily prompted a politicization (or repoliticization) of the public sphere and exerted relentless pressure on me to adopt one stance or another. Historical expertise does not automatically qualify one to analyse and comment on current political affairs, but historians are also citizens of the contemporary world, and as such they are summoned to clarify their positions amid the back and forth of conflicting interpretations – interpretations that, as it soon turned out, here became part of what has been described as a new kind of information war. To stand one's ground in the incipient controversy, one needed to keep up with the news, delve into the historical and social roots of the conflict that had erupted, and get a good sense of the altercations playing out before our eyes. What was one to think of the 'nationalism' of a 'fascist junta' in Kiev and the 'coup d'état' it had staged? How much truth was there to the allegation that anti-Semitism was rampant in Ukraine? Or to the claim that American organizations pulled the strings behind the scenes of Maidan? Who were these so-called separatists, and who might have shot down the Malaysia Airlines plane? Who opened fire on whom? Since the days of Maidan, I and everyone who takes a personal interest in the events in Ukraine has been under constant and mounting stress, a positively physical tension that permeates all fibres of thinking at all times. How am I to sit calmly through a performance of *Parsifal* when the shelling of Mariupol suggests that the attackers are trying to force a decision at any cost? With every new piece of news we hope that the tensions will subside, but over the weeks and months we have realized that we would have to live with persistent fighting for the next several years, and worse, that all indications are that Europe itself in the form into which it has coalesced in the seven decades since the war might cease to exist. The pressure exerted by unremitting and escalating military intimidation produces a situation of permanent strain that pervades life in all its manifestations and takes a heavy toll on one's health. The oppressive anxiety that the world order we have known might be overthrown lodges itself deeply in the mind. The disintegration of familiar environments and the growing distrust that makes amicable and frank exchanges of views impossible is almost physically sickening. One begins to pick up on overtones and suggestive remarks that might be clues to one's interlocutor's standpoint. One is no longer sure how colleagues, friends, one's closest associates think about Ukraine and Russia and so avoids even bringing up the subject. One watches as the increasingly acrimonious debate divides both the tight-knit circle of lifelong students of Russia and Eastern Europe and a larger public that is worried for a wide variety of reasons or else prefers to remain in denial about what is happening.

That is how it has gone for over a year now, and in that period, what we regarded as natural, normal or a given was revealed to be quite possibly the exception, one we were fortunate enough to experience by no deserts of our own: seven decades of peace in post-war Europe. Now we are facing a potential worst-case scenario for which we could not be less prepared in terms of the required conceptual instruments and repertoire of responses, not to mention the practical forms of peacekeeping, which include military defensive capabilities.

But the wound that truly smarts has been dealt not to the expert on Ukraine or Russia or Eastern Europe more generally; it cuts much deeper. It is an almost metaphysical insult that history has not progressed along what seemed to be its certain trajectory, that it defied my expectations and made a mockery of what I had envisioned as the sum of my life's work, a summation in which a life well lived would have coincided – and why should it not have? – with a history that turned out well. It seemed that the history that had brought such enormous misery upon earlier generations had rightfully come to a standstill; its upheavals had perhaps given way to a kind of calm, leaving us to turn our attention to 'normal' challenges rather than contend with emergencies of a kind we had not personally experienced. Francis Fukuyama's claim that the 'end of history' had arrived was never altogether plausible – how could it have been, shortly after 1989, the year history's wheels had sprung back into action! – but at the bottom of my heart I did believe that history, like my life, had entered a phase of conclusions and serene retrospection. The time had come to take the sum of what humanity had experienced in the twentieth century's cataclysms, to draw up the final balance, if not to put it all behind us. I felt that we had every right to entrust ourselves to the unstoppable progress of a Europe that had regained consciousness of itself, that wore its enlightenment and scepticism on its sleeves and felt fairly unshakeable – not a happy ending, exactly, but the pacification that comes with all maturation.

Europe had outgrown the escapades, the exercises in eccentricity and extremism; it reasonably took pride in the fact that it had not just survived but had got back into shape in an unimaginable success story: the traces of war had been wiped off the faces of its cities; all militancy had melted away in the bland light of civilization, had been subdued and sublimated in the shopping malls that had taken the place of the churches; the cycle of the seasons had been regularized by the steady rhythm of work and relaxation, with package deals to the world's most beautiful beaches and fulfilling careers (mass unemployment was a fading spectre). Europe had left the legendary 'century of extremes' behind and revolved in the commemorative loops of the major dates and anniversaries, when the few surviving witnesses to the great catastrophes were invited to speak even as the first generation born in peacetime already approached old age. Yet now, all of a sudden, history was back with a big bang, rending the temporal continuum; the time of an individual life and historical time stood in abrupt and stark contrast. Which image captures it best? Had we fallen into a hole, had the rug been pulled out from under our feet? What was certain was that we had reason to be deeply anxious. Something had resurfaced that an earlier age had called 'sinister'.

FURTHER READING

The following primarily lists publications I drew on for the city portraits. Extensive surveys of the literature on the history of Ukraine may be found in Paul Robert Magocsi, *A History of Ukraine: The Land and Its Peoples*, 2nd revd and expanded edn (Toronto, Buffalo, NY, and London, 2010), pp. 761–821, and Andreas Kappeler, *Kleine Geschichte der Ukraine*, 4th revd and updated edn (Munich, 2014), pp. 399–409. I could not have written this book without the broad and varied newspaper, television and online coverage of current events in Ukraine, but listing every piece of reporting would have been impractical.

GENERAL LITERATURE

Andruchovyč, Jurii, ed., *Österreichisch-ukrainische Begegnungen* (Lviv, 2013)

Andruchowytsch, Juri, and Andrzej Stasiuk, *Mein Europa: Zwei Essays über das sogenannte Mitteleuropa*, trans. Sofia Onufriv and Martin Pollack (Frankfurt, 2004)

Berkhoff, Karel C., *Harvest of Despair: Life and Death in Ukraine under Nazi Rule* (Cambridge, MA, and London, 2004)

Conquest, Robert, *The Harvest of Sorrow: Soviet Collectivization and the Terror-Famine* (New York, 1986)

Dallin, Alexander, *Deutsche Herrschaft in Russland, 1941–1945: Eine Studie über Besatzungspolitik* (Königstein im Taunus, 1981)

Fedotov, Georgii Petrovich, 'Tri stolicy' [1926], in *Litso Rossii: Stati 1918–1930*, 2nd edn (Paris, 1988), pp. 49–70

Golczewski, Frank, ed., *Geschichte der Ukraine* (Göttingen, 1993)

Grossman, Vasily, and Ilya Ehrenburg, eds, *The Black Book: The Ruthless Murder of Jews by German-Fascist Invaders throughout the Temporarily-occupied Regions of the Soviet Union and in the Death Camps of Poland during the War of 1941–1945*, trans. John Glad and James S. Levine (New York, 1981)

Hagen, Mark von, 'Does Ukraine Have a History?', *Slavic Review*, LIV/3 (1995), pp. 658–73

Jobst, Kerstin, *Geschichte der Ukraine* (Stuttgart, 2010)

Kappeler, Andreas, *Die Kosaken: Geschichte und Legenden* (Munich, 2013)

——, *Kleine Geschichte der Ukraine*, 4th revd and updated edn (Munich, 2014)

——, *Ungleiche Brüder: Russen und Ukrainer. Vom Mittelalter bis zur Gegenwart* (Munich, 2017)

Kasianov, Georgiy, and Philipp Ther, *A Laboratory of Transnational History: Ukraine and Recent Ukrainian Historiography* (Budapest and New York, 2009)

Kruglov, Aleksandr, *Khronika Kholokosta v Ukraine, 1941–1944 gg.*, Ukrainskaya biblioteka Kholokosta (Dnepropetrovsk and Zaporozhye, 2004)

Kuromiya, Hiroaki, *The Voices of the Dead: Stalin's Great Terror in the 1930s* (New Haven, CT, and London, 2007).

——, *Conscience on Trial: The Fate of Fourteen Pacifists in Stalin's Ukraine, 1952–1953* (Toronto, 2012)

Lüdemann, Ernst, *Ukraine*, 3rd edn (Munich, 2006)

Magocsi, Paul Robert, *A History of Ukraine: The Land and Its Peoples*, 2nd revd and expanded edn (Toronto, Buffalo, NY, and London, 2010)

Miroshnichenko, B. A., *Po Dnepru: Putevoditel* (Moscow, 1967)

Plokhy, Serhii, *Ukraine and Russia: Representations of the Past* (Toronto, 2008)

——, *The Gates of Europe: A History of Ukraine* (London, 2015)

Polonska-Vasylenko, Natalija, *Geschichte der Ukraine: Von den Anfängen bis 1923* (Munich, 1988)

Reid, Anna, *Borderland: A Journey through the History of Ukraine* (Boulder, CO, 2000)

Roth, Joseph, *Reisen in die Ukraine und nach Russland*, ed. and with an afterword by Jan Bürger (Munich, 2015)

Schmid, Ulrich, *UA – Ukraine zwischen Ost und West* (Zurich, 2015)

Snyder, Timothy, *The Reconstruction of Nations: Poland, Ukraine, Lithuania, Belarus, 1569–1999* (New Haven, CT, and London, 2003)

——, *Bloodlands: Europe between Hitler and Stalin* (New York, 2010)

Sotnikov, Ivan, *Dnepr moguchy: Roman* (Moscow, 1963)

Subtelny, Orest, *Ukraine: A History* (Toronto, Buffalo, NY, and London, 1988)

Trubetzkoy, Nikolai Sergeevich, 'The Ukrainian Problem', in *The Legacy of Genghis Khan and Other Essays on Russia's Identity*, ed. and with a postscript by Anatoly Liberman, preface by Viacheslav V. Ivanov (Ann Arbor, MI, 1991), pp. 245–68

Weiner, Amir, *Making Sense of War: The Second World War and the Fate of the Bolshevik Revolution* (Princeton, NJ, and Oxford, 2001)

Wilson, Andrew, *The Ukrainians: Unexpected Nation*, 4th edn (New Haven, CT, and London, 2015)

Yekelchyk, Serhy, *Ukraine: Birth of a Modern Nation* (Oxford, 2007)

Zhurzhenko, Tatiana, *Borderlands into Bordered Lands: Geopolitics of Identity in Post-Soviet Ukraine* (Stuttgart, 2010)

ON MAIDAN AND RECENT DEVELOPMENTS

Andruchowytsch, Juri, *Euromaidan: Was in der Ukraine auf dem Spiel steht*, with a photographic essay by Yevgenia Belorusets (Berlin, 2014)

'Chronik: Besetzungen öffentlicher Gebäude in der Ostukraine', *Osteuropa*, LXIV/5–6 (2014), pp. 149–56

Dathe, Claudia, and Andreas Rostek, eds, *Majdan! Ukraine, Europa* (Berlin, 2014)

Garton Ash, Timothy, 'Putin Must Be Stopped. And Sometimes Only Guns Can Stop Guns', *The Guardian*, 1 February 2015

Geissbühler, Simon, ed., *Kiew – Revolution 3.0: Der Euromaidan 2013/14 und die Zukunftsperspektiven der Ukraine* (Stuttgart, 2014)

Gusev, Gleb, ed., *#Euromaidan: History in the Making* (Kiev, 2014)

Jilge, Wilfrid, 'Geschichtspolitik auf dem Majdan: Politische Emanzipation und nationale Selbstvergewisserung', *Osteuropa*, LXIV/5–6 (2014), pp. 239–58

Kurkov, Andrey, *Ukraine Diaries: Dispatches from Kiev*, trans. Sam Taylor, with an afterword translated by Amanda Love Darragh (London, 2014)

Mitrokhin, Nikolay, 'Transnationale Provokation: Russische Nationalisten und Geheimdienstler in der Ukraine', *Osteuropa*, LXIV/5–6 (2014), pp. 157–74

Pomerantsev, Peter, 'Risse in der Kreml-Matrix: Postmoderne Diktatur und Opposition in Russland', *Transit: Europäische Revue*, 44 (Autumn 2013), pp. 179–93

——, and Michael Weiss, *The Menace of Unreality: How the Kremlin Weaponizes Information, Culture and Money. A Special Report Presented by The Interpreter, a Project of the Institute of Modern Russia* (New York, 2014)

Putin, Vladimir, 'Address by President of the Russian Federation', http://en.kremlin.ru, 18 March 2014

Raabe, Katharina, and Manfred Sapper, eds, *Testfall Ukraine: Europa und seine Werte* (Berlin, 2015)

Schuller, Konrad, *Ukraine: Chronik einer Revolution* (Berlin, 2014)

Shore, Marci, *Ukrainian Night: An Intimate History of Revolution* (New Haven, CT, 2018)

Transit: Europäische Revue, 45 (Summer 2014): 'Maidan: Die unerwartete Revolution', guest editor: Tatiana Zhurzhenko

Ukraine-Analysen, ed. Forschungsstelle Osteuropa an der Universität Bremen und Deutsche Gesellschaft für Osteuropakunde, 2006–14

Wendland, Anna Veronika, 'Hilflos im Dunkeln. "Experten" in der Ukraine-Krise: eine Polemik', *Osteuropa*, LXIV/9–10 (2014), pp. 13–33

Wilson, Andrew, *Ukraine Crisis: What It Means for the West* (New Haven, CT, and London, 2014)

KIEV, METROPOLIS

Anisimov, Aleksandr, *Privet iz Kieva* (Kiev, 2011)

Berdyaev, Nicolas, *Dream and Reality: An Essay in Autobiography*, trans. Katharine Lampert (New York, 1951)

Bulgakov, Mikhail, *White Guard*, trans. Marian Schwartz, with an introduction by Evgeny Dobrenko (New Haven, CT, 2008)

Chepelyk, Viktor, et al., eds, *Khreshchatyk: Kulturologichny putivnyk* (Kiev, 1997)

Derzhavnyi arkhitekturno-istorychnyi zapovidnyk 'Sofiisky muzei': Fotoalbom (Kiev, 1990)

Druk, Olga, and Yuliya Ferentseva, *Kiev: Istoriya, Arkhitektura, Traditsii* (Kiev, 2012)

Ehrenburg, Ilya, *Selections from* People, Years, Life (Oxford and New York, 1972)

Emchenko, A. M., *Kiev: Pamyat goroda-geroya. Fotoputevoditel* (Kiev, 1990)

Erofalov-Pilipchak, Boris, *Arkhitektura sovetskogo Kieva* (Kiev, 2010)

Hamm, Michael F., *Kiev: A Portrait, 1800–1917* (Princeton, NJ, 1993)

Kalnitskii, M. B., *Progulka po Kievu: Putevoditel* (Kiev, 2009)
——, *Biznes i biznesmeny* (Kiev, 2011)
——, *Evreiskie adresa Kieva: Putevoditel po kulturno-istoricheskim mestam* (Kiev, 2012)
——, *Zodchestvo i zodchie* (Kiev, 2012)
Khinkulov, Leonid, *Zolotye Vorota Kieva* (Kiev, 1988)
Kizny, Tomasz, *La Grande Terreur en URSS, 1937–1938* (Lausanne, 2013)
Konchakovskii, Anatolii, and Dmitrii Malakov, *Kiev Mikhaila Bulgakova: Fotoalbom* (Kiev, 1990)
Kopelev, Lev, *Education of a True Believer*, trans. Gary Kern (New York, 1980)
Kovalinskii, V., *Mecenaty Kieva* (Kiev, 1998)
Kruglov, A., *Tragediya Babego Yara v nemeckikh dokumentakh* (Dnepropetrovsk, 2011)
Kuznetsov, Anatoly, *Babi Yar: A Document in the Form of a Novel*, trans. David Floyd (Cambridge, MA, 1970)
Kyiv 1941–1943: Fotoalbom (Kiev, 2000)
Lifar, Serge, *Zhyttia dlia tantsiu* (Kiev, 2011)
Malakov, Dmytro, *Arkhitektor Horodetskyi* (Kiev, 1999)
Mandelstam, Osip, 'Kiev', in *The Collected Critical Prose and Letters*, ed. Jane Gary Harris, trans. Jane Gary Harris and Constance Link (Ann Arbor, MI, 1979)
Mikhail Bulgakov: Zhizn i tvorchestvo. Fotoalbom (Moscow, 2006)
Peisachov, Dmitrij B., *Evreiskaya zhizn v Kieve / Jüdisches Leben in Kiew*, ed. and with an introduction by Erhard Roy Wiehn (Konstanz, 1992)
Petrovskyi, Myron, *Master i gorod: Kievskie konteksty Mikhaila Bulgakova* (Kiev, 2001)
Petrowskaja, Katja, *Vielleicht Esther: Geschichten* (Berlin, 2014)
Pozniak, Pavlo, and Serhii Piaterykov, *Kyiv: Pogliad cherez stolittia. Fotoputivnyk* (Kiev, 1987)
Puchkov, Andrei, *'Kiev' Osipa Mandelshtama v intonatsiyakh, poyazneniyakh, kartinkakh* (Kiev 2015)
Rogozovskaya, Tatyana, *Dom Bulgakovykh-Turbinykh: Neputevoditel po Kievskomu muzeyu* (Kiev, 2014)
Sherotskyi, K. V., *Kyiv: Putivnyk* [1917], reprint (Kiev, 1994)
Shlenskii, Dmitrii, and Aleksei Braslavets, *Andreevsky spusk: Kulturologicheskii putevoditel* (Kiev, 1998)
Shulkevich, M. M., *Kiev: Arkhitekturno-istoricheskii ocherk* (Kiev, 1963)
Smishko, V. P., *Vozrozhdennyi Kiev*, Trudovoe Sodruzhestvo narodov SSSR v vosstanovlenii stolitsy Ukrainy, 1943–1950 gg. (Kiev, 1990)
Suprunenko, N. I., ed., *Istoriya Kieva*, 3 vols, 4 books (Kiev, 1982–6)
Terno, Valentin, *Vospominaniya o detstve: Leningrad – Kiev* (Kiev, 2011)
Volodymyrska: Kulturolohichnyi putivnyk. Istoriya odniei vulytsi (Kiev, 1999)

AH, ODESSA: A CITY IN AN ERA OF GREAT EXPECTATIONS

Aleksandrov, Rostislav, *Progulki po literaturnoi Odesse* (Odessa, 1993)
Ascherson, Neal, *Black Sea* (New York, 1995)
Atlas, D., *Staraya Odessa, ee druzya i nedrugi* (Moscow, 1992)
Babel, Isaac, 'The Story of My Dovecot', in *Collected Stories*, trans. David McDuff (New York, 1994)

Balatsky, V., *Museum in the Catacombs: Guide* (Odessa, 1986)

Boy, Ann-Dorit, 'Die Tragödie von Odessa', *Frankfurter Allgemeine Zeitung*, 7 March 2015, p. 3

Dallin, Alexander, *Odessa, 1941–1944: A Case Study of Soviet Territory under Foreign Rule* (Iaşi, 1998)

Derevyanko, Boris, *Odesskii teatr opery i baleta: Fotoocherk* (Odessa, 1990)

Deribas, Aleksandr: *Staraya Odessa: Istoricheskie ocherki i vospominaniya* [1913], reprint (Moscow, 1995)

Dolzhenkova, A., and P. Dyachenko, *Odessa: Putevoditel* (Odessa, 1978)

Est gorod u morya: Kraevedcheskii sbornik (Odessa, 1990)

Filimonov, O. V., ed., *Odesskaya pleyada: Satiricheskie proizvedeniya 20–30-kh godov* (Kiev, 1990)

Hausmann, Guido, *Universität und städtische Gesellschaft in Odessa, 1865–1917: Soziale und nationale Selbstorganisation an der Peripherie des Zarenreiches* (Stuttgart, 1998)

Herlihy, Patricia, *Odessa: A History, 1794–1914* (Cambridge, MA, 1986)

Ilf, Ilya, and Evgeny Petrov, *The Twelve Chairs*, trans. John H. C. Richardson, with an introduction by Maurice Friedberg (New York 1961)

Iljine, Nicolas V., ed., *Odessa Memories*, with an essay by Patricia Herlihy and contributions by Bel Kaufman, Oleg Gubar and Alexander Rozenboim (Seattle, WA, 2003)

Iz istorii evreiskoi Odessy: K dvukhsotletiyu goroda (Odessa, N.D.)

Jabotinsky, Vladimir [Ze'ev], *The Five: A Novel of Jewish Life in Turn-of-the-century Odessa*, trans. and annotated by Michael R. Katz, with an introduction by Michael Stanislawski (Ithaca, NY, 2005)

Koschmal, Walter, ed., *Odessa: Kapitel aus der Kulturgeschichte* (Regensburg, 1998)

Odessa: Fotoalbom (Kiev, 1994)

Odessa: Ocherk istorii goroda-geroya (Odessa, 1957)

Odessa: The Memory of the Hero-City (Kiev, 1989)

Odesskii almanakh: Deribasovskaya-Rishelyevskaya (Odessa, 2000)

Odesskii gosudarstvennyi literaturnyi muzei: Putevoditel (Odessa, 1968)

Ostrovskii, G., *Odessa, more, kino: Stranitsy istorii dalekoi i blizkoi* (Odessa, 1989)

Penter, Tanja, *Odessa 1917: Revolution an der Peripherie* (Cologne, 2000)

Pilyavskii, Valentin, *Zdaniya, sooruzheniya, pamyatniki Odessy i ikh zodchie: Spravochnik* (Odessa, 2010)

——, *Zodchie Odessy: Istoriko-arkhitekturnye ocherki* (Odessa, 2010)

Richardson, Tanya, 'Odessa's Two Big Differences (and a Few Small Ones)', *Eurozine*, www.eurozine.com, 1 September 2014

Sarkisyan, K., and M. Stavnicer, *Ulicy rasskazyvayut . . .* (Odessa, 1986)

Timofeenko, V. I., *Odessa: Arkhitekturno-istoricheskii ocherk* (Kiev, 1984)

Vlasishen, Yurii, *Odessa: Oranzhevyi gid* (Moscow, 2011)

Zinko, Feliks, *Koe-chto iz istorii Odesskoi ChK* (Odessa, 1998)

Zipperstein, Steven J., *The Jews of Odessa: A Cultural History, 1794–1881* (Stanford, CA, 1985)

PROMENADE IN YALTA

Ascherson, Neal, 'Die Krim – eine Einleitung', in *Die Krim – Goldene Insel im Schwarzen Meer: Griechen – Skythen – Goten*, exh. cat., Landeskunde Museum Bonn (Darmstadt, 2013), pp. 21–35

Jobst, Kerstin S., *Die Perle des Imperiums: Der russische Krim-Diskurs im Zarenreich* (Constance, 2007)

Magocsi, Paul Robert, *This Blessed Land: Crimea and the Crimean Tatars* (Toronto, 2014)

Popov, Arkady, 'Krymskie mify', http://arkadiy-popov.blogspot.ru, 24 May– 7 June 2015

Sasse, Gwendolyn, *The Crimea Question: Identity, Transition, and Conflict* (Cambridge, MA, 2007)

LOOK UPON THIS CITY: KHARKOV, A CAPITAL OF THE TWENTIETH CENTURY

Bosse, George, *Jene Zeit in Charkow, 1936–1941: Eine Jugend unter Stalin* (Berlin, 1997)

Carrère, Emmanuel, *Limonov: A Novel*, trans. John Lambert (London, 2014)

Chekhunov, N. V., and G. A. Dubovis, *Gosprom. Vremia. Sudba* (Kharkov, 2004)

Drobitskii Yar: Memorial-muzei (Kharkov, 2008)

Friedrich, Gunter, *Kollaboration in der Ukraine im Zweiten Weltkrieg: Die Rolle der einheimischen Stadtverwaltung während der deutschen Besetzung Charkows 1941 bis 1943*, doctoral thesis, Ruhr Universität Bochum (2008)

Hausmann, Guido, 'Lokale Öffentlichkeit und städtische Herrschaft im Zarenreich: Die ukrainische Stadt Charkiv', in *Stadt und Öffentlichkeit in Ostmitteleuropa 1900–1939: Beiträge zur Entstehung moderner Urbanität zwischen Berlin, Charkiv, Tallinn und Triest*, ed. Andreas R. Hofmann and Anna Veronika Wendland (Stuttgart, 2002), pp. 213–34

Kevorkyan, Konstantin, *Pervaya stolitsa: Ocherki, proza* (Kharkov, 2007)

Kharkiv: Visitor's Guide, 3rd edn (Kharkov, 2012)

Kharkov: Kratkii putevoditel (Kharkov, 2012)

Kolovrat, Yu., *Spasov skit: Krushenie tsarskogo poezda i istoriya khrama Khrista Spasitelya. Putevoditel* (Kharkov, 2013)

Kopelev, Lev, *Education of a True Believer*, trans. Gary Kern (New York, 1980)

Kosarev, Borys, *Modernist Kharkiv, 1915–1931*, exh. cat., The Ukrainian Museum, New York (Kiev, 2012)

Kotelevskii, Vladimir, and Igor Kotelevskii, *Kharkov: XXI vek. nachalo. Photoalbom / Kharkov: XXI ct. Beginning* (Donetsk, 2012)

Lyubavskyi, Roman G., *Povsiakdenne zhyttia robitnykiv Kharkova v 1920-ti – na pochatku 1930-kh rokiv* (Kharkov, 2014)

Machulin, Leonid, *Ukrainskaya stolitsa dlya krasnogo imperatora* (Kharkov, 2009)

Ploticher, E. A., *Slovo o rodnom gorode* (Kharkov, 2009)

Rozenfeld, Maksim, *Kharkov: Retrogeografiya. Fotoalbom* (Kharkov, 2013)

Shkodovskii, Yu. M., I. N. Lavrentyev, A. Yu. Leybfreyd and Yu. Yu. Polyakova, *Kharkov vchera, segodnya, zavtra* (Kharkov, 2002)

Staging the Ukrainian Avant-garde of the 1910s and 1920s, exh. cat., The Ukrainian Museum, New York, Myroslava M. Mudrak, Tetiana Rudenko, consultative curators (Kiev, 2015)

Starovynnyi Kharkiv u poshtovykh kartkakh: Albom (Kharkov, 2004)

Weissberg-Cybulski, Alexander, *The Accused*, trans. Edward Fitzgerald (New York, 1951)

Yatsina, O. A., *Arkhitekturnaya simfoniya Kharkova* (Kharkov, 2008)

Zhadan, Serhii, *Voroshilovgrad*, trans. Reilly Costigan-Humes and Isaac Wheeler (Dallas, TX, 2016)

Zhurzhenko, Tatiana, '"Capital of Despair": Holodomor Memory and Political Conflicts in Kharkiv after the Orange Revolution', *East European Politics and Societies*, xxv/3 (August 2011), pp. 597–639

——, 'The Fifth Kharkiv', *New Eastern Europe*, 7 July 2015

DNEPROPETROVSK: ROCKET CITY ON THE DNIEPER AND CITY OF POTEMKIN

Dnipropetrovskyi istorychnyi muzei im. D. I. Yavornytskoho: Putivnyk (Dnepropetrovsk, 1971)

Kabakov, Ilya, *L'album de ma mère / My Mother's Album* (Paris, 1995)

Kavun, Maksim, *Sady i parki v istorii Ekaterinoslava / Dnepropetrovska: Park imeni T. B. Shevchenko* (Dnepropetrovsk, 2009)

Kravchenko, Victor, *I Chose Freedom: The Personal and Political Life of a Soviet Official* (Garden City, NY, 1947)

Lazebnik, Valentina, *Neizvestnaya Ekaterinoslavshchina: Istoricheskie ocherki* (Dnepropetrovsk, 2012)

Lindner, Rainer, 'Städtische Modernisierung im südlichen Zarenreich: Ekaterinoslav und Žitomir, 1860–1914', in *Städte im östlichen Europa. Zur Problematik von Modernisierung und Raum vom Spätmittelalter bis zum 20. Jahrhundert*, ed. Carsten Goehrke and Bianka Pietrow-Ennker (Zurich, 2006), pp. 281–316

——, *Unternehmer und Stadt in der Ukraine, 1860–1914: Industrialisierung und soziale Kommunikation im südlichen Zarenreich* (Konstanz, 2006)

Moroz, V. S., *Pamyatnye mesta revolyutsionnoi slavy Dnepropetrovshchiny: Putevoditel* (Dnepropetrovsk, 1985)

Portnov, Andrii, 'Dnepropetrovsk: Tam, gde nachinaetsya Ukraina', www.gefter. RU, 27 June 2014

Romanov, Evgenii, *V borbe za Rossiyu: Vospominaniya* (Moscow, 1999)

Shatrov, Mikhail, *S vershiny poluveka: Kniga o posleoktyabrskom Dnepropetrovske* (Dnepropetrovsk, 1968)

——, *Gorod nakh trekh kholmakh: Kniga o starom Ekaterinoslave* (Dnepropetrovsk, 1969)

Shchupak, Igor, *Evrei v Ukraine: Voprosy istorii i religii s drevneishikh vremen do Kholokosta* (Dnepropetrovsk, 2009)

Vatchenko, A. F., and G. I. Shevchenko, *Dnepropetrovsk: Putevoditel-Spravochnik* (Dnepropetrovsk, 1974)

Zhuk, Sergei I., *Rock and Roll in the Rocket City: The West, Identity and Ideology in Soviet Dnepropetrovsk, 1960–1985* (Washington, DC, and Baltimore, MD, 2010)

DONETSK: TWENTIETH-CENTURY URBICIDES

Batenin, E. S., ed., *Donbass: Juzhnyi gorno-promyshlennyi raion* (Moscow, 1928)

Białoszewski, Miron, *A Memoir of the Warsaw Uprising*, trans. and with an introduction and notes by Madeline G. Levine (New York, 2015)

Donetsk: Ot poselka do megapolisa / Donetsk: From Obscure Village to Global City (Donetsk, 2010)

Friedgut, Theodore H., *Iuzovka and Revolution*, vol. i: *Life and Work in Russia's Donbass, 1869–1924*, and vol. ii: *Politics and Revolution in Russia's Donbass, 1869–1924* (Princeton, NJ, 1989–94)

Grigorenko, Petro, *Memoirs*, trans. Thomas P. Whitney (New York, 1982)

Janion, Maria, *Die Polen und ihre Vampire. Studien zur Kritik kultureller Phantasmen*, ed. and with an introduction by Magdalena Marszalek, trans. Bernhard Hartmann and Thomas Weiler (Berlin, 2014), especially the section 'Der Tod der Stadt', pp. 199–207

Kuromiya, Hiroaki, *Freedom and Terror in the Donbas: A Ukrainian-Russian Borderland, 1870s–1990s* (Cambridge, 1998)

——, 'The Enigma of the Donbas: How to Understand Its Past and Future', www.hi-phi.ua, 24 August 2015

Mitrokhin, Nikolay, 'Bandenkrieg und Staatsbildung: Zur Zukunft des Donbass', *Osteuropa*, LXV/1–2 (2015), pp. 5–19

Penter, Tanja, *Kohle für Stalin und Hitler: Arbeiten und Leben im Donbass, 1929–1953* (Essen, 2010)

Skibenko, A. K., *Donetskaya oblast: Putevoditel* (Donetsk, 2008)

——, *Putevoditel: Gorod na beregakh Kalmiusa! Kraevedcheskie progulki po rodnomu gorodu* (Donetsk, 2013)

Staraya Yuzovka (Donetsk, 2014)

Styopkin, V., *Illyustrirovannaya istoriya Yuzovki-Stalino-Donetska* (Donetsk, 2007)

——, *Degtyaryov: Khozyain oblasti* (Donetsk, 2013)

——, and S. Tretyakov, *Stalino glazami soldata vermakhta* (Donetsk, 2013)

Zhadan, Serhii, *Anarchy in the UKR* (Kharkov, 2005)

Zhadan, Serhiy, *Depeche Mode*, trans. Myroslav Shkandrij (London, 2013)

——, *Voroshilovgrad*, trans. Reilly Costigan-Humes and Isaac Wheeler (Dallas, TX, 2016)

Zimmer, Kerstin, *Machteliten im ukrainischen Donbass: Bedingungen und Konsequenzen der Transformation einer alten Industrieregion* (Berlin, 2006)

CZERNOWITZ: CITY UPON A HILL

Bilek, Vasyl, Orest Kryvoruchko, Oleksandr Masan and Ihor Chekhovskyi, *Vitannia z Chernivtsiv* (Chernivtsi, 1994)

Braun, Helmut, ed., *Czernowitz: Die Geschichte einer untergegangenen Kulturmetropole* (Berlin, 2005)

Coldewey, Gaby, ed., *Zwischen Pruth und Jordan: Lebenserinnerungen Czernowitzer Juden* (Cologne, 2003)

Corbea-Hoisie, Andrei, *Czernowitzer Geschichten: Über eine städtische Kultur in Mittelosteuropa* (Vienna, 2003)

Husar, Yukhim, and Serhii Rozumnyi, *Chernivtsi: Shcho? De? Yak? Fotoputivnyk* (Kiev, 1991)

Koepp, Volker, *Herr Zwilling und Frau Zuckermann: Episoden aus dem jüdischen Leben in Czernowitz*, film (Germany, 1999)
——, *Dieses Jahr in Czernowitz*, documentary film (Germany, 2003)
Pollack, Martin, et al., *Mythos Czernowitz: Eine Stadt im Spiegel ihrer Nationalitäten* (Potsdam, 2008), with a bibliography, pp. 239–51
Pomerantsev, Igor, *Czernowitz, Chernovtsy, Chernivtsi: Proza, esse* (Chernivtsi, 2012)
Rezzori, Gregor von, *An Ermine in Czernopol*, trans. Philip Boehm, with an introduction by Daniel Kehlmann (New York, 2011)
Rychlo, Peter, and Oleg Liubkivskyj, *Literaturstadt Czernowitz*, 2nd improved edn (Chernivtsi, 2009)
Wichner, Ernest, and Herbert Wiesner, eds, *In der Sprache der Mörder: Eine Literatur aus Czernowitz, Bukowina*, exh. cat., Literaturhaus Berlin (Berlin, 1993)
Yavetz, Zvi, *Erinnerungen an Czernowitz: Wo Menschen und Bücher lebten*, 2nd revd edn (Munich, 2007)

LVIV: CAPITAL OF PROVINCIAL EUROPE

Amar, Tarik Cyril, *The Paradox of Ukrainian Lviv: A Borderland City between Stalinists, Nazis, and Nationalists* (Ithaca, NY, and London, 2015)
Bartov, Omer, *Erased: Vanishing Traces of Jewish Galicia in Present-day Ukraine* (Princeton, NJ, 2007)
Czaplicka, John, ed., *Lviv: A City in the Crosscurrents of Culture* (Cambridge, MA, 2002)
Dohrn, Verena, *Reise nach Galizien: Grenzlandschaften des alten Europa* (Frankfurt am Main, 1993)
Fässler, Peter, Thomas Held and Dirk Sawitzki, *Lemberg – Lwów – Lviv: Eine Stadt im Schnittpunkt europäischer Kulturen* (Cologne, 1995)
Gross, Jan T., *Revolution from Abroad: The Soviet Conquest of Poland's Western Ukraine and Western Belorussia* (Princeton, NJ, 1988)
Henke, Lutz, Grzegorz Rossoliński, and Philipp Ther, eds, *Eine neue Gesellschaft in einer alten Stadt: Erinnerung und Geschichtspolitik in Lemberg anhand der Oral History / Nove suspilstvo v davnomu misti: Pamyat ta istorychna polityka zasobamy oral history* (Wrocław, 2007)
Hrytsak, Yaroslav, 'Lviv: A Multicultural History through the Centuries', *Harvard Ukrainian Studies*, XXIV/1/4 (2000), pp. 47–73
Images of a Vanished World: The Jews in Eastern Galicia, exh. cat. (Lviv, 2003)
Kotłobułatowa, Irina, *Lwów na dawnej Pocztówe* (Kraków, 2002)
Longolius, Sonja, and Katharina Schubert, *Lemberg / Lviv: Jüdische Erinnerungsorte in Lemberg – eine Bestandsaufnahme* (Berlin, 2007)
Lvivshchyna: Istoryko-kulturni ta kraieznavchi narisi (Lviv, 1998)
Melnyk, B. V., *Vulytsiamy starovynnoho Lvova* (Lviv, 2002)
Mick, Christoph, *Kriegserfahrungen in einer multiethnischen Stadt: Lemberg, 1914–1947* (Wiesbaden, 2010)
Nowak, Janusz T., Stanisław Sroka and Ryszard Terlecki, *Historyczny Lwów: Przewodnik* (Kraków, 1993)
Pollack, Martin, *Galizien: Eine Reise durch die verschwundene Welt Ostgaliziens und der Bukowina* (Frankfurt am Main, 2001)

——, *Kontaminierte Landschaften: Unruhe bewahren* (Salzburg, 2014)

Purchla, Jacek, and Krzysztof Broński, eds, *Mythos Galizien*, exh. cat., Wien Museum, Vienna, and Międzynarodowe Centrum Kultury, Kraków (Vienna, 2015)

Roth, Joseph, 'Lemberg, die Stadt', in *Reisen in die Ukraine und nach Russland*, ed. and with an afterword by Jan Bürger (Munich, 2015), pp. 15–25

Struve, Kai, 'Tremors in the Shatterzone of Empires: Eastern Galicia in Summer 1941', in *Shatterzone of Empires: Coexistence and Violence in the German, Habsburg, Russian, and Ottoman Borderlands*, ed. Omer Bartov and Eric D. Weitz (Bloomington, IN, 2013), pp. 449–62

Turystychny putivnyk: Lviv / Lviv: A Guidebook for the Visitor (Lviv, 1999)

Yamash, Yurii, *Arkhitektura teatriv Lvova (kinets XVIII st. – persha pol. XIX st.)* (Lviv, 2003)

Wendland, Veronika, *Die Russophilen in Galizien: Ukrainische Konservative zwischen Österreich und Rußland, 1848–1915* (Vienna, 2000)

Wittlin, Józef, and Philippe Sands, *City of Lions*, trans. Antonio Lloyd-Jones, with a preface by Eva Hoffman and photographs by Diana Matar (London, 2016)

Wolff, Larry, *The Idea of Galicia: History and Fantasy in Habsburg Political Culture* (Stanford, CA, 2010)

ACKNOWLEDGEMENTS

A PROFESSIONAL HISTORIAN relies on the longstanding relationships he has built with colleagues and contacts. Sometimes, however, he owes sudden eye-opening insights to chance encounters: the train conductor – the daughter of a Russian Ukrainian family, she was raised in Vinnytsia, spent her youth in Tashkent, studied in Moscow, and moved to Kharkov with her husband – who came out to me as a Ukrainian patriot; or the interlocutor in a café in Kharkov one Sunday morning, a piano tuner by profession but a sniper by vocation, a highly decorated Afghanistan veteran, who was on his way to the war in the Donbass – a precision mechanic of death, you might say. I am grateful to everyone who spoke to me and helped me better understand what was going on. Needless to say, what I have made of these encounters – which I have rendered to the best of my knowledge and belief – is my responsibility alone.

Crucial encouragement to go back to school, as it were, to travel to Ukraine and see for myself, came from Timothy Snyder, whom I met in Leipzig in 2012 and then again in Kiev in May 2014, as well as from Hiroaki Kuromiya, whose decades-long dedication to his 'object of research', the Donbass, I can only admire. During my time in Vienna, I was fortunate to speak to Andreas Kappeler on several occasions. His seminal works on the history of Ukraine have been indispensable to me as I sought to understand the country's evolution, and I am delighted to know that his readership has grown considerably. If there is one person to whom I owe a greater debt of gratitude, it is Martin Pollack, who opened my eyes to Galicia over thirty years ago and still keeps me up to date on the various intellectual and literary tendencies in this world that he knows better than virtually anyone.

As I went about exploring Ukraine's cities, numerous individuals provided me with important advice and information. For Kharkov, they were Tatiana Zhurzhenko, Vienna; Antje Rempe, Nuremberg; and Igor Solomadin and Yevhen Zakharov in Kharkov itself. Several visits to Dnepropetrovsk would not have been possible without the information volunteered by Andrii Portnov, Berlin, and the initiative of Igor Shchupak of the Ukrainian Holocaust Institute and Museum, Dnepropetrovsk. Stefania Ptashnyk, Bohdan Cherkes, Yurko Prokhasko and Yaroslav Hrytsak were inexhaustible founts of knowledge on Lviv. Igor Pomerantsev and Petro Rykhlo kept me in touch with Chernivtsi. In Kiev, I am most grateful to Konstantin Sigov, Andreas Umland, Mark Belorusets and Rabbi Alexander Dukhovny.

Acknowledgements

Konrad Tschäpe, who has assisted me since my days at the Europa-Universität Viadrina in Frankfurt an der Oder, edited the manuscript with his customary diligence. The book could not have come out in time without the patience and encouragement of my collaborator of many years Tobias Heyl.

Vienna, that wonderful city, where I had the opportunity to work during the spring of 2015 as a fellow at the Internationales Forschungszentrum Kulturwissenschaften, proved a privileged vantage point from which Ukraine was suddenly not so distant at all. I am deeply grateful to the centre's director, Helmut Lethen, and to everyone who helped make my stay so stimulating and productive.

PHOTO ACKNOWLEDGEMENTS

THE AUTHOR AND THE PUBLISHERS wish to express their thanks to the below sources of illustrative material and /or permission to reproduce it.

Alamy: p. 206 (Chronicle); Alexandr Il'in: p. 92; iStockphoto: p. 81 (Kuklev); Library of Congress, Washington, DC: pp. 87 (bottom), 120, 124, 128, 138, 155, 261; Mary Evans Picture Library: pp. 215, 263 (Sueddeutsche Zeitung Photo); REX Shutterstock: pp. 6 (Emeric Fohlen), 16 (Alexander Zemlianichenko/AP), 36 (Maxim Shipenkov), 53 (Max Black/AP), 68 (Sipa USA); Shutterstock: pp. III (Versh), 144 (Viacheslav Lopatin).